The Kurdish Spring

Kurdish Regions of the Middle East

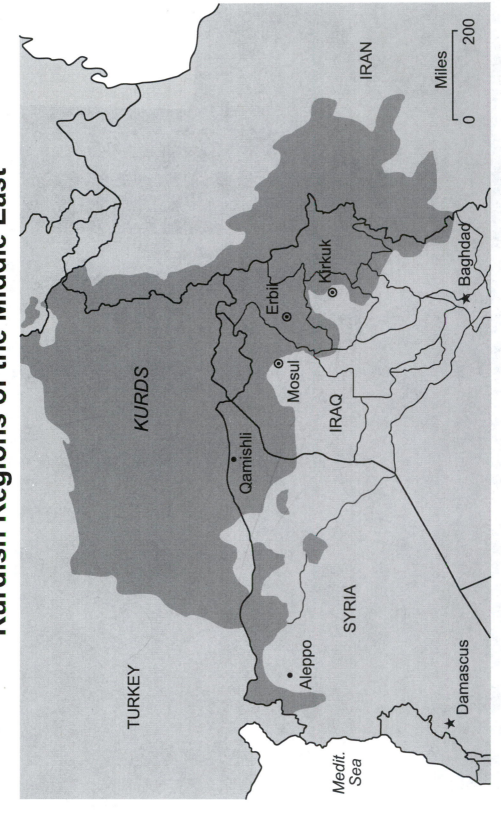

The Kurdish Spring

A New Map of the Middle East

David L. Phillips

With a foreword by **Bernard Kouchner**

Transaction Publishers
New Brunswick (U.S.A.) and London (U.K.)

ISBN: 978-1-4128-5576-1 (cloth); 978-1-4128-5680-5 (paper)
Printed in the United States of America

To Tara and Maya Phillips, my darling daughters. They remind me to live your dream. For the Kurds, the dream is independence. Everyone's dream is peace.

Contents

Part Four: Peril and Opportunity

Foreword

The Activist Professor

Political science keeps events at bay and touches upon them with caution. David L. Phillips loves to embrace them. If you get lost in the day-to-day confusion of events, read his book and you will be able to distinguish what is important from the mundane.

The Berlin Wall, 9/11, the Ukraine crisis, HIV-AIDS, Ebola—experts have seldom forecast the major events of our time. Phillips is not your ordinary professor: he is a human rights activist. And he recognizes that he can be fallible.

We live through foggy times, aggravated as they are by the frenzy of the news cycle. Who are the enemies of the rule of law? What terrorism lurks behind the masks of religion? Why does geopolitical change lead to more barbarism? David L. Phillips deciphers all the figures of contemporary threats and crisis. He also believes in the resources of our democracies, however threatened they may be. He knows how to turn international law into an instrument for peace. His capacity for analysis acts as a detector of conflicts to come.

Rather than retreating to the quiet of his reading rooms, predicting the past and lamenting about done deeds, Phillips likes to travels to the most forlorn places on the planet, an active witness of current turmoil.

Our paths have crossed many times, from the Middle East to Latin America, from Eastern Ukraine to Southeast Asia. The Columbia professor has his own ring of informers to assess the tactics of ISIS and the chances of the Kurds—the only champions of local democracy—to hold them back in Iraq and in Syria. From day to day, he has followed the massacres, the violence upon women and children, compelling us all to convince our governments it is never too late to react.

Phillips knows how to project the real world into stale lecture rooms. To commentators and diplomats alike, he is a reality detector, and for us all, a lightning rod in times of confusion.

Bernard Kouchner
Founder of MSF (Nobel Peace Prize–winning Médecins
Sans Frontières, or Doctors without Borders)
Former French foreign minister

Author's Note

The Kurdish Spring draws on my experience as a practitioner and scholar of Kurdish issues for over twenty-five years. I have been engaged in various capacities, working with the US Congress, as a US official, at think tanks, institutes, and universities. Based on my experience, Kurds are one of America's best and most reliable friends in the Middle East.

Dr. Najmaldin Karim, a Kurdish neurosurgeon from Maryland, who would become Governor of Kirkuk, visited my office in the Rayburn House Office Building in 1988. He brought gruesome photos of Kurdish civilians who perished during a chemical weapons attack in the village of Halabja. These photos depicted old men in traditional Kurdish garb sprawled in piles. Kurdish women and girls in colorful clothes and headscarves lay dead in the streets, faces twisted in anguish, foam running from their mouths, pained expressions frozen in death.

On February 27, 1991—the day the Gulf War ended—Senator Claiborne Pell, chairman of the Senate Foreign Relations Committee, invited prominent Kurds to Capitol Hill for an International Conference on the Future of Democracy in Iraq. The conference was organized by the Congressional Human Rights Foundation, which I headed. Pell opened the session, followed by Edward M. Kennedy and other senators. Congressmen Tom Lantos and John Porter, cochairmen of the Congressional Human Rights Foundation, spoke next. Pell gave me the gavel to chair the meeting. The chairman's gavel, well worn at the handle and chipped around the head, was a historic item. Handling the gavel was a reminder of my significant responsibility during the day's discussion.

President George H. W. Bush encouraged the Kurds to rebel against Saddam Hussein, but the Iraqi regime did not collapse. Bush turned a blind eye when Saddam launched a counterattack, driving more than 1.5 million Kurds across the borders of Iran and Turkey. Kurdish militia—peshmerga—tried to defend Kurds from Saddam's superior forces. The term *peshmerga* means "those who face death."

In February 1992, Jalal Talabani convened a meeting of the Patriotic Union of Kurdistan (PUK) in Sulaimani. Karim and I made the long drive from Diyarbakir in Southeast Turkey across the Habur Gate into Iraqi Kurdistan. The road was covered with a long slick of black crude. Oil drums were strapped underneath the carriages of trucks, smuggling crude in exchange for food needed in Iraqi Kurdistan.

The mood was celebratory. Saddam's forces had been expelled; Kurds enjoyed self-rule. They erupted in wild cheers when I called for freedom, democracy, and human rights (Azadi, Demokrasi, and Buji). At Masoud Barzani's meeting of the Kurdistan Democratic Party (KDP) in August 1993, I proposed that the United States establish a consulate general in Erbil. Kurds enthusiastically welcomed an "American flag in Kurdistan." The US Department of State set up a consulate in Erbil after Saddam was overthrown.

During a trip to Southeast Turkey, where most of the population is Kurdish, I was detained by Turkey's gendarmerie. The police interrogated me for travelling through Mardin, Silopi, and other towns under martial law. They wanted to know if I was in contact with the Kurdistan Worker's Party (PKK). That night, I met board members of the Diyarbakir Human Rights Association at the Caravanserai Inn on the ancient Silk Road. They described detention, torture, and the abuse of Kurds by Turkish security services. Quickly, narrative became reality. The gendarmerie was waiting outside and hustled members of the association into police vans. Diyarbakir's "super-governor" nonchalantly promised to look into the incident.

Marc Grossman, the US Ambassador to Turkey, introduced me to Dr. Dogu Ergil, chairman of the Political Science Department at Ankara State University. Ergil had recently completed a sociological survey that debunked the characterization of Kurds as separatist and militant. An overwhelming majority of Kurds rejected PKK violence, preferring to realize their goals through Turkey's continued democratization and integration into Euro-Atlantic institutions. Ergil wanted to operationalize his research through a dialogue and reconciliation project. We organized meetings of prominent Turks and Kurds at a chateau in France, a lakeside villa in Switzerland, and at a monastery in Belgium. They issued a charter, Walking Together in History, that called for political and cultural rights, and economic development.

Turkey suffered financially from sanctions imposed by the international community on Iraq after the Gulf War. Moreover, it was concerned that Iraqi Kurdistan's progress would inspire unrest among Kurds in Turkey. Ankara did not support Saddam, nor did it support foreign intervention to get rid of him, which Turkish officials feared would destabilize the region.

Toppling Saddam was a clear priority for President George W. Bush after 9/11. Ambassador William J. Burns, assistant secretary of state for Near Eastern Affairs (NEA), encouraged me to get involved in Iraq's political transition. Qubad Talabani, the PUK representative in Washington, arranged my visit to Iraqi Kurdistan in July 2002. I flew to Qamishli, a Kurdish city in Northeast Syria. In a cinder-block building on the Tigris River, a Syrian official served me tea and checked my authorization to transit from Syria to Iraq. Sure enough, my name and passport number were handwritten in his registry. Qubad provided a four-digit code: 3462. The official checked to see if the code matched his registry and issued a letter of passage.

Crossing the Tigris in a fishing boat, I could see a Kurdish flag across the river and a sign: "Welcome to Iraqi Kurdistan." Our convoy sped off to a meeting with Masoud Barzani. Kurds were developing a plan for future governance in Iraq. Their draft described "internal independence." It envisioned a federal, democratic republic of Iraq with local control of security and natural resources. The central government was assigned limited authority for border security and fiscal policy. The draft was a pit stop on the path to independence.

I briefed Burns and Ambassador Ryan C. Crocker back in Washington. NEA recruited me to join The Future of Iraq Project, an interagency effort engaging hundreds of Iraqis in planning a post-Saddam Iraq. Crocker, who served as US ambassador to Iraq from 2007 to 2009, was the point man. He asked me to assist the Democratic Principles Working Group, which Iraqis called the "mother of all working groups." It considered the most contentious issues: power sharing, resource ownership, local security, religion, and the status of Kirkuk, an oil-rich city contested by Kurds, Arabs, and Turkmen.

Neighboring states influenced events in Iraq. In 2005, Javad Zarif, Iran's Permanent Representative to the UN, invited me to address the Institute for Political and International Studies, a Foreign Ministry think tank in Tehran. I met privately with officials, intellectuals, and other Iranians working on Iraq's transition. Iranian intelligence officers hosted me at their villa to discuss Iraq's future. I presented my views on the role of Kurds in Iran and Iraq, suggesting common areas of interest between the United States and Iran.

Developments in Turkey also had a significant impact on Iraqi Kurdistan. My report, "Disarming, Demobilizing, and Reintegrating the

Kurdistan Workers Party" was published in October 2007.[1] A dialogue between Turks and Iraqi Kurds led to another report, "Confidence Building between Turks and Iraqi Kurds." In August 2009, Turkey's opposition parties held back-to-back press conferences accusing Prime Minister Recep Tayyip Erdogan of conspiring with the United States to normalize relations with Iraqi Kurdistan. They named me as the architect of America's plan to sell out Turkish interests.

Deluged with unwanted publicity, I tried to keep a low profile while writing opinion pieces in the Turkish and international media, speaking at the National Press Club and the European Parliament, and testifying at a hearing of the US House of Representatives Committee on Foreign Affairs.

The outbreak of civil war in Syria was a call to action. Kurds in Syria were targeted both by government and al-Qaeda affiliated groups. Kurds found refuge in Rojava, a patchwork of Kurdish-populated territory on Syria's border with Turkey. The State Department was struggling to establish meaningful contact with the Syrian opposition. I pitched Ambassador Robert S. Ford, the US special envoy to Syria, on a two-step process: convene Kurds from Syria to discuss governance arrangements, then broaden the circle to include other minorities. About forty Syrian Kurds attended a Paris Conference on Post-Assad Syria in March 2013. Participants described atrocities by the regime: indiscriminate shelling, scud missile, and aerial attacks. They described pressure from jihadis and foreign fighters. Participants complained about America's role, asserting that US inaction had allowed extremists to hijack the revolution.

Though the Democratic Union Party (PYD) was the leading Kurdish group in Syria, its representatives were excluded from the Paris conference. The meeting was financed by the US government's Middle East Partnership Initiative. Though the PYD is ideologically aligned with the PKK, it is not listed as a Foreign Terrorist Organization (FTO). The decision to exclude the PYD was a political decision rather than a legal requirement.

The PYD was also excluded from the Geneva peace talks in January 2014. I invited the PYD head, Salih Moslem Mohamed, to the United States, but he could not get a visa. Even if US agencies agreed, Washington would seek a green light from the Turkish government. Giving Ankara a veto of US policy was shortsighted, undermining an inclusive political settlement in Syria.

The Kurds are at a historic crossroads. This book tells their story. There are many scholars knowledgeable about Kurdish issues and the Middle East. However, few have been involved in Kurdish issues for as long as I have. Few have my experience working with Kurds across party lines and in different countries. Few have been engaged as both a scholar, activist, and as an official. These pages describe the tragic history of betrayal and abuse experienced by the Kurds. They also tell a hopeful story of progress, with Kurds poised to realize their rights and national aspirations.

David L. Phillips
New York City
October 1, 2014

Note

1. Phillips, David L. "Disarming, Demobilizing and Reintegrating the Kurdistan Workers Party." *National Committee on American Foreign Policy*. N.p., n.d. Web. 16 Feb. 2014. <https://www.ncafp.org/report-on-disarming-demobilizing-and-reintegrating-the-kurdistan-workers-party/>.

Introduction

Kurds are the largest stateless people in the world. An estimated 32 million Kurds live in what is called Kurdistan, a geographic area consisting of Turkey (North Kurdistan), Iraq (South Kurdistan), Syria (West Kurdistan), and Iran (East Kurdistan). The Kurds were divided by Western powers in the twentieth century and subjugated by Arabs, Ottomans, and Persians. According to a Kurdish proverb, "Kurds have no friend but the mountains." Today, however, Kurds are evolving from a victimized people to a coherent political community with viable national aspirations.

The Kurdish Spring is a contemporary political history, describing the struggle of Kurds for rights and statehood. It chronicles their betrayal and abuse in the twentieth century. The 1980s was a low point. In Iraq, Saddam Hussein used chemical weapons to kill up to 182,000 Iraqi Kurds, including 5,000 in a single day at Halabja; 4,500 Kurdish villages were destroyed during the Anfal Campaign between 1986 and 1988.[1] In Turkey, since 1988, 40,000 people have died as a result of conflict with the PKK. The government's aggression drove one million people from their homes but failed to drain the swamp of support for the PKK. In Syria, Kurds were denied citizenship. Punished for expressing their Kurdish identity, Syrian Kurds suffered Arabization and ethnic cleansing. Iranian Kurds, like most Iranians, were repressed and denied basic human and minority rights.

Kurds rebounded. After the Gulf War, the US-led Operation Northern Watch successfully protected Iraqi Kurds and created conditions for their return and self-rule. Iraqi Kurdistan became an island of stability, compared to other parts of Iraq where sectarianism and violence are rampant. Beginning in 2012, Turkey and the Kurdistan Regional Government (KRG) developed a strategic partnership based on common commercial and energy interests. Their rapprochement animated greater political and cultural rights for Kurds in Turkey. The Democratic Union Party (PYD), the dominant Kurdish group in Syria, tried to protect Syrian Kurds caught in the crossfire of Syria's civil war. The PYD declared autonomy in Rojava, encompassing territories in the districts of Kobane, Al-Jazeera, and Afrin. Iran is also evolving. President Hasan Rouhani has spoken about minority rights and floated the idea of allowing Kurdish-language instruction in schools. Successful negotiations on Iran's nuclear program could have the added benefit of advancing Iran's democratization and autonomy for minorities.

Iraqi Kurdistan is at the center of events in the region. It is a critical bulwark against the Islamic State (IS), which occupied a third of Iraq including parts of Iraqi Kurdistan, declared a caliphate, and established a terror state. Turkey recognized that its interests are served through a strategic partnership with Iraqi Kurdistan, which exports oil and gas via Turkey to international markets and acts as a moderate security buffer against spiraling sectarian violence in Iraq. However, Turkey proved to be a false friend.

History is being written, but its outcome is uncertain. Down the path to independence for Iraqi Kurdistan lies greater stability, democratic development, and enhanced energy flows. Down the other path lies instability and violence. As evidenced by the IS's lightening strike on Iraqi Kurdistan in July 2014, the way forward is fraught with both peril and opportunity.

Ethnicity, Culture, and Language

No accurate census data exists for Kurds. Many Kurds have a nomadic and tribal tradition in remote and rugged lands. It is estimated that 22.5 million Kurds live in Turkey.[2] Another 8 to 10 million are in Iran, 4.5 million in Iraq, and 2.5 million in Syria.[3] Kurdish refugees have migrated to Europe (over two million), Russia, and ex-Soviet states—Armenia, Georgia, and Azerbaijan (over half a million).

The Montevideo Convention of 1933 established necessary characteristics for statehood: a permanent population, a defined territory, a government, and the capacity to enter into relations with other states. Though Iraqi Kurdistan meets some of these criteria, Kurds are still organized along tribal lines. Kinship ideology defines Kurdish identity, accentuating tribal, linguistic, and religious differences.

Pious Kurds trace their roots to the Islamic General Khalid ibn al Walid, a companion of the Islamic Prophet Mohammad,[4] who conquered Iraq and Syria in the seventh century. Kurds also have lineage to Saladin, the first Sultan of Egypt and Syria, who conquered Jerusalem during the Second Crusade and negotiated a truce with King Richard the Lionheart allowing Muslim control of the Holy City.[5] It is written, "Saladin was victorious and became an Arabic hero. If Saladin had lost he would have become a Kurdish Spy."[6]

Mullah Mustafa Barzani is a unifying figure who founded the Kurdistan Democratic Party (KDP) and served as the commander of the Kurdish Republic of Mahabad in 1946. He is seen as a modern version of Saladin. As a military leader, Mustafa Barzani defended Kurds from the Iraqi and Iranian regimes until his death in 1979. The Jaffs, the largest South Kurdish tribe, live in the Zagros area between Iraq and Iran, and reach as far south as Sulaimani. Their most emblematic figure is Lady Adela Khan, known by the British as "the Princess of the Braves." She ruled a principality near Halabja at the start of the twentieth century. The Talabani group originated in Kirkuk and migrated to Koya. Its name is derived from Riza Talabani, a celebrated Kurdish poet from Sulaimani.

Jalal Talabani broke with the KDP and established the Patriotic Union of Kurdistan (PUK) in 1975. Differences exist between KDP and PUK loyalists. KDP supporters are typically more rural and conservative, with aristocratic and landlord leanings. PUK backers tend to be more urban and cosmopolitan. Erbil, the KDP's hub, is orderly and efficient. Sulaimani is more freewheeling and diverse. The Gorran movement recently emerged as a force for political reform in Iraqi Kurdistan, demonstrating diversity in Kurdish political culture. "Gorran" means change.

Language distinguishes Kurds from one another. Kurmanji predominates in North and West Kurdistan, while Sorani is spoken in South and East Kurdistan. They are the main dialects, while Zaza and Gorani are local ones. Zaza is spoken in pockets of North, South, and East Kurdistan. Gorani, and its sub-dialects—Laki and Hawrami—are spoken in the deep parts of South Kurdistan. South Kurmanji and Gorani use a Persian alphabet, whereas North Kurmanji uses a Latin alphabet. The Kurdish language belongs to the Indo-European family and is distinct from Arabic (Semitic) and Turkish (Ural-Altaic), most closely resembling Farsi.

In religious terms, 75 percent of Kurds are Sunni Muslims. Most are socially moderate and pro-Western, except for a small group of Islamist Sunni Kurds who live in the high mountains above Halabja in Iraqi Kurdistan. They established the Union of Religious Scholars, which morphed into the Islamic Movement of Kurdistan. Though the Islamic Party of Kurdistan has seats in the Kurdistan Parliament, only about 5 percent of Kurds associate themselves with the Islamic Movement.[7] The balance of Kurds includes Shia, Alevi, Sufis, Yazidi, and Christian. About 30 percent of the ten million Kurds in Iran are Shia, similar to Iran's majority. These Shia come primarily from Kermanshah, Bijar, Ilam, and Khorassan. Alevis comprise a religious group within Shia Islam. Their esoteric Sufi practice is linked to Zoroastrianism. Most Kurdish Alevis come from Dersim in Turkey's Tunceli Province. There are also Alevis villages stretching east from Bingöl to Muş, Varto, and Kars in Eastern Turkey. Yazidi Kurds are mostly Zoroastrian and have mystical tendencies.[8] An estimated quarter million Yazidis are in Iraq's Nineveh Province and across the border in Turkey. A small number of Christian Kurds are based in Armenia and have ties to the Armenian Orthodox Church. Some Christian Kurds live in villages adjoining the Christian Assyrian community. An ancient Jewish community also exists in Kurdistan, with synagogues in Erbil, Koya, Sulaimani, and Zakho.

Kurds have a long legacy of pluralism given their mixed origins. There are many differences, but Kurds draw together becoming one people when they are under duress or attack.

The Land

The Zagros mountain range is the spine of Kurdistan. Kurdish villages adorn its steppes, which gradually transform into rolling hills and the plains of Mesopotamia. Kurdistan has nine major mountains. The highest points are Mt. Alvand in Iran at 3,580 meters, Mt. Halgurd in Iraq at 3,734 meters, Mt. Munzur in Syria at 3,840 meters, and Mt. Ararat in Turkey at 5,165 meters.[9] The total area of Kurdistan is about 595,700 square kilometers, roughly equal to the size of France.[10] Kurds are a mountain people.

Temperatures fluctuate along extremes: bitter cold in the winter and very hot in the summer. Snow is the primary form of precipitation in Kurdistan. The average annual precipitation is 150–200 centimeters in the central mountain regions and 50–100 centimeters in the plains. Melting snow flows into great rivers.[11] The Euphrates River, which originates in Turkey, is augmented by the Great Zab, the Little Zab, and the Adhaim rivers before it finally joins the Euphrates River.[12] The Euphrates also originates in Turkey and then enters Syria, where it combines with the Balikh and Khabur Rivers, crosses into northwestern Iraq, winding through a scenic gorge, and joins the Tigris, creating the Shatt-al-Arab in the Persian Gulf.

Rivers are used for irrigation and hydroelectric power generation. They also supply alpine lakes, such as Lake Dukan in Iraq, Lake Urmia in Iran, and Lake Van in Turkey. Nestled beneath snow-capped peaks, these beautiful lakes are tourist destinations for Arabs seeking summer escape from the hot plains of Mesopotamia. Iraqi Kurdistan used to be thickly forested before Saddam Hussein denuded the region as part of Iraq's scorched-earth policy toward the Kurds. The KRG planted many seedlings after 1992, reforesting the region to restore its natural beauty. Pastures in the plains are also used for basic agriculture and nomadic herding.

Energy Supplies

Exploration and production of oil and gas impact Kurdish and regional relations. Energy transport is crucial to relations between Kurds and the states where they reside. Iraqi Kurdistan possesses an estimated forty-five billion barrels of recoverable oil. It ranks tenth among the world's largest oil-holding territories.[13] Its largest oilfields are Tawke, Taq Taq, and Shaikan near Kirkuk and Khaniqin. Currently, the KRG produces about two hundred thousand barrels per day (BPD).[14] A KRG-built pipeline to Turkey exported about four hundred thousand BPD in 2014. One million BPD will be exported in 2015, and two million barrels per day by 2019.[15] Iraqi Kurdistan also has gas reserves of around 110 trillion cubic feet.[16]

Turkey is Iraqi Kurdistan's largest trading partner.[17] It is a large consumer of energy supplies but only produces 6.7 percent of its total oil consumption. Oil fields in Batman and Silvan yielded only about ten million barrels in 2011, making Turkey deeply dependent on foreign suppliers. Turkey acquires about 30 percent of its oil from Iran, which has the fourth-greatest proven oil reserves worldwide. Iraq supplies 19 percent of its oil via the Kirkuk-Ceyhan pipeline. Turkey imports 98 percent of its natural gas from Iraq and Iran.[18] Syria is in a similar predicament, with only 2.5 billion barrels of proven oil reserves and a nationwide production of about 350,000 barrels per day. Reserves are split between Hassake in the far northeast, where Kurds are a majority, and Deir Ezzor to the south.[19]

Oil fields in Iranian Kurdistan at Sarpilie Zahaw, Qasr-e Shirin, and Islam Awa have great potential. Nearby natural gas fields have estimated reserves of about 260 billion square meters.[20] The government expects that sanctions relief would stimulate research and development for domestic energy supplies and facilitate transport from Iraq via Iran to the Persian Gulf. Trucks from Iraqi Kurdistan are already transporting up to 30,000 barrels per day across the border destined for Iran's Bandar Imam Khomeini terminal.[21] In 2013, the KRG and Iran announced plans to build two pipelines that will allow Iraqi Kurdistan to supply 25,000 tons of oil per day.[22]

Identity Politics

"Good Kurds" are those who do what the United States wants. "Bad Kurds" are those who do not. Kurds are rewarded for compliant behavior. Rewards are withheld when they do not comply. US officials, especially "Arabists" in the State Department, treat Kurdish issues as a minority-rights concern rather than a matter of democracy, self-determination, and justice. In this way, Kurds are often taken for granted, rather than appreciated as one of America's most important allies in the Middle East. The West has sympathy for Kurds, whose history of victimization includes being gassed, murdered, and tortured. But sympathy is no longer sufficient. Kurds increasingly resist subordinating their national aspirations to the will of the international community.

The twentieth century was a graveyard for Kurdish aspirations. The 1923 Lausanne Treaty betrayed US President Woodrow Wilson's Fourteen Points and denied the Kurds a homeland. The 1975 Algiers Accord, brokered by National Security Adviser Henry Kissinger, settled a border dispute between Iran and Iraq at the expense of Kurds. In 1991, the Kurdish uprising was spurred on by President George H. W. Bush, who abandoned the Kurds to Saddam's brutal counteroffensive.

US policy in the Middle East prioritizes stability and energy flows. The United States propped up Saddam Hussein as a bulwark against Iran. It muted criticisms of Turkey's human rights abuses and President Recep Tayyip Erdogan's authoritarianism. As the eastern flank of NATO, Turkey is a critical security partner and a valuable bridge between the West and Central Asia. Time and again, the United States found it expedient to sell out the Kurds. Caught between foreign policy pragmatists and pro-democracy ideologues, Kurds were collateral damage to more important Western interests.

President George W. Bush wanted to refashion the Middle East by ousting Saddam as the first step toward democratic transformation in the region. Though Saddam cultivated an aura of invincibility, he was easily overthrown. Saddam was found hiding in a dirt hole and executed. Bush's advisers sought solace in the Arab Spring of 2011 and 2012, believing that the Iraq War was a catalyst for pro-democracy movements. However, they did not foresee the consequences of sudden and dramatic change. Pro-democracy forces criticized the Obama administration for waiting too long to support them. US allies in the Persian Gulf had the opposite view. They were deeply concerned when President Barack Obama abandoned Egypt's Hosni Mubarak. Inaction in Syria's civil war was seen as a betrayal of American principles, and détente with Iran as naïve.

Obama delivered inspirational speeches about democracy to audiences in Istanbul and Cairo. However, America's overt participation in the Arab Spring risked discrediting local leaders. Obama's ambivalence led to charges that he was on the wrong side of history. Regimes criticized the United States for its hidden hand manipulating events, while welcoming its security assistance and diplomatic support. The Arab Spring became democracy's winter.

In today's Middle East, America has no better friend than the Kurds.[23] Instead of trying to placate its adversaries, the United States should stand with its friends. America's strategic, commercial, and security interests are advanced through solidarity with the Kurds. Its approach to the Middle East must be reality based. The map of the Middle East is changing. Rather than be passive or reactive, the United States should get in front of events and proactively manage change. It must see things as they are, not as they were, or how the West wants them to be.

Notes

1. "KRG Representation in the United Kingdom." *KRG Representation in the United Kingdom.* N.p., n.d. Web. 16 Feb. 2014. <http://uk.krg.org/genocide/pages/page.aspx?lngnr=12&smap=170000&pnr=48>.

2. "Over 22.5 million Kurds live in Turkey, new Turkish statistics reveal." *Over 22.5 million Kurds live in Turkey, new Turkish statistics reveal.* N.p., n.d. Web. 16 Feb. 2014. <http://www.ekurd.net/mismas/articles/misc2012/9/turkey4166.htm>.

3. "The Kurdish Experience. Middle East Research and Information Project." *The Kurdish Experience. Middle East Research and Information Project.* N.p., n.d. Web. 09 May 2014.

4. Mcdowell, David. "A Modern History of Kurds." *Google Books.* I.B. Tauris, 2007. Web. 09 May 2014.

5. "Medieval Sourcebook: De Expugatione Terrae Sanctae per Saladinum: Capture of Jerusalem by Saladin, 1187." *Internet History Sourcebooks Project.* N.p., n.d. Web. 16 Feb. 2014. <http://www.fordham.edu/halsall/source/1187saladin.asp>.

6. Mella, Jawad. "The Colonial Policy of the Syrian Baath Party in Western Kurdistan." *Docstoc.com.* N.p., n.d. Web. 21 May 2014.

7. "Islamic Movement of Kurdistan." *Stanford University.* N.p., n.d. Web. 16 Feb. 2014. <https://www.stanford.edu/group/mappingmilitants/cgi-bin/groups/view/25>.

8. Smith-Spark, Laura, Andrew Carey, Hamdi Alkhshali, Jason Hanna, Richard Allen Greene, and Mariano Castillo. "UK Raises Terror Threat Level, Citing Risks out of Syria, Iraq." CNN. Cable News Network, 01 Jan. 1970. Web. 10 Sept. 2014. <http://www.cnn.com/2014/08/29/world/meast/isis-iraq-syria/index.html>.

9. "Kurdistan's Geography and Climate." *Kurdistan's Geography and Climate.* N.p., n.d. Web. 9 May 2014.

10. "Kurds and Kurdistan: Facts and Figures." *Kurdish Studies, An International Journal.* N.p., n.d. Web. 16 Feb. 2014. <http://www.oswego.edu/~baloglou/anatolia/kurds.html>.

11. Ibid.

12. "Kurdistan's Geography and Climate." *Kurdistan's Geography and Climate.* N.p., n.d. Web. 9 May 2014.

13. "Kurdistan's vast reserves draw oil majors." *Financial Times.* N.p., n.d. Web. 17 Feb. 2014. <http://www.ft.com/cms/s/0/8d15816c-4929-11e2-9225-00144feab49a.html#ixzz2sZDKXdDr>.

14. "Oil majors shy away from first major Kurdish export deal." *Financial Times.* N.p., n.d. Web. 16 Feb. 2014. <http://www.ft.com/cms/s/0/429f1102-7ddf-11e3-95dd-00144feabdc0.html#axzz2tWynRziS>.

15. Briant Swint, "Kurdistan's Oil Ambitions." Bloomberg Business Week, 14 Nov. 2013.

16. "Iraqi Kurds pump oil to Turkey amid fears of new clash." *UPI.* N.p., n.d. Web. 17 Feb. 2014. <http://www.upi.com/Business_News/Energy-Resources/2013/12/19/Iraqi-Kurds-pump-oil-to-Turkey-amid-fears-of-new-clash/UPI-96341387470215/#ixzz2sZEiWzZr>.

17. "Weighing up the Kurds." *Investors Chronicle* . N.p., n.d. Web. 16 Feb. 2014. <http://www.investorschronicle.co.uk/2014/01/22/shares/news-and-analysis/weighing-up-the-kurds-CFOMjwmY9uREOzJlMDL0eN/article.html>.

18. International Energy Administration. 2013 Oil and Gas Security.

19. Josh Wood, "Syria's oil resources are a source of contention for competing groups." The New York Times. 13 March 2013.

20. "Kurdistan Region-Iraq News in brief. November 22, 2013." *Kurdistan Region-Iraq News in brief. November 22, 2013.* N.p., n.d. Web. 17 Feb. 2014. <http://www.ekurd.net/mismas/articles/misc2013/11/kurdlocal1436.htm>.

21. "Kurdistan Opens Oil Trade Route via Iran | Iraq Business News." *Kurdistan Opens Oil Trade Route via Iran | Iraq Business News.* N.p., n.d. Web. 17 Feb. 2014. <http://www.iraq-businessnews.com/2013/08/11/kurdistan-opens-oil-trade-route-via-iran/>.

22. Seal, S. "Two Oil Pipelines Will Soon Connect Iraqi Kurdistan and Iran." *Two oil pipelines will soon connect Iraqi Kurdistan and Iran.* Dailt Sabeh. 10 May 2014. Web. 15 May 2014. <http://www. Iraqdirectory.com/en/2014/05/10/27093/two-oil-pipelines-will-soon-connect-iraqi-kurdistan-and-iran.aspx>.

23. Israel is an exception.

Part One

1

Betrayal

The twentieth century was a period of false promises, betrayal, and abuse for Kurds. The Kurds had national aspirations as the Ottoman Empire started to wane. They sought political support and protection from the Great Powers. Promises were made, but Kurds were ultimately abandoned. Hopes dashed, Kurds rebelled and were suppressed, their political rights and cultural identity brutally denied.

End of the Ottoman Empire

The Ottoman Empire reached its zenith in 1453 with the conquest of Constantinople by Sultan Mehmed II. Its peak continued until the late sixteenth century under the sons of Suleiman Kanuni ("the Magnificent").[1] Yavuz Selim seized the Holy Cities in 1517, legitimizing the Ottoman Sultan as a caliph, a head of state. As the Ottoman Empire expanded, it created the millet system to manage relations with Christian and other minorities.[2] "Millet" is derived from the Arabic word meaning "nation." This system bestowed religious freedom on religious minorities as long as they swore fealty and paid taxes to Constantinople ("The Porte"). To manage its far-flung territories, the millet system allowed a degree of decentralization, feeding the empire's coffers and ensuring stability. The millet system also allowed self-rule for ethnic minorities, who flourished under Ottoman rule. Many of the sultan's viziers were ethnic Greeks, Arabs, or Persians.

The sultan was called "the shadow of God on earth." He held absolute power.[3] During the sixteenth and seventeenth centuries, especially during the rule of Suleiman the Magnificent, the Ottoman Empire expanded and prospered. The Porte extended control from Southeast Europe into Central Asia and Mesopotamia. It ruled from the Caucasus on the North Black Sea coast to the Maghreb and the Horn of Africa. The string of conquests ended with defeat at the Battle of Vienna in 1683. The Treaty of Karlowitz in 1699 ceded large swaths of territory in

Central Europe. After centuries of successful expansion by the Ottoman Empire, a period of retrenchment and stagnation ensued.

Sultan Mahmud II, followed by his son Abdulmecid, tried to stem the Ottoman Empire's decline, initiating Tanzimat reforms through the Imperial Decree of Gulhane in 1839.[4] "Tanzimat" means reorganization. Tanzimat reforms were a response to nationalist movements, including demands of the Kurds. The 1856 Reform Decree was intended to provide modern citizenship rights. It sought to enhance Ottomanism by requiring submission to a single code of laws—in effect centralizing power. The Porte thought that Tanzimat would restore the loyalties of Greeks, Armenians, and Kurds. It also believed that modernization would deter European powers from trying to interfere in the Ottoman Empire's internal affairs. However, Tanzimat did not deter Europe's meddling or enhance the loyalty of groups under the millet system, which included the Kurds. Instead of fostering loyalty and coherence, it fueled dissent. Kurds, Greeks, Serbs, and Russian-backed Armenians rebelled.[5]

During the Russo-Turkish War of 1828–29, the fourth of seven wars between the Ottoman and Russian empires, the Kurds initially acted as a bulwark against Russian expansionism. Bedr Khan Beg, a Kurdish tribal leader and emir from Djazireh, was a powerful hereditary feudal chieftain of the Bokhti tribe. Since the fourteenth century, his clan enjoyed uninterrupted rule of Cizre-Botan, a wealthy and prosperous emirate. He was given the title of "Pasha," in recognition of his contributions to the empire and his help fighting Armenians.[6] But Bedr Khan rebelled against the Porte, demanding an independent Kurdistan in 1834. He organized Kurdish tribes into a disciplined army and struck an alliance with the chieftains of Kars in North Kurdistan and with Emir Ardelan in Eastern Kurdistan. Bedr Khan established control over a large part of Ottoman Kurdistan by 1840.

The Ottoman army launched a counterattack. English and American missionaries turned the Christian tribes against Bedr Khan. In 1847, Osman Pasha persuaded Yezdan Sher, Bedr Khan's nephew, to join the Ottoman side. With the eastern flank exposed, Bedr Khan fled Djazireh for the more easily defensible fortress of Eruh. He was finally defeated, exiled to Crete in 1850, and died in Damascus in 1868.[7]

The Ottoman Empire was challenged again during the Russo-Turkish War of 1877–78. The Porte faced a growing insurrection by Armenians. Sheik Ubeydullah, a member of the powerful Kurdish Semdinan clan, took advantage of the empire's diverted attention. He declared an independent Kurdish principality and demand recognition by both the Porte and Persia's Qajar dynasty.[8] Initially, the Ottomans supported Sheik Ubeydullah, who stood against Armenian separatists fighting for independence. But the Porte reversed its stance in 1880, violently suppressing Sheik Ubeydullah's bid for self-rule.[9] In response to the rise of Armenian Committees, it recruited irregular Kurdish militias to fight Armenian pro-independence groups beginning in 1891. The Kurdish cavalry was called "Hamidieh," after Sultan Abd-ul-Hamid II. Under instructions from the Porte, the Hamidieh took an active part in the massacre of Armenians at Sasun and other Armenian-populated villayets between 1894 and 1896. Kurds sought regional autonomy in exchange for their service, demanding the appointment of Kurdish-speaking officials and the use of the Kurdish language in local government and education systems. They also sought the right to practice Shari'a and customary law.

Russia played a double game. It supported both Armenian and Kurdish nationalism, as part of its strategy to diminish the Ottoman Empire. In fact, Moscow did not want either an independent Armenia or Kurdistan. It had its own expansionist designs on Eastern Anatolia. The young Turks who seized power in 1908, targeted populations they thought were sympathetic with Russia. Armenians and other Christian communities were suspected of treason or espionage and deported. Kurds were allowed to take over Armenian properties. Enver, Cemal, and Talat Pasha—the so-called "three pashas" who led the Committee of Union and Progress (CUP)—issued orders in support of the Armenian Genocide.[10]

Empire's End

World War I marked the end of the Austria-Hungarian and the Ottoman Empires. The Russian Empire also collapsed through pressure from Bolsheviks, which led to the abdication of Czar Nicholas II. During the early twentieth century, ethno-nationalism replaced allegiance to distant monarchs. "Kurdish nationalism was the illegitimate child of Turkish nationalism."[11]

Istanbul entered into a secret alliance with Germany in August of 1914. It joined the Central Powers, Germany and the Austria-Hungarian Empire, against the Allies—France, Britain, and Russia, who were joined by Japan and the United States.[12] Washington entered the war in April 1917, after the German practice of unrestricted submarine warfare sunk merchant ships with Americans on board. Turkish forces engaged on multiple fronts. They fought Greeks, Assyrians, and Armenians in Asia Minor. Turkish forces engaged the Russian Army in the Caucasus. Turkish forces were also in the East. They launched a Sinai offensive, challenging Britain's control of the Suez Canal and its holdings in South Asia.

The tide turned against the Turkish army after initial victories. Russia fought fiercely, despite the gathering storm of its civil war. In June 1916, Britain instigated Arab tribes to revolt. British forces conquered Damascus, Mecca, and Medina after a two-year siege. They captured Palestine in January 1917, Baghdad and Mesopotamia in March 1918. Finally, the Kirkuk garrison surrendered in May 1918. All Arab-populated regions of the Ottoman Empire, including Mosul, had succumbed to British or French forces.

Final defeat of the Ottoman Empire was enshrined with the Mundros Armistice of October 30, 1918. The CUP cabinet resigned; Enver, Cemal, and Talat Pasha fled the country on November 7. Mundros marked the Ottoman Empire's humiliating and unconditional surrender. The Allies established the right to occupy any area of the empire. The Straits, the Dardanelles, and the Bosphorus were opened to Allied warships, allowing control over transportation and maritime activity. Except for the gendarmerie, all Ottoman forces were demobilized. Food, coal, and other materials were relinquished to the Allies. Ottoman finances were subject to regulation by an Allied commission, with a portion of revenues dedicated for reparations.[13] Mundros made allowances for Armenians, Georgians, and Azerbaijanis.[14] Ottoman security forces, including the gendarmerie, were removed from the six Armenian-populated eastern provinces. All detained Armenians were immediately released.[15]

Britain developed a plan for administering the Kurdistan region. British officers with extensive experience in Kurdish affairs, E. B. Sloane and E.W.C. Noel, initiated talks with local Kurdish leaders. They recommended the establishment of a British-sponsored Kurdish tribal council to Britain's High Commissioner in Baghdad, Sir Percy Cox. He endorsed the proposal to Britain's Foreign Office on October 30, 1918. Cox went even further, proposing the establishment of a Kurdish state in South and West Kurdistan. Kurds were unified, for the moment, motivated by fear of punishment for crimes they committed against Armenians and Assyrians. However, divisions between Kurdish leaders soon surfaced. Throughout late 1919 and most of the following year, British troops were engaged on the Northern frontiers of Mesopotamia. Revolts flared up everywhere. Some were inspired by the Turks in an attempt to drive

British troops out of the Mosul area. Some were simply a reaction by Kurds to the imposition of yet another outside authority.[16]

Cox's recommendation was entirely consistent with Britain's practice of arbitrary decisions impacting peoples in the region. With the war still underway, Sir Mark Sykes of Britain and George Picot of France started secret negotiations in November 1915. The Sykes-Picot Agreement, officially called the Asia Minor Agreement, was finalized on May 16, 1916. The accord divided Ottoman Asia into British and French zones of influence. The Baghdad and Basra villayets were assigned to Britain. Sykes-Picot assigned the Mosul villayet to France.[17] Kurds received no favor. Britain and France viewed them as peoples subject to exploitation by Great Powers.

The Fourteen Points

US President Woodrow Wilson's progressive ideas for self-determination and free trade were published as "Fourteen Points" on January 8, 1918, during the final year of World War I. It was a detailed legal treatise and statement of principles based on research by a team of 150 advisers led by Wilson's counselor, Edward M. House. Wilson's egalitarian worldview was a dramatic departure from Sykes-Picot. The Points were directed to multiple audiences, including the German government and people. Wilson was the first head of state to address a global audience through radio transmission. Hard copies of his speech were also dropped behind enemy lines. Wilson sought support from the Allies for his vision, as well as establishment of the League of Nations. He also sought to persuade a skeptical US domestic audience of the need for America's robust role in world affairs.

Eight of Wilson's Fourteen Points addressed territorial issues. Five of the Fourteen Points addressed human rights and democratic principles, including the right to self-determination. Point Five called for "A free, open-minded, and absolutely impartial adjustment of all colonial claims, based upon a strict observance of the principle that in determining all such questions of sovereignty the interests of the populations concerned must have equal weight with the equitable claims of the government whose title is to be determined."[18] Point Ten maintained, "The peoples of Austria-Hungary, whose place among the nations we wish to see safeguarded and assured, should be accorded the freest opportunity of autonomous development."[19] According to Point Twelve, "The Turkish portions of the present Ottoman Empire should be assured a secure sovereignty, but other nationalities which are now under Turkish rule should be assured an undoubted security of life and an absolutely unmolested opportunity of autonomous development."[20] Point Fourteen proposed the creation of the League of Nations to ensure "Political independence and territorial integrity [of] great and small states alike."[21]

Wilson addressed a joint session of the US Congress on February 11, 1918. "Peoples and provinces are not to be bartered about from sovereignty to sovereignty as if they were mere chattels and pawns in a game, even the great game, now forever discredited."[22] He continued, "Peoples may not be dominated and governed only by their own consent. 'Self-determination' is not a mere phrase. It is an imperative principle of actions which statesmen will henceforth ignore at their peril."[23] Wilson repudiated Sykes-Picot, stating, "Every territorial settlement involved in this war must be made in the interest and for the benefit of the populations concerned, and not as a part of any mere adjustment or compromise of claims amongst rival states."[24] He also addressed Germany with both threat and promise:

> For such arrangements and covenants we are willing to fight and to continue to fight until they are achieved; but only because we wish the right to prevail and desire a just and stable peace such as can be secured only by removing the chief provocations to war, which this program does remove. We have no jealousy of German greatness, and there is nothing in this program that impairs it. We grudge her no achievement or distinction of learning or of pacific enterprise. We do not wish to injure her or to block in any way her legitimate influence or power. We do not wish to fight her either with arms or with hostile arrangements of trade if she is willing to associate herself with us and the other peace-loving nations of the world in covenants of justice and law and fair dealing. We wish her only to accept a place of equality among the peoples of the world – the new world in which we now live—instead of a place of mastery."[25] The Fourteen Points became the basis for German armistice and surrender, as negotiated in the Paris Peace Conference of 1919.

Wilson's Fourteen Points surprised the Allies. There was no coordination or prior consultation. France's foreign minister, George Clemenceau, cynically responded, "Even the good Lord contented Himself with only Ten Commandments, and we should not try to improve upon them."[26] France finally concluded that her priorities could be advanced through cooperation with the United States and accepted the Fourteen Points on November 1, 1918.

Britain also had a tepid response. Britain's foreign secretary, Lord Arthur Balfour, was concerned that Wilson's idealistic support for self-determination could hinder its territorial ambitions and mercantile interests. Moreover, Britain wanted the Fourteen Points to endorse reparation payments for damage during the war. Britain would later agree to all points except freedom of the seas. German Chancellor Count von Hertling welcomed Wilson's proposals in remarks to the Reichstag. However, Von Hertling qualified his support, insisting that Germany's presence in Belgium and Alsace-Lorraine should be negotiated.[27] Balfour scorned von Hertling's "lip service" to Wilson's proposals.[28] "There is no question of Alsace-Lorraine to go before a peace conference."[29] Wilson's Fourteen Points set the stage for the armistice of Villa Giusti between Italy and the Austria-Hungarian Empire on November 3, 1918.[30] Turks focused on their own self-determination, not those of minorities and other groups. Self-determination meant sovereignty over territories they retained at the war's end.

Wilson also had to address a war-weary public in the United States. There were 320,174 casualties from the war, including 116,628 deaths.[31] In financial terms, the war cost $32 billion.[32] All told, nine million people died. The Republican Party had a strong isolationist platform. Republicans scorned Wilson's vision of the world, and America's role in it.

Beyond his tangible accomplishments, Wilson was heralded for his commitment to "the principle of justice to all peoples and nationalities and their right to live on equal terms of liberty and safety with one another, whether they be strong or weak."[33] The Nobel Committee awarded him the Nobel Prize for Peace in 1919.

The Paris Peace Conference

World leaders convened to establish the terms for peace after World War I and, in the process, to redraw the map of Europe and the Middle East. The conference was held at Versailles, just outside of Paris. It lasted six months, from January to July of 1919. Thirty nations attended, but discussions were dominated by the Big Four: Britain, France, Italy, and the United States. Prime Minister David Lloyd George represented Britain, along with notables including Sir Winston Churchill and economist John Maynard Keynes. George Clemenceau represented France, and Prime Minister Vittorio Orlando represented Italy. Russia was invited, but its new Bolshevik government declined to attend. The vanquished Central Powers—Germany, Austria-Hungary, Turkey, and Bulgaria—were not invited. There were two

Turkish administrations at that time: the Sultanate in Istanbul and the national parliament in Ankara. Neither was included.

Wilson headed the US delegation, but he fell ill at the outset. As the host, and with Wilson at half mast, Clemenceau asserted a dominant role. He was a formidable figure who thought that self-determination was far less important than reparations and justice. France was pragmatic, less interested in high-minded principles than recovering its losses from the war. Specifically, Clemenceau sought security guarantees and territories. He also demanded a guilt clause assigning full responsibility to Germany for the war and establishing the principle of reparations by Germany to the Allies.

Nations aspiring to statehood were invited to make their case at the Paris Peace Conference. Lawrence of Arabia attended as a member of the Arab delegation. Ho Chi-Minh petitioned the conference to give independence to Vietnam. Kurds were also represented. However, they disagreed over demarcation of the political and administrative boundaries of Kurdish territories. Kurds were also divided on lines of their national aspiration. Some sought an independent Kurdistan. Others wanted a place in Turkey, which was envisioned as a rump state of the Ottoman Empire. They viewed inclusion in Turkey as a vehicle for achieving equal citizenship as a part of the Muslim majority. Another group emphasized the need for protection from Great Powers, regardless of demarcation. Overall, Kurds failed to articulate a clear vision for the future, nor were they able to organize a credible leadership delegation at the Paris Peace Conference. Kurdish local chiefs pursued local interests rather than a broad national vision.

Şerif Pasha attended on behalf of the Istanbul-based Society for the Ascension of Kurdistan (KTJ). He proposed boundaries for North Kurdistan: "The frontiers of Turkish Kurdistan, from an ethnographical point of view, begin in the north at Ziven, on the Caucasian frontier, and continue westwards to Erzurum, Erzincan, Kemah, Arapgir, Besni, and Divick; in the south they follow the line from Harran, the Sinjihar Hills, Tel Asfar, Erbil, Sulaimani, Akk-el-man, Sinne; in the east, Ravandiz, Başkale, Vezirkale, that is to say the frontier of Persia as far as Mount Ararat."[34] Some Kurds objected to Pasha's demarcation, demanding more territory. Emin Ali Bedirhan, head of a hardline faction of the KTJ, proposed an alternative map that included Van and sea access.[35] Factions debated independence versus autonomy. Serif Pasha strongly supported the creation of an autonomous Turkish Kurdistan. The Bedirhan faction demanded independence. It condemned Şerif Pasha's concessions, demanding his resignation and the dismissal of KTJ's president, Seyyid Abdulkadir. Amidst intense acrimony, Serif Pasha resigned. His departure meant there was no Kurdish representation at the Paris Peace Conference. Seyyid Abdulkadir sent a cable reserving the right to protest any decision affecting Kurds.

Kurdish-Armenian relations were also contentious, especially in light of the role played by Kurds in the expulsion and killing of Armenians. Kurds demanded control of ancient Armenian centers Agri and Mus, while accepting Armenian claims to the Erzurum villayet and Sasun.[36] Despite stark differences between the Kurds and Armenians, they managed to reach consensus and issue a joint statement.

Turks deeply resented the break-up of Ottoman territories. The Fourteen Points became the basis for German armistice and surrender, as negotiated in the Paris Peace Conference of 1919,

> The Society for the Defense of the Rights of Eastern Anatolia convened a two-week meeting in Erzerum on July 23, 1919. The society issued a declaration affirming that the six eastern villayets were an inviolable part of the Ottoman Empire and should remain a constituent part of Turkey. Article VI rejected "dividing lands and separating peoples who are within the boundaries established by the armistice signed by the Allies on October 30, 1918 and in eastern Anatolia, as well as in other regions, inhabited by a majority of Muslims and dominated by Muslims culturally and economically."[37]

Most Kurds did not want Kurdistan to fall within Turkey. While rejecting Turkish rule, Kurds also rejected the division of Kurdistan into British and French zones of influence. But after four long years of war, Britain lacked the troops, resources, and political will to establish Kurdistan as a unified territory and single protectorate under its control. It only wanted to retain Mesopotamia, present-day Iraq. Kurds had no good options. In one scenario, Kurds would have autonomy within Turkey. In the other, Kurdistan would be divided between Britain and France. A federation of Kurdish territories was also considered. Either way, Kurds were looking at a partition. Britain and France offered no alternative vision to Sykes-Picot.

Negotiations at the Paris Peace Conference did not occur in a vacuum. They were affected by events on the ground, beyond the control of negotiators. The Allies occupied Istanbul on March 16, 1919. Italian forces landed at Antalya on March 28, 1919. Greek forces landed at Smyrna in May of 1919, initiating the Greco-Turkish War (1919–1922). These attacks precipitated Turkey's War of Independence.

Mustafa Kermal Ataturk, the founder and first president of the Republic of Turkey, issued the Sivas Declaration in September of 1919.[38] The Sivas Declaration was a statement of nationalist principles that took direct aim at Kurdish separatists. It affirmed plans for a unified Turkey. Sivas endorsed measures to limit Kurdish political and cultural identity. When Kurds sought to establish a Kurdish Democratic Party, Ataturk denied the party's registration. Kurds were arrested and executed for secessionist activities. While confronting Kurds, Ataturk was also trying to entice them with appeals for Muslim solidarity. He cynically drew parallels between the killing of Muslims by Greeks in Smyrna and conflict between Muslim Kurds and Armenians in eastern Anatolia.

The Treaty of Sevres

The Treaty of Versailles was finalized on June 28 and published on October 21, 1919. Versailles reconfigured the map of Europe, creating nine new states: Poland, Finland, Austria, Hungary, Czechoslovakia, Yugoslavia, Estonia, Latvia, and Lithuania. In addition, Versailles divided the Middle East into zones of influence, as envisioned by Sykes-Picot. The Baghdad and Basra villayets were assigned to Britain; Britain took Transjordan, Palestine, and what are now Iraq and Kuwait. France gave up the Mosul villayet and took what are now Syria and Lebanon. The United States was offered a mandate over the Kurds, but Wilson declined the responsibility. He did not want the United States to become a colonial power in the Middle East. Dealing with the Kurdish question was deferred to future negotiations between Britain and France. The League of Nations was envisioned as an international collective security arrangement intended to prevent future wars and handle matters of international justice.

The treaty sowed the seeds of future conflict by subjugating Germany and depriving it of assets for reconstruction. Article 231, the "war guilt clause," established Germany's responsibility for World War I and enshrined the principle of reparations. The Supreme Council of the Principal Allied Powers—Great Britain, France, and Italy—met in Italy at San Remo in April of 1920. The San Remo Conference was an opportunity to achieve a unified position on the disposition of Ottoman territories and the terms of a peace treaty with Turkey. Ataturk insisted that the Allies negotiate only with Ankara, not the Ottoman Sultanate. On April 23, 1920, Ataturk abolished the Ottoman sultanate, declared Ankara as the capital of a new Turkish state, and convened the Turkish Grand National Assembly (TGNA).[39]

Kurds wanted a voice in negotiations. The KTJ sent a memorandum to delegates of the San Remo Conference demanding independence for Kurdistan. In an attempt to preempt the possible extension of Armenia's boundaries, its annex included a map of Kurdistan.[40] The Allies agreed on a process to address the Kurdish question. "A Commission appointed by the British, French and Italian Governments" was authorized to develop "a scheme of local autonomy for the predominantly Kurdish areas, east of the Euphrates, south of the boundary of Armenia, north of the northern frontier of Syria, and Mesopotamia." They agreed that Kurds should be given the right to appeal for independence to the League of Nations within one year and that the Mosul villayet would adhere to Kurdistan in the event of independence.[41] The accord was presented as a fait accompli to Ottoman representatives on May 11, 1920.

The treaty's first section included notable details. Article 62 stated:

> A Commission sitting at Constantinople and composed of three members appointed by the British, French and Italian Governments respectively shall draft a scheme within six months of the present Treaty's coming into force of local autonomy for the predominantly Kurdish areas lying east of the Euphrates, south of Armenia as it may be determined hereafter, and north of the frontier of Turkey with Syria and Mesopotamia.[42]

It envisioned Kharput, Dersim, Hakkari, and Siirt lying within Kurdistan, and Diyarbakir as Kurdistan's capital. Kurdish-populated territories west of the Euphrates, such as Adiyaman, Malatya, Elbistan, Darende and Divrik, were assigned to a French zone of interest.

Article 63 issued: "The Turkish Government hereby agrees to accept and execute the decisions of both Commissions mentioned in Article 62 within three months from their communication to the said Government."[43] Article 64 further worked out terms:

> If within one year of the present Treaty's coming into force, the Kurdish peoples within the areas defined in Article 62 shall address themselves to the Council of the League of Nations in such a manner so as to show that the majority of the population of these areas desire independence from Turkey. If the Council then considers these people's capability of such independence and recommends that it should be granted to them, Turkey hereby agrees to execute such a recommendation, and to renounce all rights and title over these areas. If and when such a renunciation takes place, no objection will be raised by the Principal Allied Powers to the voluntary adhesion to

such an independent Kurdish state of the Kurds inhabiting that part of Kurdistan which has hitherto been included in the Mosul villayet.[44]

The thorny issue of Armenia's frontier with Kurdistan was deferred. A demarcation commission was also planned to establish the frontier between Kurdistan and Persia. Lastly, Article 89 stipulated:

> Turkey, Armenia and the other signatories agree that the frontier between Armenia and Turkey in the villayets of Erzurum, Trebizonde, Van, and Bitlis be subject to the arbitration of the President of the United States. They agree to accept his decision and any measures he might recommend concerning Armenia's access to the sea and the demilitarization of any Ottoman territories adjacent to the said frontier.[45]

Sevres recognized the multiethnic character of Kurdistan. The treaty included a clause guaranteeing the protection of racial and religious minorities, with specific reference to Chaldo-Assyrians. Sevres did not, however, offer a specific definition of minority rights in the form of self-government, control of natural resources, or cultural rights such as use of minority languages.[46]

The Treaty of Sevres was signed on August 10, 1920. It officially abolished the Ottoman Empire. Sevres required that Turkey renounce all claims to territories in Arab Asia and North Africa. Greece was given control of Eastern Thrace, the Aegean Islands, and the west coast of Anatolia. The rump of Anatolia was all that remained for Turkey.

Rejection

The Treaty of Sevres was negotiated with representatives of Farid Pasha, who was installed as vizier by Britain in March 1919. Ataturk mocked him as a "prisoner of the allies, rejecting his authority to negotiate on behalf of Turkey." Sevres was signed by Pasha's proxies, Minister Resid Halis, Ambassador Hadi Pasha, Riza Tevfik, and Damad Ferid Pasha. Ataturk immediately denounced Sevres, and used it to animate the War of Independence.

The National Pact, also known as the National Oath was declared during the last session of the Ottoman parliament, on January 28, 1920.[47] It expanded on declarations of the Erzurum Congress and the Sivas Congress, affirming Turkey's sovereignty and self-determination. It demanded independence from the Great Powers and control of all non-Arab territories. "The territories of the Ottoman Empire, excluding countries inhabited by an Arab majority, which, in accordance with the declarations of the Allied Powers will be called upon to exercise their right to self-government, form an indivisible whole. Turkey must enjoy in these territories full sovereign rights, primary conditions for the existence and the development of every independent state."

It consisted of six points. Article one was a repudiation of Britain's control of Mesopotamia and a direct challenge to the postwar order that was being orchestrated by the Allies. Article two rejected the creation of an independent Armenian state under American mandate in northeastern Anatolia. Article three repudiated Greek claims. Article four challenged Britain's demands for maritime control of the Straits. Article five asserted the rights of Muslim minorities, alongside the rights of Christians. Finally, Article six rejected occupation in all its forms. Ataturk declared, "It is the nation's iron fist that writes the Nation's Oath which is the main principle of our independence to the annals of history."[48]

The National Oath reflected facts on the ground. Ataturk's forces rolled up victories on the battlefield. They repelled the Greek army in Western Anatolia and Eastern Thrace, massacring civilians and turning Smyrna to ashes. General Ismet Inonu declared final victory over the Greek army in January 1921. Ataturk's forces targeted Armenian bands, recapturing Kars and other lands on the north coast of the Black Sea and Far West that had been lost to Russia in 1877. Ankara and the Bolsheviks, who had consolidated control in Russia, signed a Treaty of Friendship in March 1921.

France and Britain could no longer ignore Turkey's nationalist agenda or its battlefield victories. They faced a fork in the road. Either France would commit a huge force to defend Cilicia and retain its holdings, or she would abandon Sevres and negotiate a new treaty accommodating Turkish nationalism. Britain's envoy, Sir M. Cheetham, wrote to the Marques Curzon of Keddleston:

> The Treaty of Sevres is no longer practicable in view of the enormous military and financial burdens involved. . . . France must choose between continued latent hostility with Turkey—in which case it would be better to finish the matter at once by a war—and resumption of former friendly relations; in the latter case, frontier questions would become of secondary importance and Syrian question would no longer exist.[49]

The Allies invited both the Ottoman and Ankara governments to discuss options for revising the Treaty of Sevres to the London

Conference, which started on February 21, 1921. A delegation from Greece was also invited. Bekir Sami Kunduh, the first Turkish minister of foreign affairs, headed the delegation from Ankara. Rejecting participation by Ottoman representatives from Istanbul, he demanded recognition of Turkey's independence. Bekir Sami Kunduh repudiated Sevres, reaffirming principles of the National Pact. "The populations of Kurdistan possessed complete representation in the Grand National Assembly. The Kurds had always proclaimed that they constituted an indivisible whole with Turkey. The two races [Kurds and Turks] were united by a common feeling, a common culture and a common religion." Only a "small committee" of Kurds sought sovereignty, and this minority "in no way represented the populations for whom they claimed to speak."[50]

Meanwhile, French envoys were engaged in secret negotiations with Ankara. Talks concluded with the Franklin-Bouillion Accord, otherwise known as the Ankara Agreement, on October 20, 1921. Franklin-Bouillon was a material and strategic victory for Ataturk. Except for Syria, France effectively relinquished its claims to Ottoman Lands. Turkey gained Cilicia and other parts of northern Syria, such as Nusaybin and Jazira bin Umar. Bilateral negotiations culminating in the accord also provided Ataturk's Ankara-based government with legitimacy and international recognition.[51]

Later, on March 16, 1921, the Treaty of Moscow was signed between the TGNA and Bolshevik Russia. The treaty defined Turkey's borders, as well as the borders of Georgia, Armenia, and Azerbaijan. Commitments were reaffirmed by the Treaty of Kars of October 13, 1921. These treaties refute Turkish claims that Armenia seeks to establish "Greater Armenia."

Turkish troops redeployed along the border with Mesopotamia, freed from the battlefield with France in Cilicia and with Russia on the Black Sea coast. By 1922, Britain was losing confidence in Sevres, and reconsidering its commitment to the Kurds. Hashemite King Faysal I feared that Iraqi Kurds would join their fellows in Turkey and Persia to challenge Iraq. Faysal also wanted to include Kurds in Iraq to ensure a Sunni majority in the Assembly. Cox endorsed Faysal's recommendations to Winston Churchill, Britain's colonial secretary.[52]

Peace with Turkey would require giving Ankara control of Northern Kurdistan. Doing so would narrow Britain's options in Mesopotamia. Britain could not credibly sponsor an independent Kurdish entity in Southern Kurdistan, while abandoning other parts of Kurdistan to

Turkey. Lord Arthur Balfour was also concerned about the lack of unity and political organization among Kurds. According to Balfour, "The question of the wording of this article [Article 64] has already been raised by the Turkish delegates in the course of the Conference here, and that there is a possibility of the article being modified in such a way as to omit all mention of a future independent Kurdish state and therefore of the right of the Kurds of Southern Kurdistan [within the frontier of Mesopotamia] to join such a state."[53]

Halil Bedirhan turned to Percy Cox. He requested weapons for an armed rebellion in Dersim, Diyarbakir, Bitlis, and Van. "We are heart and soul pro-British," maintained Bedirhan. "We want a British Mandate, and if Britain will assist us we on our part will be her buffer state between her Iraq and her enemies in Russia and Turkey." Cox suggested to Churchill that, in the event that talks with Turkey failed, Britain would be "justified in seeking other means to secure what is vital to our existence—in other words, supporting Kurdish nationalists against the Kemalists."[54] Cox's suggestion was firmly rejected. Britain's coffers had been drained by the war. The British public was tired of conflict and averse to new entanglements in the Middle East.

The Treaty of Lausanne

Armed resistance cells, called Defense of Rights Committees, were the core of a broader Turkish National Movement. In 1920–1921, Ataturk consolidated power in Anatolia and Northern Kurdistan, setting the stage for negotiations. By the time delegations met in Lausanne, Switzerland, Ataturk had succeeded in marginalizing the Ottoman sultanate in Istanbul and was the sole representative of Turkey. Ataturk also gained leverage over Britain and France through the Chanak Crisis of September 1922. Ataturk threatened to attack British and French troops guarding the Dardanelles, the strait linking the Sea of Marmara with the Aegean Sea. A military standoff ensued. Prime Minister David Lloyd George resigned in humiliation, giving way to a new government. The Chanak incident made clear the limits of Britain and France. The Allies were victors of World War I. However, Britain and France wanted to avoid a renewed conflict with Turkey. They would not fight to enforce the Treaty of Sevres.

The TGNA sent a delegation to Lausanne headed by Foreign Minister Ismet Pasha. Lord Curzon chaired the conference. His opening remarks asserted Britain's control of the Mosul villayet. Curzon's claim was a flashpoint. Curzon and Ismet Pasha clashed repeatedly over the Eastern question. With Britain and Turkey maintaining intractable positions, the Lausanne conference agreed to establish a special commission on territorial issues.

Relinquishing the Mosul villayet was a non-starter, but Kurds in other areas were expendable. Cox suggested,

> It might considerably ease the frontier negotiations if we could give preliminary official pledge to Turkey that in the changed circumstances we have abandoned the idea of Kurdish autonomy included in the Treaty of Sevres, and that our aim is to incorporate in Iraq as far as may be feasible under normal Iraqi administration all the Kurdish areas which may fall on the Mosul side of the frontier as the result of the negotiations.[55]

Even with Britain showing flexibility on Kurdistan's autonomy, the two sides were at an impasse over the Mosul villayet. With negotiations deadlocked over the status of Mosul, Britain proposed arbitration by the League of Nations. Turkey opposed involvement by the League, fearing it would get short shrift. Not only was Turkey not a member of the League, Sir Eric Drummond, a British diplomat, was secretary-general of the League of Nations. Turkey rejected arbitration by the world body, proposing a plebiscite instead.

Britain conspired with Faysal, the leader of the 1916 Arab Revolt, to arrange an uprising of Kurdish tribes along the Turkish border. A security crisis would underscore the antipathy of Kurds to rule by Ankara. Ataturk's unflinching commitment to secularism undermined previous appeals of pan-Islamism against British rule. With Kurds in rebellion, Curzon enlisted the help of French Prime Minister Raymond Poincaré. Curzon pointed to Kurdish unrest, warning Poincaré that renewed hostilities in Iraq risked undermining existing agreements between France and Turkey, as well as negotiations in Lausanne. Poincaré urged Ismet Pasha to accept Curzon's proposal, which included a demarcation process confirming the so-called Brussels Line that divided the Mosul villayet from Turkey's border. Ismet Pasha refused to cede Southern Kurdistan, but agreed to refer the Mosul question to the League of Nations.

The second session of the Lausanne Conference ended on July 24, 1923. Lausanne was the product of negotiations, as opposed to Sevres, which was imposed. Turkey signed the Lausanne Treaty on one side. On the other side it was signed by Britain, France, Italy, Japan, Greece, Romania, and the Kingdom of Serbs, Croats, and Slovenes. The Allies recognized Turkey within its current frontiers, abandoning the idea of an independent Armenian state. Turkey surrendered its claims to former Arab provinces, including Libya, Sudan, and Egypt. Britain was awarded Cyprus.[56] Italy was given possession of the Dodecanese Islands.[57] The Dardanelles were declared free and open to commercial maritime activities.[58] Lausanne enshrined the rights of religious and ethnic minority rights, assuring local administration and local police (Article 13); freedom of religion (Article 38); free use minority languages (Article 39); local control of education (Article 40); employment rights in the civil service (Article 41); and customary law (Article 42).

References to "Kurds" or "Kurdistan" were conspicuously absent from the Lausanne Treaty.[59] The Allies decided to sacrifice the national aspirations of Kurds. From Lausanne onward, the Kurdish issue became an issue of minority rights in Turkey, Iran, Iraq, and Syria.[60]

The Treaty of Lausanne also failed to resolve the Mosul question, delaying a final decision and bureaucratizing the decision-making process. Lausanne stipulated that "The frontier between Turkey and Iraq shall be laid down in friendly arrangement to be concluded between Turkey and Great Britain within nine months. In the event of no agreement being reached between the two Governments within the time mentioned, the dispute shall be referred to the Council of the League of Nations."[61] Lausanne prevented a military confrontation between Britain and Turkey over Mesopotamia.

Turkey ratified the Treaty of Lausanne on August 23, 1923. It was ratified by Greece, Italy, and Japan over the next ten months. Britain was the last to ratify, on July 16, 1924. The Treaty of Lausanne came into force on August 6, 1924. Peace was restored and official diplomatic relations established between the signatories. Ataturk celebrated the outcome: "This treaty is a document declaring that all efforts, prepared over centuries, and thought to have been accomplished through the Sevres Treaty to crush the Turkish nation have been in vain. It is a diplomatic victory unheard of in the Ottoman history!"[62] Ismet Pasha was awarded the title of national chief in 1938 after Ataturk's passing.

The United States did not engage Turkey militarily during World War I. It was not a signatory to the Treaty of Sevres or the Treaty of Lausanne. The United States and Turkey did sign a Treaty of Friendship and Commerce in Lausanne on July 24, 1923. However, diplomatic relations between Turkey and the United States were not established until 1927. Armenian-Americans objected relations with Turkey, in light of the Armenian Genocide.

Lausanne's failure to address Mosul's status fuelled violence along the Brussels line. Britain adopted a "forward policy," using force to stabilize the situation. Its garrisons were instructed to hold the line until the frontier delimitation commission could get in place and complete its task. Meanwhile, stakeholders jockeyed for position. Turkey wanted to create facts on the ground. Kurds sought to control local affairs, strengthening their case for maximum autonomy. Britain wanted to preserve stability in Iraq. The security situation along the Brussels line deteriorated dramatically between 1923 and 1924, with combined attacks by Turkish and Kurdish forces. The decision on Mosul's status was referred for arbitration by the League of Nations in June 1924.

A fact-finding delegation of the commission arrived to assess local conditions and gauge the aspirations of directly affected populations. The commission was charged with determining whether residents wanted to remain a part of Iraq or join Turkey. The commission emphasized the welfare of both Kurds and Christian minorities as well as Yazidi Kurds who practice an esoteric religion based on Zoroastrianism. Kurds represented 75 percent of the population. Arabs, Turkmen, and Assyrians represented the balance. Differences also existed between Kurds. Those living north of the Zab were culturally and linguistically similar to Kurds in Turkey, while Kurds south of the Zab bore similarities to Kurds in Iran.[63]

The Mosul villayet was awarded to Britain on December 18, 1925. Upholding the Brussels line, the report also required Britain to finalize a bilateral agreement with Iraq within six months, extending its mandate over Iraq for twenty-five years. The League required that "officials of the Kurdish race must be appointed for the administration of their country, the dispensation of justice, and teaching in the schools, and that Kurdish should be the official language of all these services."[64] Turkey contested the commission's recommendation, referring the final settlement to the Permanent Court of International Justice at The Hague. On July 18, 1926, the Court upheld the League's determination as binding on Britain and Turkey.[65]

Oil Politics

Events were shaped by the discovery of oil. The Turkish Petroleum Company (TPC) was registered in 1912. Said Halim, Turkey's grand vizier, gave TPC permission to explore for oil in the Mosul and Baghdad villayets. TPC was initially capitalized at £160,000. British investors held 50 percent of its shares; 25 percent was owned by Deutsche

Bank, and 25 percent by Royal Dutch-Shell. Turks had no ownership position in TPC. It was just a territorial name designed to minimize Turkish feelings of exploitation.

In 1920, Britain and France agreed that France would assume Deutsche Bank's ownership position. Woodrow Wilson objected to the deal, demanding an "open-door policy" on oil concessions and other commercial opportunities in the Middle East. Wilson sought equal access for American capital, technology, and commercial interests as sought by the New Jersey Standard Oil Company.

The Baba Gurgur oil field north of Kirkuk was discovered in October 1927. It was a gusher, spurting oil and gas uncontrollably for nine days. The Kirkuk oil field is one hundred kilometers long and twelve kilometers wide, stretching from Kirkuk to Mosul, with huge estimated reserves. Baba Gurgur means "Father of Flames" in Kurdish. Its discovery marked the beginning of a tragic period of exploitation for the Kurds.

Notes

1. *BBC News*. BBC. Web 14 May 2014.
2. "Levy, Jews of the Ottoman Empire." *Levy, Jews of the Ottoman Empire*. N.p., n.d. Web. 13 May 2014.
3. "List of Sultans of the Ottoman Empire." *Wikipedia*. Wikimedia Foundation, 28 May 2014. Web. 29 May 2014. http://en.wikipedia.org/wiki/List_of_sultans_of_the_Ottoman_Empire.
4. "The Gulhane Decree and the Beginning of the Tanzimat Reform Era in the Ottoman Empire, 18391." Sitemaker.umich.edu. Modern Middle East Sourcebook Project, 2004. Web 13 May 2014.
5. Lost Islamic History. The Decline of the Ottoman Empire: Part 3 Nationalism.
6. http://www.iranicaonline.org/articles/bedir-khan-badr-khan-d.
7. Nezam Kendal, in A People without a Country, pp. 20–21.
8. Ozoglu, Hakan. Kurdish Notables and the Ottoman State: Evolving Identities, Competing Loyalties, and Shifting Boundaries. Feb 2004. p. 75.
9. http://www.thesis.bilkent.edu.tr/0002450.pdf.
10. Enver Pasha, Talaat Pasha, and Djemal Pasha.
11. Interview with Dogu Ergil by the author. August 9, 2014.
12. "THE TRIPLE ALLIANCE. » 11 Oct 1913 » The Spectator Archive." *The Spectator Archive*. N.p., n.d. Web. 13 May 2014.
13. Kili 1982 : 84 86; Shaw and Shaw 1977: 356.
14. Andersen, Andrew, and Georg Egge. "Armenia in the Aftermath of Mudros: Conflicting Claims and Strife with the Neighbors." *Http://www.conflicts. rem33.com/images/Armenia/restoration%20and%20terr%20issue/T3.html*. N.p., n.d. Web.
15. Kili 1982: 5 8; Lewis 1968: 239 242; Shaw and Shaw 1977: 327–328.
16. The Kurdish Problem and the Mosul Boundary: 1918–1925, By Peter Sluglett. Excerpt from *Britain in Iraq: 1914–1932* (London: Ithaca Press, 1976). pp. 116–125.

17. http://cnsnews.com/blog/patrick-j-buchanan/unraveling-sykes-picot#sthash.ZulbBWJt.dpuf.
18. US State Department. Office of the Historian. https://history.state.gov/milestones/.../fourteen-points (accessed 17 Feb 2014).
19. Ibid.
20. Ibid.
21. Ibid.
22. President Woodrow Wilson's Address to Congress, Analyzing German and Austrian Peace Utterances (Delivered to a Joint Session of the US Congress, February 11, 1918).
23. Ibid.
24. Ibid.
25. Ibid.
26. ww1ha.org/france/clemenceau.htm (accessed 17 Feb. 2014).
27. Remarks by German Chancellor Count Hertling to the Reichstag (24 Jan. 1918 and 25 Feb. 1918).
28. Speech by Foreign Secretary Arthur Balfour to Parliament (27 February 1918).
29. *Source Records of the Great War, Vol. VI,* ed. Charles F. Horne, *National Alumni 1923.*
30. Keegan, John (1998). *The first World War.* London: Random House (UK). ISBN 0-09-1801788.
31. www.pbs.org/greatwar/.../casdeath_pop.html (accessed 17 Feb. 2014).
32. https://www.fas.org/sgp/crs/.../RS22926.pdf (accessed 17 Feb. 2014).
33. US State Department. Office of the Historian. https://history.state.gov/milestones/.../fourteen-points (accessed 17 Feb. 2014).
34. "Map of Kurdistan in 1919 Paris Peace Conference. By Alan Rawand." Web. 14 May 2014.
35. Alan Abdulla. "Map of Kurdistan in 1919 Paris peace conference." March 15, 2012. Ekurd.net www.ekurd.net/mismas/articles/misc2012/3/state5992.htm.
36. Ibid.
37. Article 6. Translated by Shaw and Shaw, *History,* vol. ii, p. 345.
38. Harris, George S. *Studies in Atatürk's Turkey the American dimension.* Leiden: Brill, 2009. Print.
39. Davidson, "The Turkish Diplomacy to Lausanne," Pg. 182u.
40. (FO371/5068 E4396/11/44).
41. Karabell, Zachary. "San Remo Conference (1920)." *Encyclopedia.com.* High-Beam Research, 01 Jan. 2004. Web. 29 May 2014. <http://www.encyclopedia.com/doc/1G2-3424602380.html>.
42. "Section I, Articles 1 - 260." - *World War I Document Archive.* N.p., n.d. Web. 14 May 2014. <http://wwi.lib.byu.edu/index.php/Section_I,_Articles_1_-_260>.
43. Ibid.
44. Ibid.
45. Ibid.
46. Satalkar, Bhakti. "Treaty of SÃ¨vres." *Buzzle.* Buzzle.com, 7 Jan. 2011. Web. 19 Feb. 2014. <http://www.buzzle.com/articles/treaty-of-sevres.html>.
47. Published on 12 Feb. 1920.

48. Butler, Daniel Allen. *Shadow of the sultan's realm the destruction of the Otto-man Empire and the creation of the modern Middle East.* Washington, D.C.: Potomac Books, 2011. Print.

49. (FO371/6343/E7957, Telegram from Sir M. Cheetham to the Marques Curzon of Keddleston, 11 July 1921).

50. Mesopotamian Intelligence Report, No. 4, December 31, 1920.

51. (FO371/7781, Cable from the Colonial Office to Foreign Office, March 1922)

52. The Kurdish Problem and the Mosul Boundary: 1918–1925, By Peter Slu-glett. Excerpt from *Britain in Iraq: 1914–1932* (London: Ithaca Press, 1976). pp. 116–125.

53. (FO371/6346/E3042, The Under-Secretary of State, Foreign Affairs).

54. (FO371/6347/E12643, The Residency, Baghdad, 28 October 1921).

55. Azad Aslan. "Revision of the Treaty of Sevres and Incorporation of South Kurdistan into Iraq: History Revisited." The Kurdish Globe. 4 March 2010. kurdishglobe.net/article/4675CBA36FFCCAC84FA4D422721ED321/ Revision...

56. Article 15.

57. Article 20.

58. Article 23.

59. Azad Aslan. *The Kurdish Globe.* "Revision of the Treaty of Sevres and Incorporation of South Kurdistan into Iraq: History Revisited." 4 March 2010. kurdishglobe.net/article/4675CBA36FFCCAC84FA4D422721ED321/ Revision... (Accessed 17 Feb. 2014).

60. Ibid.

61. Article 23 [item 2].

62. M. Kemal Ataturk. The Great Speech of 1927. http://www.mfa.gov.tr/ lausanne-peace-treaty.en.mfa.

63. Commission report, Pg. 57.

64. Commission report. Pg. 89–90.

65. The Kurdish Problem and the Mosul Boundary: 1918–1925, By Peter Slu-glett. Excerpt from *Britain in Iraq: 1914–1932* (London: Ithaca Press, 1976). pp. 116–125.

Part Two

Abuse

2

Kurds in Iraq

Great Britain received the mandate for Iraq at the San Remo Conference in April 1920.[1] The mandate was intended as a transitional authority to facilitate the independence of former Ottoman territories. However, directly affected populations viewed the British mandate as another form of imperialism. Tribal leaders resented land ownership laws imposed by British administrators. They also balked at the burial tax in Najaf, a sacred destination for Shiites.[2] The Grand Mujtahid of Karbala, Imam Shirazi, insisted that Muslims could not be ruled by non-Muslims. He issued a fatwa: "Service in the British administration was unlawful."[3]

Mesopotamian tribes who fought with the British against Ottoman armies demanded a state of their own. They launched the Great Iraqi Revolution of 1920. Friday prayers morphed into mass protests against the British administration. Sir Percy Cox received a petition from tribal leaders making the case for independence. Violence erupted when Cox dismissed their appeal in June 1920.[4] The revolt started in Mosul, but soon British garrisons were overrun in the mid-Euphrates region. Anarchy spread across Iraq. Winston Churchill ordered the Royal Air Force to join the battle, turning the tide. Rebels in Najaf and Karbala surrendered in October 1920.

At the Cairo Conference of March 1921, Faysal ibn Husayn, a Hashemite, was installed as king of Iraq. In appointing Faysal, the British government made a tactical decision to step back from day-to-day administration. Faysal had good credentials. He was a descendent of the Prophet Muhammad. His family held positions in Mecca and Medina for over a thousand years. He gained credibility with Arab tribes through his prominent role in the 1916 Arab Revolt against the Turks, and close cooperation with T. E. Lawrence ("Lawrence of Arabia"). Faysal proved himself on the battlefield, leading the charge against Damascus in October 1918. Churchill and Cox intended to keep Faysal on a short leash. They were concerned about his pan-Arab ambitions and desire to reconcile Sunni and Shiite sects. Faysal was a proponent of an Arab state in the Fertile Crescent that included territories of modern day Iraq, Syria, and Palestine. After Faysal's appointment, the Kingdom of Iraq was founded on August 23, 1921.

*****

The British appointed Mahmud Barzanji—sheikh of a Qadiriyah Sufi family of the Barzanji clan from Suleimani—governor of South Kurdistan in 1920.[5] The Foreign Office envisioned Kurdish territory in Iraq as a buffer between the Arab tribes of Mesopotamia and Ataturk's forces, who were waging a war of independence to restore Turkey's control over former Ottoman lands. Churchill thought Barzanji would do Britain's bidding, but Barzanji pursued his own agenda to establish an independent Kurdish state. In 1920, he rebelled against Britain. Barzanji was, however, injured in battle on the road between Kirkuk and Suleimani, captured, and sentenced to death.

Britain imprisoned Mahmud Barzanji in India, where he remained in exile until 1922. Barzanji avoided capital punishment because he showed mercy to British officers whom he had captured. Moreover, the British needed Barzanji. With Ataturk's forces making inroads into Southern Kurdistan, Cox argued for Barzanji's release. Barzanji was Britain's best bet to prevent Turkish incursions and stabilize the region. Oil had been discovered in Kirkuk, raising the stakes in Northern Iraq. Barzanji was brought back from exile to head a Kurdish government.

The Anglo-Iraq Declaration was signed on December 20, 1922, and ratified in 1924. It affirmed Britain's authority over Iraq's fiscal and foreign policy. King Faysal felt betrayed by the accord and chafed under Britain's control. Though he threatened to block Iraq's ratification of the declaration, he ultimately succumbed to British coercion. Faysal agreed to follow instructions on fiscal policy until Iraq made good on its balance of payments to Britain. He also accepted the embedding of British officials as advisers in eighteen government departments.

Iraqi Prime Minister Abd al-Muhsin al Saadun warned, "This nation cannot live unless it gives all Iraqi elements their rights. Their officials should be from among them: their tongue should be their official language and their children should learn their own tongue in the schools. It is incumbent upon us to treat all elements, whether Muslim or non-Muslim, with fairness and justice."[6] The Anglo-Iraq Declaration was envisioned as a step toward an independent Iraqi Kurdistan. But Cox made the creation of a Kurdish government contingent upon Kurdish factions agreeing to the demarcation of boundaries and a constitution. He was convinced Kurds could not reach consensus on these critical and contentious issues and would never become independent.

Doubting Cox's commitment to an independent Iraqi Kurdistan, Barzanji played a double game. He went through the motions of complying with Britain's demands while secretly reaching out to the Turks. Mahmud Barzanji unilaterally declared himself king of Kurdistan. When Cox learned of this duplicity, he abruptly cancelled the Anglo-Iraqi Declaration. Mahmud Barzanji refused to vacate his throne and launched a guerilla war. The Royal Air Force responded by attacking with chemical bombs on August 16, 1923.[7] Barzanji was finally defeated and exiled to the deserts of Southern Iraq in May 1932. The Kingdom of Iraqi Kurdistan was short-lived.

*****

A new Anglo-Iraq Treaty was promulgated in June 1930. The treaty would expire either in twenty-five years or when Iraq became independent, whichever came first. Iraq gained independence on October 3, 1932. Britain and Iraq agreed on security cooperation; Iraq was required to assist Britain in the event of war. The Royal Air Force maintained its base in Shaibah, near Basra and at Habbaniya and between Ramadi and Fallujah. Britain wanted a military presence to protect its petroleum interests. Britain found vast oil supplies in 1927, the year the Iraqi Petroleum Company (IPC) was founded. Britain retained complete authority to develop Iraq's energy resources. It agreed to pay the Iraqi government a small royalty after twenty years.

Mosul was a flash point in the North. Both Iraq and Turkey claimed Mosul and parts of Nineveh Province. Kurds, Arabs, and Turkmen all had historical claims to the oil-rich region. Its status would be determined by the League of Nations, of which Iraq was now a member. In exchange for Britain's support of Mosul's accession to Iraq, King Faysal granted the IPC a seventy-five-year oil concession.[8] IPC was a consortium of the British, French, and US companies that succeeded the Turkish Petroleum Company.

King Faysal's commitment to pan-Arabism helped bridge divisions between Shiites and Sunni. By 1933, however, Iraqi Shiites were growing restless under the rule of Sunni Arab Hashemites. The Hashemite government targeted potential adversaries from different ethnic and sectarian groups. Approximately, three thousand Assyrians were killed in the Simele Massacre in August 1933. A Kurdish uprising in the north and a Yazidi revolt in the Shengal Mountains were suppressed in 1935.[9] Shiite tribes in the mid-Euphrates region were massacred in 1935 and 1936.

King Faysal died in September 1933. Ghazi, his playboy son, replaced him. Ghazi wanted to unite Iraq and Kuwait. Sectarian and ethnic divisions threatened to destabilize Iraq. Bakr Sidqi, a general and Iraqi nationalist from Kirkuk, launched a military coup in 1936, with Ghazi's backing, and became prime minister. Bakr Sidqi adopted socialist views, rejecting British rule. He was a Kurd, but not a Kurdish nationalist,[10] nor was he a proponent of pan-Arabism. Despite his attempts, Bakr Sidqi failed to stabilize Iraq. He was assassinated in Mosul on August 12, 1937. Instability worsened when Ghazi died in a car crash and was succeeded by his infant son, Faysal II, in 1939. A second military coup in 1941 tried to overthrow 'Abd al-Ilah, the regent and uncle of Faysal II. Britain dispatched a temporary force to restore its position and order.

In World War II, many Iraqis sided with Germany as an opportunity against British colonialism. Iraqi Prime Minister Rashid Ali al-Gaylani seized power in 1941. Palestine was divided and in turmoil.[11] Under pressure from the Foreign Office, he broke off diplomatic relations with Germany, but he refused British demands that Iraq declare war on the Axis Powers. He defiantly expelled pro-British politicians and civic leaders from Iraq. He also nurtured close cooperation with Italy's Fascist government in order to advance his Arab nationalist agenda. On April 17, 1941, Rashid Ali proposed a mutual defense agreement between Iraq and Italy. In May, British forces reoccupied Iraq and restored 'Abd al-Ilah to power. The renewed presence of British forces fueled resentment by Iraqis. It also intensified Kurdish nationalism.

Iraq became a staging ground for military operations by the Allies and a launch point for attacks against the Vichy-French administration in Syria. British and Soviet forces invaded Iran in 1941, preventing Iran from entering World War II on Germany's side. They divided the country into two zones of control, with Kurds in the Soviet zone enjoying de facto independence. Mullah Mustafa Barzani rebelled against the Hashemite government in 1943. Mustafa Barzani's revolt was suppressed with the help of the British Royal Air Force. Mustafa Barzani and his older brother, Ahmed Barzani, head of the Barzan tribe, fled to Iran in October 1945. Mustafa Barzani joined forces with

Qazi Mohamed, who led the Kurdistan Democratic Party of Western Kurdistan (Iran) and established the Kurdish Republic of Mahabad.

Mustafa Barzani is the godfather of Kurdish nationalism.[12] He was a charismatic tribal chieftain with a lifelong commitment to the Kurdish cause. He was born in the village of Barzan on March 14, 1903. As a three-year old, he and his mother were imprisoned in Mosul by the Ottoman administration.[13] He joined the Kurdish armed movement as a sixteen-year-old in the ranks of Sheikh Mahmud Barzanji. In 1925, he was sent as an envoy by the Barzan clan to visit Sheikh Said Piran in Northern Kurdistan. He commanded Barzan peshmerga during the uprising of 1932. Mustafa Barzani's valiant lifelong struggle for Kurdish national identity is a source of pride for Kurds to this day.

Mustafa Barzani turned to the Soviet Union to assist the Kurdish Republic of Mahabad. He asked Soviet officials for tanks and heavy weapons but only received a few rifles and a printing press. Moscow was aloof to Kurdish entreaties. The Soviet Union was no champion of Kurdish rights. Its real interest was gaining oil concessions in Iran. To this end, it manipulated separatist activity by Kurds and ethnic Azeris to gain leverage over the Iranian government. Iran agreed to provide the Soviet Union with oil concessions in May 1946. Russian forces withdrew, abandoning the Kurds. When the Iranian army entered Tabriz, many tribal chiefs switched sides, and the pro-Soviet Kurdish Republic of Mahabad collapsed. Barzani and four hundred of his best fighters fled and took refuge in the Soviet Union, where they founded the Kurdistan Democratic Party (KDP) on August 16, 1946.

Cold War politics dominated regional issues, including the cause of Kurdish nationalism. Britain reasserted its influence in Iraq through the Anglo-Iraqi Treaty of 1948. It revised the 1930 version and extended its term to 1973. This angered Arab nationalists and led to the Al-Wathbah uprising in 1948. Years later, in 1955, Iraq entered into an alliance with Britain and later, formally, the United States by joining the Baghdad Pact with Iran, Turkey, and Pakistan. The following year, Egypt nationalized the Suez Canal. Seizing the Suez Canal was a strong statement of Arab nationalism and a rejection of Western influence in Egypt. Through its obligation under the Baghdad Pact, Iraq was compelled to join Britain, France, and Israel when they attacked Egypt to regain control of the Suez Canal. Iraqis strongly objected. They were also uncomfortable fighting on behalf of Israel. Egyptian President Gamal Abdel Nasser's pan-Arab ideology resonated with Iraq's Arab majority.

The CIA was busy with covert operations in the region. In 1953, it orchestrated the overthrow of Iranian Prime Minister Mohammed Mossadegh, who had nationalized Iran's oil. The British Intelligence Agency, MI6, was also behind Mossadegh's overthrow. Nationalization of Iran's oil industry was a blow to Britain, which controlled a disproportionate share of the profits under the Anglo-Iranian Oil Company (AIOC). The AIOC had refused Iran's proposal for a 50/50-profit split, modeled on the arrangement with Aramco in Saudi Arabia.

The CIA and MI6 engineered another coup in Iraq, on July 14, 1958. The 14th of July Revolution was led by General Abdel Karim Qasim and Colonel Abdul Salam Arif. King Faysal II was executed, ending thirty-seven years of Hashmite rule. Qasim became the sole leader and prime minister.[14] Iraq was run by a Revolutionary Council headed by a committee of the country's communal and ethnic groups. The committee was intended to function as a co-presidency but was deeply dysfunctional. Iraq drifted toward anarchy as rival groups competed for control.

The United States was concerned about Qasim's Communist leaning. Qasim confirmed Washington's fears by withdrawing from the Baghdad Pact in 1959 and seeking an alliance with the Soviet Union. He also lifted the ban on Iraq's Communist Party, the most powerful Communist party in the Arab world, which was founded in the 1930s and lasted until the 1960s. Qasim cancelled the mutual security agreement with Britain, evicting British forces from their air base at al-Habbaniyya. He supported Algeria's rebels fighting France. Qasim disputed Iran for control of Shatt al-Arab waterway. He contested the Arabic-speaking Khuzestan region in Iran. The United States stood with Iran, its most important ally in the region, and a bulwark against Communism.

Qasim also antagonized Iraqis. Between 1958 and 1962, there were twenty-nine coup attempts against the Qasim government. A coup by Baathist officers failed on October 7, 1959. Saddam Hussein, a young Baathist coup plotter, fled the country when pro-Qasim Communist militia launched violent reprisals against the armed forces. The garrison in Mosul was manned by pro-Nasser officers, who rebelled against Qasim. Mustafa Barzani and his peshmerga were invited to return from exile for the purpose of suppressing pan-Arab rebels. Mustafa Barzani was lured by promises of autonomy; Qasim declared Kurds as "one of the two nations of Iraq."[15]

By 1961, Iraqi Kurds were in full revolt. Mustafa Barzani consolidated his position, defeating the Lolans and Harki tribes that supported

Qasim. Using guerilla tactics, Barzani's force of approximately 15,000 fighters vanquished the Iraqi armed forces and gained control of 25,000 square miles in Iraqi Kurdistan.[16] Iraqi Kurdistan achieved de facto independence under Mustafa Barzani's leadership. Battlefield victories came with a cost. In 1963, Qasim ordered the Arabization of Kurds in Kirkuk who had migrated in the 1920s to work in the oil fields and settled alongside the predominant population of Turkmen. Tens of thousands of Kurds were forcibly displaced and their property seized as a result of Qasim's plan to systematically change Kirkuk's demography. Kurds were relocated to impoverished parts of southern Iraq, and poor Arabs shifted from the south with the promise of inexpensive housing and jobs in the oil sector.

Conflict in Iraqi Kurdistan contributed to unrest in the armed forces, mobilizing opposition to Qasim by the Arab Renaissance (Baath) Socialist Party. In 1963, Baathists overthrew Qasim and went on a rampage executing Kurds and communists. By November 1963, however, Abdul Salam Arif and his military cohorts regained control and came back to power.

In 1966, Abdul Salam Arif died in a helicopter crash and was succeeded by his brother, Abdul Rahman Arif. Abdul Rahman Arif rejoined the battle with Mustafa Barzani but suffered a humiliating defeat at the Battle of Mount Handrin in May 1966. The Iraqi-Kurdish conflict lasted from 1961 until 1970 and claimed up to one hundred thousand lives. It ended when Mustafa Barzani agreed to the March Manifesto, a twelve-point autonomy agreement. The agreement envisioned an autonomous Kurdish region in northern Iraq. Kurds would have proportional representation in the national legislature, and Iraq would have a Kurdish vice president. The agreement also recognized Kurds as one of two nations constituting Iraq.

Abdul Rahman Arif was overthrown by Major General Ahmed Hasan al-Bakr who was elected president and prime minister of Iraq by the Revolutionary Command Council (RCC) on July 17, 1968. His nephew, Saddam Hussein, was appointed vice president and deputy chairman of the RCC. Bakr was largely a figurehead; Saddam wielded power behind the scenes.

The Baathist government moved vigorously to implement its socialist policy and consolidate popular support among Arabs. It nationalized the IPC in 1972. With world oil prices increasing tenfold after the October 1973 Arab-Israeli war, Iraq was flush with oil revenue. The government invested heavily in social and economic programs. Priority was given to the national steel and iron industries, as well as petrochemical facilities. The government also built schools and hospitals. Literacy and girls' education were priorities. Living standards improved as Iraq's economy expanded.

The Autonomy Agreement was a tactical maneuver by Baghdad. It was never implemented. When Mustafa Barzani reverted to demands for independence, violent conflict resumed in the spring of 1974. The Iraqi armed forces were bolstered by Soviet tanks and warplanes. Kurdish villages were bombed and strafed. Kurds were also attacked with phosphorous shells, the first use of chemical weapons by Iraq against the Kurds.[17] Mustafa Barzani was the target of at least a dozen assassination attempts by the government's intelligence agency, the Mukhabarat. Two assassination attempts nearly succeeded.[18]

Jalal Talabani, founded the Patriotic Union of Kurdistan (PUK) on June 1, 1975. The PUK attracted intellectuals from Sorani-speaking and urban parts of southern Kurdistan, while Mustafa Barzani drew support from rural Kurmanji-speaking Kurds in northern Iraqi Kurdistan. Mustafa Barzani and Talabani practiced different brands of Sufism. Talabani was part of the Qadiri Sufi order, whereas Mustafa Barzani was an adherent of Naaqshbandi Sufism.

*****

Pro-West and anti-Communist, the Shah of Iran, Mohammed Reza Pahlavi, was a pillar of US policy in the region. Mustafa Barzani was supported by the Shah, who used the Kurds as a wedge in Iran's geopolitical rivalry with Iraq. Concerned about the Soviet Union's influence in Baghdad, the United States supported Mustafa Barzani's rebellion. It provided financing. The Shah gave money and supplies, including antitank weapons and mortars. Israel offered training. By 1975, the peshmerga were over one hundred thousand strong.[19] Iraqi Kurds were pawns in the Cold War.

The peshmerga ("those who stand before death") protected Kurds. Beyond security, the peshmerga set up media outlets, including newspapers and radio. Its public diplomacy reached out to Kurds in rural areas, using both Kurdish and Arabic. It broadcasted music and poetry. The peshmerga even formed their own traditional music band named Kazan. Every village had a secret council that provided the peshmerga with food, clothing, and shelter. The councils worked closely with peshmerga to organize schools and provide grassroots education about the

Kurdish cause. Rural health clinics were set up for wounded fighters and civilians.

Outreach focused not only on recruits but also targeted youth and women. Many women joined secret cells supporting the resistance. They appeared with their husbands, brothers, and sons on the battlefield. Others served in field hospitals or as battlefield messengers. Kurdish civil society paid a steep price. Villages were destroyed, cattle killed and dumped in wells. Whole forests were incinerated, schools and universities attacked. On April 24, 1974, Qaladize, a city in the Pishdar region and a focal point of the Kurdish rebellion, was bombed with napalm rockets.

America's political support was far more important than its material supplies. In the Middle East, "the enemy of my enemy is my friend." Mustafa Barzani knew that Iran could abandon him but was convinced that America's involvement was a safeguard against being cut off by Tehran.[20] However, Barzani overestimated the degree of America's commitment to the Kurds. According to a classified House Select Intelligence Committee report,

> The recipients of US arms and cash were an insurgent ethnic group fighting for autonomy in a country bordering our ally [Iran]. . . . The President, Dr. Kissinger, and the foreign head of state [Mohammed Reza Pahlavi] hoped that our clients would not prevail. They preferred instead that the insurgents simply continue a level of hostilities sufficient to sap the resources of our ally's neighboring country [Iraq]. . . . Even in the context of covert action, ours was a cynical enterprise.[21]

While urging the Kurds to rebel, Washington was also encouraging Iraq and Iran to resolve their differences. The Shah and Saddam Hussein talked on the margins of the 1975 meeting of the Organization of Petroleum Exporting Countries in Algiers. They agreed to continue negotiations on border demarcation and navigation rights. The United States worked behind the scenes with Algeria and Jordan to facilitate a deal. The Algiers Accord was finalized on March 5 and signed on June 13, 1975. Saddam relinquished Iraq's claim to territory in order to gain Iran's support against the Kurds. As part of the deal, the Shah agreed to discontinue all forms of assistance to Mustafa Barzani and seal the border between Iraq and Iran.

Mustafa Barzani and the peshmerga were squeezed. The Iraqi army was ramping up an offensive, sealing Kurdistan to the south and west.[22] Turkey also closed its border. Barzani turned to US officials, but his appeal fell on deaf ears. The United States helped the Kurds at the request of the Shah, and it withdrew support in parallel to the Shah's decision. Betrayed by Washington and abandoned by Tehran, Barzani was left without a patron. The Kurdish rebellion was crushed. Iraq's conquest broke Barzani's spirit. It also inflicted huge suffering on Kurdish society. Many villages were destroyed and tens of thousands of Iraqi Kurds were forcibly resettled.[23]

Mustafa Barzani became the Shah's "guest."[24] He was detained in a Tehran villa owned by SAVAK, Iran's secret police agency. Barzani was diagnosed with lung cancer and transported by the CIA to the Mayo Clinic in August 1975. US doctors found that his cancer had spread and was inoperable. Mustafa Barzani was overcome by a sense of failure and died in 1979. He was initially buried in Iran, but his mortal remains were relocated to his ancestral village of Barzan in 1993.

Mustafa Barzani's son, Masoud, was born the same day that the KDP was founded, August 16, 1946. Massoud inherited the Kurdish national cause. "I was born in the shadow of the Kurdish flag in Mahabad," said Barzani. "I am ready to serve and die for the same flag."[25] Inheriting leadership of the KDP from his father, he became secretary general in 1979.

*****

The fourth president of Iraq, Ahmad Hasan al-Bakr, initiated discussions with Syria about unifying Iraq and Syria. Both were under Baath leadership. Syrian President Hafez al-Assad would become vice president as a result of the merger. Saddam recognized that merging Iraq and Syria would diminish his authority. He marshaled support in Iraq's Baath Party and forced Bakr to resign. Despite never having served in the military, Saddam became secretary general of Iraq's Baath party, commander-in-chief of the armed forces, and president on July 16, 1979.[26]

Saddam imagined that opponents in the military and party hierarchy were conspiring against him. His first act was to purge the Baath party. In a chilling episode, the names of purported opponents were ceremoniously read out loud at the Baath Party Congress on July 22, 1979. These people were dragged from the plenary hall and arrested. For dramatic effect, some were executed in the hallway. That day, sixty-eight people were arrested, tried before a political court, and executed. Those who remained were petrified. Saddam congratulated them for their present and future loyalty.[27] He cultivated a cult of personality, commissioning statues and paintings of himself across the country as a reminder to Iraqis of his omnipotent rule. Saddam turned Iraq into a republic of fear.

The 1979 return of Ayatollah Khomeini to Iran represented a challenge to Saddam's leading role in the region. Shiites represented a majority of Iraq's population, and many of the holiest Shiite shrines were in Iraq. The Imam Ali Mosque in Najaf contains the tomb of Ali, the cousin and son-in-law of Muhammad and the fourth caliph. The Imam Hussein Shrine in Karbala stands on the grave of Hussein ibn Ali, who was martyred during the Battle of Karbala in AD 680. The Day of Ashura, which marks the anniversary of Hussein's death, is commemorated by Shiite pilgrims from far and wide who march to the shrine whipping their bloodied bodies. Mosques in Kufa and Samarra are also revered holy sites for Shiites.

Ayatollah Khomeini summoned Iraq's Shiites to rebel against Saddam's secular regime. Saddam scoffed at Khomeini's threats, determined not to show any sign of weakness. A territorial dispute over the Shatt al-Arab waterway was the ostensible reason for the Iran-Iraq War. However, the conflict was essentially a regional rivalry between Saddam Hussein and Ayatollah Khomeini played out on the battlefield. Both wanted to depose the other, asserting their brand of governance and Islam. Iran and Iraq had a legacy of border disputes, which both leaders used to incite nationalism.

Iraq invaded Iran on September 22, 1980. US officials were ambivalent about choosing sides. Ronald Reagan became president in 1981 and welcomed a stalemate. The United States was content to let each side bloody the other. When Israel launched a surprise air raid destroying the Iraqi nuclear reactor at Osirak, the United States condemned the attack for violating Iraqi sovereignty. The powerful pro-Israel lobby in Washington backed Israel's action, warning the Reagan Administration to be wary of Saddam. But wariness did not translate into support for Iran. The United States was still traumatized by the events of 1979, when Iranian radicals had seized the US Embassy in Tehran and held Americans hostage for 444 days.

By 1982 Iran managed to regain territory it had lost. Thousands of young Iranians formed a human wave, dashing through minefields on the Iraq-Iran border chanting religious slogans. Saddam used chemical weapons against Iranian forces. Iraqi and Iranian cities were bombed. Oil tankers and merchant ships were attacked in the Persian Gulf to deprive the other of trade. Saddam targeted Iraqis he suspected of sympathizing with Iran, executing three hundred officers for questioning his conduct of the war. By war's end on August 20, 1988, as many as 1.5 million people had died and 750,000 were injured. Ultimately, Saddam claimed victory, but all he accomplished was staving off defeat. The Iraq-Iran border was intact. Both Saddam Hussein and Ayatollah Khomeini remained in power.[28]

Iraq made diplomatic gains during the eight years of war with Iran. Iraq's relations improved with Arab Sunni countries, Kuwait, Saudi Arabia, and Egypt. Wealthy Gulf States bankrolled the war, giving both financial and military aid. France and the Soviet Union provided weapons. Baghdad and Washington restored diplomatic relations, which were cut in 1967 to protest US support for Israel in the Six-Day War. Washington provided food and commodities to Iraq. Western firms also sold Iraq precursors that were transformed into chemical weapons used against Iran, as well as Iraqi Kurds. Saddam turned the international community's fear of Khomeini to his advantage.

*****

The UN Security Council passed Resolution 598, calling for an end to the war, on July 20, 1987.[29] Iran ignored appeals from the international community. Instead of a ceasefire, Iran attacked northern Iraq in the spring of 1988. Saddam accused the Kurds of acting as a fifth column, supporting Iran's offensive. Iraq intensified its attacks on the Kurds right after the cease-fire with Iran in July 1988. After the Iraq-Iran War, Saddam launched a military campaign of extermination and looting that was called Anfal. The campaign took its name from Suratal-Anfal in the Qur'an. *Al Anfal* literally means the "spoils" (of war).[30] The Anfal Campaign is also known as the Kurdish genocide.

Saddam appointed a cousin, Ali Hassan al-Majid, secretary-general of the Baath Party's Northern Region on March 29, 1987. Majid was instructed to "take care" of the Kurds using all necessary measures to clear a twenty-kilometer buffer on the Iraqi side of the Iraq-Iran border of its Kurdish residents.[31] The campaign targeted civilians in Badinan, a four-thousand-square-mile territory in the Zagros Mountains, with Turkey to the north and the Great Zab River to the east. The Anfal Campaign was not an event. It was a systematic attack against Kurds that occurred over several years. It culminated in mass killings using weapons of mass destruction between February 1987 and August 1988.

Anfal had eight stages. The first seven targeted PUK-controlled territory in Northeast Kurdistan along the Iranian border. The final stage targeted KDP-controlled territory in the Northwest during August and September 1988. Majid signed directive SF/4008 on June 20, 1987. Clause 5 established "prohibited zones."[32] Majid ordered that "all persons captured in those villages shall be detained and interrogated by the security services, and those between the ages of 15 and 70 shall be executed after any useful information has been obtained from them, of which we should be duly notified."[33] Majid signed a subsequent directive on September 6, 1987, calling for "the deportation of . . . families to the areas where there saboteur relatives are . . ., except for the male [members], between the ages of 12 inclusive and 50 inclusive, who must be detained [and killed]."[34]

Up to two hundred thousand Iraqi soldiers, including members of the elite Republican Guard, were deployed with air support. Helicopter gunships inflicted heavy casualties. In addition, the Iraqi army collaborated with state-sponsored Kurdish militias called Jash. The term means "donkey's foal" in Kurdish. Jash were mercenaries paid by Saddam to kill their own people. Jash looted livestock and raped Kurdish women.[35] Majid also issued directive SF/4008, which targeted men of so-called battle age. They were rounded up, executed, and their bodies dumped in mass graves.[36]

Majid was known as Chemical Ali for deploying weapons of mass destruction against civilians. The most notorious incident occurred in Halabja on March 16, 1988. Up to five thousand Kurds—mostly women and children—were killed by an aerial bombardment using sarin and mustard gas. Many victims of chemical weapons still suffer severe health problems. Chemical and biological weapons burned the skin, eyes, and lungs, and caused cancer, deformities, and neurological damage in its victims. As many as, 182,000 Kurds were killed during the Anfal. Approximately 4,500 Kurdish villages and at least 31 Assyrian villages were destroyed.[37] Kurds worldwide annually commemorate the Halabja anniversary in solemn ceremonies of remembrance.

*****

Iraq had the fourth-largest army in the world, but its military expenditures caused a fiscal crisis. Iraq owed almost $200 billion to its Arab and Sunni neighbors who bankrolled Iraq's war with Iran. Saddam threatened Iraq's creditors, including Kuwait. "Iraqis will not forget the maxim that cutting necks is better than cutting the means of living. Oh, God almighty, be witness that we have warned them."[38]

Saddam was true to his word. He claimed the rich Rumaila oil field that ran underground between Iraq and northern Kuwait. With the Iraqi Army poised to attack Kuwait, President George H. W. Bush drew a line in the sand, indicating that an attack on Kuwait would be seen as an attack against the United States. Bush feared that Iraq would occupy Kuwait and Saudi Arabia, thereby monopolizing the world's oil supplies. Saddam ignored Bush's warning. Claiming Kuwait as Iraq's nineteenth province, Iraq invaded on August 2, 1990. Kuwait's defense forces collapsed on the second day. Iraq annexed Kuwait less than a week later.

Bush warned, "This will not stand, this aggression against Kuwait." The United States led an international coalition to liberate Kuwait.[39] The air campaign to denigrate Iraq's forces was launched on January 17, 1991. During six weeks, coalition forces dropped more bombs than during World War II. When the ground assault started on February 24, Iraqi forces were quickly overwhelmed. With infantry in hot pursuit, Iraqi armored vehicles fleeing north were shot like fish in a barrel.

Bush's national security team debated an end to the war. Chairman of the Joint Chiefs of Staff Colin Powell narrowly defined US war aims: liberate Kuwait and destroy Saddam's offensive capability. Secretary of Defense Dick Cheney argued against marching on Baghdad:

> The idea of going into Baghdad . . . or trying to topple the regime wasn't anything I was enthusiastic about. I felt there was a real danger here that you would get bogged down in a long drawn-out conflict, that this was a dangerous, difficult part of the world; if you recall we were all worried about the possibility of Iraq coming apart, the Iranians restarting the conflict that they'd had in the eight-year bloody war with the Iranians and the Iraqis over eastern Iraq. We had concerns about the Kurds in the north. The Turks get very nervous every time we start to talk about an independent Kurdistan.[40]

Cheney continued,

> If you're going to go in and try to topple Saddam Hussein, you have to go to Baghdad. Once you've got Baghdad, it's not clear what you do with it. It's not clear what kind of government you would put in place of the one that's currently there now. Is it going to be a Shia regime, a Sunni regime or a Kurdish regime? Or one that tilts toward the Baathists, or one that tilts toward the Islamic fundamentalists? How much credibility is that government going to have if it's set up by the United States military when it's there? How long does the United

States military have to stay to protect the people that sign on for that government, and what happens to it once we leave?[41]

The United States declared a cease-fire for 8 a.m. on February 28, 1991.

*****

Some Bush Administration officials deplored the idea of leaving Saddam in power. Bush called on Iraqis to overthrow Saddam. He spoke to the Iraqi people via Voice of America on February 15, 1991, inciting them to rebel: "There is another way for the bloodshed to stop: and that is, for the Iraqi military and the Iraqi people to take matters into their own hands and force Saddam Hussein, the dictator, to step aside and then comply with the United Nations' resolutions and rejoin the family of peace-loving nations."[42]

Shiites in the South were the first to rise up against Saddam, on March 4, 1992. Their insurgency was called the Sha'aban Intifada. The Kurdish National Uprising broke out the next day in the town of Rania. Peshmerga and army deserters seized Mosul and Kirkuk. They chanted pro-democracy slogans and clamored to attack Baghdad. Cease-fire terms forbade Iraq to use fixed-wing aircraft, but they counterattacked with helicopter gunships. Panic stricken by Iraq's artillery and aerial bombardment, 1.5 million Kurds fled to Iran and Turkey. Tens of thousands of Shiites were killed in the south. The Iraq government drained marshes in the Tigris–Euphrates river system. US armed forces were ordered not to oppose Saddam's counterattack. According to Undersecretary of Defense for Policy Paul Wolfowitz, US forces were, "idly watching a mugging."[43]

Iran's supreme leader ordered Iranians to open their homes to refugees, who were given haven in Iran. However, Turkey sealed its border. It feared that a million Kurdish refugees flooding its territory would cause instability and incite Kurds in Turkey. President Turgut Ozal advocated a return strategy rather than resettlement. He urged the United States and Britain to create the conditions for Iraqi Kurds to go back safely to their homes and villages. After urging the Kurds to rise up, Bush was shamed into action.

Turkey played an indispensable role in Operation Provide Comfort, which mobilized the international community to deliver life-saving supplies of food, water, and shelter to Kurds in the mountains. But a million Kurds could not remain perched on the Iraqi-Turkish border. They needed protection before returning to their villages. The UN

Security Council endorsed Operation Northern Watch, establishing a no-fly zone north of the thirty-sixth parallel in the skies above Iraqi Kurdistan, and below the thirty-second parallel, where Shiites were under assault.

In addition, US forces established a safe area sixty miles into Iraq on April 17. They built camps and centers to distribute relief supplies, which served as a magnet for the return of Kurds. In October, Iraq agreed to withdraw its forces from Iraqi Kurdistan. A green line was established as the internal boundary for Iraqi Kurdistan. It encompassed the provinces of Suleimani, Erbil, and Dohuk. However, the city of Kirkuk was excluded. The Bush Administration wanted to prevent the Kurds from controlling Kirkuk's oil supply, which would give it the economic means for independence.

Iraqi armed forces manned the green line. They enforced sanctions against the Kurds, blocking the delivery of food, fuel, and other essential supplies. The international community adopted a containment strategy toward Iraq. In addition to the no-fly zones, the UN Security Council authorized weapons inspections and economic sanctions. The Kurds suffered a double embargo. Iraq blockaded the internal boundary, and sanctions closed Iraq's frontier with Turkey. Saddam thought Massoud Barzani and Jalal Talabani would seek a return to the *status quo ante*. He was convinced that Iraqi Kurdistan could not survive without Baghdad. He also thought that the international community would lose interest in Iraq now that Kuwait was liberated and the war was over.

Notes

1. "San Remo Resolution." *Council on Foreign Relations*. Council on Foreign Relations, 25 Apr. 1920. Web. 15 May 2014. <http://www.cfr.org/israel/san-remo-resolution/p15248>.
2. Litvak, Meir, and Ofra Bengio. *The Sunna and Shi'a in history: division and ecumenism in the Muslim Middle East*. New York, NY: Palgrave Macmillan, 2011. Print.
3. Tripp, Charles. A History of Iraq. Cambridge University Press, 2007, Pg. 41.
4. Vinogradov, Amal. "The 1920 Revolt in Iraq Reconsidered: The Role of Tribes in National Politics," International Journal of Middle East Studies, Vol.3, No.2 (Apr., 1972): Pg. 135.
5. "Kurdsat english news." *Kurdsat english news*. N.p., n.d. Web. 29 May 2014. <http://www.kurdsat.tv/news.php?id=16&type=biography>.
6. Yasin Aziz. Kurdistan Tribune. A Few Days Life of Revolution in Halabja: Introduction. November 4, 2013 http://kurdistantribune.com/2013/few-days-life-of-revolution-halabja-introduction/ (accessed April 25, 2014).
7. "British Use of Chemical Weapons in Iraq, Killing Kurds in the Old Days." Americans Against World Empire, n.d. Web. 15 May 2014. <http://www.againstbombing.org/chemical.

8. "Operation Desert Storm Timeline." N.p., n.d. Web. 15 May 2014. <http://www.history-of-american-wars.com/operation-desert-storm.html>.

9. "Sinjar Mountains - InfoRapid Knowledge Portal." *Sinjar Mountains - InfoRapid Knowledge Portal.* N.p., n.d. Web. 16 May 2014.

10. Natali, Denise. *The Kurds and the State: Evolving National Identity in Iraq, Turkey, and Iran.* Syracuse, NY: Syracuse UP, 2005. Print.

11. "The Iraq Coup of 1941, The Mufti and the Farhud." *The Iraq Coup of Raschid Ali in 1941, the Mufti Husseini and the Farhud (Farhoud).* N.p., n.d. Web. 16 May 2014.

12. Lawrence, Quil. *Invisible Nation: How the Kurds' Quest for Statehood Is Shaping Iraq and the Middle East.* New York: Walker, 2008. Print.

13. Ibid.

14. Romero, Juan. *The Iraqi Revolution of 1958: A Revolutionary Quest for Unity and Security.* Lanham, MD: U of America, 2011. Print.

15. Ezgi, Doug. "A Comparative Case Study: Kurdish Secessionism in Iraq and Turkey." *Https://files.nyu.edu/de339/public/Ezgi%20Kurdish%20Case%20Study%20Chapter.pdf.* New York University, n.d. Web.

16. "The Kurdish Rebellion." *The Harvard Crimson.* William A. Nitze, October 3, 1962.

17. "Who Really Used Chemical Weapons?" *Who Really Used Chemical Weapons?* N.p., n.d. Web. 16 May 2014.

18. *PBS.* PBS, n.d. Web. 16 May 2014.

19. "JUNE 1994 VOLUME I: NUMBER 2." *The Last Years of Mustafa Barzani.* Web. 16 May 2014.

20. David Korn. "The Last Years of Mustafa Barzani. *The Middle East Quarterly.* June 1994. Vol. I: No. 2.

21. Published in *The Village Voice,* February 16, 1976.

22. David Korn. "The Last Years of Mustafa Barzani. *The Middle East Quarterly.* June 1994. Vol. I: No. 2.

23. Darius Kadivar. Persian Realm. "Diplomatic History: Shah and Saddam Sign 1975 Algiers Agreement." January 3, 2009. http://iranian.com/main/blog/darius-kadivar/diplomatic-history-shah-and-saddam-sign-1975-algiers-agreement.html (accessed April 28, 2014).

24. "JUNE 1994 • VOLUME I: NUMBER 2." *The Last Years of Mustafa Barzani.* Web. 16 May 2014.

25. "Masoud Barzani." *Masoud Barzani.* N.p., n.d. Web. 1 May 2014. <http://www.kdp.se/mbhp.html>.

26. "How Did Saddam Hussein Became President of Iraq?" *WikiAnswers.* Answers Corporation, n.d. Web. 29 May 2014. <http://wiki.answers.com/Q/How_did_Saddam_Hussein_became_president_of_Iraq>.

27. Ibid.

28. Roger Hardy. "The Iran-Iraq war: 25 years on." BBC. September 22, 2005. http://news.bbc.co.uk/2/hi/4260420.stm (accessed April 29, 2014).

29. "UN Security Council Resolution 598, Iran / Iraq." *Council on Foreign Relations.* Council on Foreign Relations, 20 July 1987. Web. 16 May 2014.

30. "8. Surah Al-Anfal (The Spoils of War)." *Translation of Surah Al-Anfal.* Web. 16 May 2014.

31. Tran, Mark. "Iraq Executes Chemical Ali." *The Guardian.* Guardian News and Media, 26 Jan. 2010. Web. 16 May 2014.

32. Cited in *Iraq's Crime of Genocide*, pp. 11.
33. Cited in *Iraq's Crime of Genocide*, pp. 11, 14.
34. Cited in *Iraq's Crime of Genocide*, p. 298.
35. "Researcher: Kurdish Women Are Victims of a Legacy of Violence." *Rudaw*. Web. 16 May 2014.
36. *'Iraq's crime of genocide' by Human Rights Watch 1994, p.266 – 268*
37. Human Rights Watch. (1993) 'Genocide in Iraq - The Anfal Campaign Against the Kurds.' http://www.hrw.org/legacy/english/docs/2006/08/14/iraq13979_txt.htm.
38. http://www.pbs.org/wgbh/pages/frontline/shows/longroad/etc/cron.html (accessed May 1, 2014)
39. "George Bush (Sr) Library." *Bush Library*. Web. 16 May 2014.
40. Ibid
41. http://www.slate.com/articles/news_and_politics/chatterbox/2002/10/dick_cheney_dove.html (accessed May 1, 2014).
42. "Articles: Rise Up and Die: Hillary Clinton on Aleppo in February." *Articles: Rise Up and Die: Hillary Clinton on Aleppo in February*. N.p., 10 Aug. 2012. Web. 16 May 2014.
43. "Chapter 13 Breaking Up Is Hard to Do: Nations, States, and Nation-States A. Logistics." *Religion/Language Summary -*. Web. 16 May 2014.

3

Kurds in Turkey

Deeply disappointed by their betrayal at Lausanne, Kurds intensified their armed rebellion in February 1925. Sheikh Said Piran established Azadi, the Kurdish Independence Society. He led a force of 15,000 Kurdish rebels against 52,000 well-armed Turkish troops. The rebels had some initial success with hit-and-run operations in Diyarbakir and Mardin, until Turkish warplanes joined the battle. Outmanned and outgunned, the rebels were unable to defend Silvan, Hani, Palu, Piran, and Lice. Attacks by Turkey's air force destroyed 206 villages and killed 15,200 people, including women and children. Within a month, the Azadi rebellion was put down. Sheikh Said Piran and thirty-six of his deputies were hung in Diyarbakir's Mountain Gate (Dag Kapi) on June 29, 1925. Another 75,000 of Sheikh Said's compatriots were arrested.[1] Neither their mortal remains nor personal belongings were handed over to the families.[2]

Sheikh Abdurrahman, Sheikh Said's brother, renewed the struggle. He attacked Turkish garrisons in the fall of 1927, capturing the districts of Lice, Bingol, and Bayazid. Sheikh Abdurraham controlled remote mountain passes south of Erzurum. When Turkish warplanes attacked Kurdish positions, rebels took refuge in their high-altitude encampments. Kurds, led by solider and politician Ihsan Nuri Pasha, declared an independent Kurdistan in December 1927. They named it the Republic of Ararat. Kurds managed to control Agri Province until June 1930. However, they were overwhelmed by a force of 66,000 troops and one hundred aircraft at Zilan on July 21.[3] The Kurdish rebellion was defeated by September, and fully disbanded early the next year.[4]

Mustafa Kemal Ataturk, whose name means "the father of Turks," institutionalized a policy of "Turkification." Ankara actively promoted the cult of Ataturk, which was called Kemalism. Ataturk viewed himself as a modernizer. He sought to Europeanize Turkey and bring it in line with Western, secular, industrial, and progressive standards. He abolished the caliphate and banned Muslim garb. He changed the script from Arabic to Latin. The glorification of "Turkishness" was the core of Kemalism. Ataturk exalted the power of the State.

Kurdish identity represented a challenge to Ataturk's ideology of exclusive racialism. Ataturk declared martial law, assigned Turkish administrators to the Southeast, and issued land grants to Turkish war veterans. Resettling Turks in the Southeast was driven by a strategy to change the region's demography and subdue the indigenous population. Kurdish cultural rights were restricted through ordinances forbidding the use of Kurdish language in official proceedings and in court. Kurdish-language instruction in schools was banned. Limitations were imposed on formal education opportunities to Kurdish youth. Newborn Kurds were not allowed to have Kurdish names. Kurdish village names were changed to Turkish ones. Kurdish cultural festivals such as Newroz, the celebration of Kurdish New Year, and singing Kurdish folk songs were forbidden.[5]

The Turkish Grand National Assembly (TGNA) passed the Resettlement Law on June 14, 1934. The bill authorized local authorities to collect taxes, seize property, and relocate Kurds who were deemed a risk to state security.[6] On November 1, 1936, Ataturk addressed TGNA about the threat of Kurds in Dersim, demanding tough law and order.[7] His remarks set the stage for adoption of the Tunceli law, which authorized the government to set up military posts in the districts of Kahmut, Sin, Karaoglan, Amutka, Danzik, and Haydaran. It allowed local courts to relocate Kurds. The Kurdish name Dersim was changed to Tunceli.

British Foreign Secretary Anthony Eden, known for his opposition to appeasement in the 1930s, warned:

> The government has tried to assimilate the Kurdish people for years, oppressing them, banning publications in Kurdish, persecuting those who speak Kurdish, forcibly deporting people from fertile parts of Kurdistan to uncultivated areas of Anatolia where many have perished. The prisons are full of non-combatants, intellectuals are shot, hanged or exiled to remote places. Three million Kurds, demand to live in freedom and peace in their own country.[8]

Seyid Riza, an Alevi religious figure and leader of the Hesenan tribe, initiated the Dersim rebellion in response to Ataturk's Turkification program. The military governor of Erzincan Province invited Seyid Riza for talks on September 10, 1937. When Seyid Reza and his delegation arrived, they were shackled and sent to a detention center in Elazig. Seyid Riza, his sixteen-year old son, and compatriots were hung on November 15. Three days after Seyid Riza's execution, Ataturk attended a ribbon-cutting ceremony at the Singeç Bridge at Pertek. To protest Seyid Riza's betrayal and murder, Kurdish militants blew up the bridge and severed communications lines.

Ataturk intensified the crackdown against Kurds in Tunceli. The counterinsurgency campaign occurred over a year. It involved three offensives by Turkish ground forces, indiscriminate attacks by Turkey's air force against Kurdish villages, and a final sweep to cleanse Tunceli of rebels. According to the Turkish government's official report, 13,160 Kurds were killed, and 11,818 exiled during the Dersim rebellion.[9] The actual figures were much higher. As many as 70,000 people may have been killed.[10] Widespread atrocities were reported, including the alleged bombing of Kurdish villages with poison gas. Torture was widespread.[11] Women and children perished in caves when the army bricked up entrances and lit fires to suffocate families in hiding. When they attempted to flee, Turkish troops were waiting with bayonets.[12] Ataturk proudly acknowledged issuing the order for Turkish troops to wipe out the Kurdish population of Dersim.[13]

Ataturk's Republican People's Party (CHP) adopted draconian security measures targeting Kurds after Dersim. The very existence of Kurds in Turkey was denied. They were called "Mountain Turks." The ban on Kurdish language, culture, and geographical place names was fully enforced. In addition, the CHP undertook a project of "historic revisionism."[14] Mention of the Dersim massacre was excluded from "official history."[15]

Prime Minister Recep Tayyip Erdogan addressed the events in Dersim at a meeting of his Justice and Development Party (AKP) in 2011. "Is it me who should apologize or you [CHP leader Kemal Kilicdaroglu]? If there is an apology on behalf of the state and if there is such an opportunity, I can do it and I am apologizing. But if there is someone who should apologize on behalf of the CHP, it is you, as you are from Dersim. You were saying you felt honored to be from Dersim. Now, save your honor."[16] Erdogan was motivated by politics, not contrition. His statement was an acknowledgement of the mass killing of Kurds, but not an apology. Erdogan invoked the memory of Dersim as an attack against Ataturk's CHP and its secularist policies.

*****

Ataturk died in 1938, a year after the Dersim Massacre. The CHP vowed to fulfill Ataturk's legacy by strengthening Turkish nationalism and secularism. During the Cold War, however, Soviet and socialist ideologies emerged as an alternative to Kemalism. Idea Clubs, a left-leaning student consortium, was founded at Ankara University on January 3, 1956, and became a federation in 1965.[17] Idea Clubs emerged at a time when Turkey was becoming increasingly polarized. Leftist intellectuals, students, and trade unionists called for land reform, nationalization of industries, and restrictions on foreign capital. The CHP and proponents of the status quo adamantly resisted reforms.

Leftists also protested Turkey's economic ties and security cooperation with the West. In 1952, Turkey joined the North Atlantic Treaty Organization (NATO), and in 1955, it joined the Baghdad Pact.[18] After the overthrow of Iraq's King Faysal II in 1958, Turkey emerged as a critical bridge between NATO and the Central Treaty Organization (CENTO), which succeeded the Baghdad Pact. CENTO was a bulwark against the Iraqi Communist Party, which enjoyed support from Arab and Kurdish oil workers. CENTO was also a vehicle to counter Kurdish nationalism, which was on the rise in the region.[19]

Security officials were increasingly concerned about radicalism at universities as a challenge to the State. Politically motivated violence escalated in frequency and intensity. In February, 117 student demonstrators were tried and sentenced.[20] Police fired on students in Istanbul on April 28, 1960.[21] The military organized a coup on May 27. Chief of the General Staff Cemal Gürsel arrested President Celal Bayar, Prime Minister Adnan Menderes, and other cabinet members. Turkey's new constitution, approved by a referendum on July 9, 1961, established the Second Republic. It enshrined supremacy of the State, declaring: "The Turkish Republic is a nationalistic, democratic, secular, and social state . . . ." (Article 2).[22] "The Turkish State is an indivisible whole comprising its territory and people. Its official language is Turkish" (Article 3).[23] "Sovereignty is vested in the nation without reservation and condition" (Article 4).[24]

*****

Abdullah Ocalan, a sympathiser of the leftist movement, was born on April 4, 1948, to a Turkish mother in the southeastern village of Omerli.[25] He received a degree from a vocational school in Ankara, took a job at the Diyarbakir Title Deeds Office, and enrolled at the

Istanbul University's Law Faculty. After a year, he transferred to Ankara University to study political science. On campus, Ocalan joined the Turkish Revolutionary Youth Federation (Dev-Genc), a Marxist-Leninist student debating society, which inspired the formation of the Kurdistan Worker's Party (PKK).[26] Chief of the General Staff Memduh Tagmac implemented a sweeping set of socioeconomic measures banning radical Leftist groups like Dev-Genc. Revolutionary Path (Devrimci Yol) and the Revolutionary Workers and Peasants Party of Turkey, the initial offshoots of Dev-Genc, were also banned. Rather than direct coercion, Turkey's armed forces conducted a soft coup in 1971. They called it "guided democracy."

Ocalan was befriended by Haki Karer, a charismatic Kurdish student leader at Ankara University and founder of the People's Liberation Party of Turkey (THKO). He would later become Ocalan's housemate. The THKO was part of a Leftist coalition that opposed Süleyman Demirel and his conservative Justice Party, which came to power in 1975. The Justice Party entered into coalition with ultranationalist parties, the Nationalist Front, the National Salvation Party, and the far-right Nationalist Movement Party of Alparslan Turkes. The coalition formed an alliance with the State Security Services, targeting leftists.

Political violence was widespread, claiming about five thousand lives between 1976 and 1980. There were many incidents, including the May Day massacre of 1977. The Socialist Workers Party of Turkey gathered half a million people in Taksim Square on May 1, 1977. Armored vehicles and water cannons occupied the square. Shots were fired from the rooftop of the Marmara Hotel. According to the Confederation of Revolutionary Trade Unions, thirty-six people died during the riot.[27]

To decentralize the struggle, Haki Karer went on a recruitment trip to Gaziantep, a city in the southeast with a large Kurdish population. He encountered members of another Kurdish faction, Sterka Sor (Red Star), at a coffee shop. They argued about ideology and tactics. Haki Karer was slain on May 18, 1977, allegedly by Red Star.[28] According to Abdullah Ocalan, "We realised that we were face to face with a war that we were not at all ready for it when Haki was massacred. It was such a situation that the whole sky and ground opened up to pour death on us. Our movement could end that day, and we had to act responsibly." Ocalan continued, "We neither had a single gun or any money to take revenge. We had no power in our hands other than our naked hearts. . . ."[29]

The Siverek and Hilvan rebellions followed Haki Karer's killing. Siverek is a multiethnic community in Sanliurfa Province, populated by Kurds, Turkmen, and Arabs. The Siverek campaign was directed against Kurdish feudal landlords. Ataturk sought to transform Turkey from a feudal monarchy into a modern, secular, and sovereign state. His efforts largely succeeded, except in rural areas of the Southeast, where feudalism was deeply entrenched. Rather than eradicate feudal lords or "beys," Ataturk tried to coopt them. Members of the Bucak clan fought alongside Turkish troops against Sheikh Said during the uprising of 1925. Sedat Bucak, a Zaza, the notorious leader of the Bucak clan, was a member of parliament with close ties to Turkey's security establishment. In the 1990s, he was the point man for enlisting members of the Bucak clan as village guards. The Village Guard System was a network of local militias hired by the Turkish state. They were involved in kidnappings, disappearances, and assassinations of Kurds.

Halil Cavgun founded the Riha Yuksek Education Association. He was admired by Kurds for standing up to feudal oppression. Halil Cavgun was killed exactly a year after the death of Haki Karer, while hanging a poster memorializing Haki.[30] His murder sparked the Hilvan Siverek Resistance Initiative. Its founder, Mehmet Karasungur, led the resistance. He was born in Hasret village in Cewlik to a poverty-stricken family of twelve. He established the Cewlik Branch of the All Teachers' Unity and Solidarity Association. Like the struggle against the Bucak clan in Siverek, the Hilvan resistance targeted Kurdish feudal landlords, especially the Suleyman clan. The Suleymans and Bucaks acted as an extension of the State. The Hilvan resistance was the first successful rebellion by Kurds against feudal landlords who were condemned for "exploiting the peasants" and "collaborating" with the Turkish State against the Kurdish people.[31]

The PKK (Partiya Karkeren Kurdistan) was officially established at a congress of Kurds in the village of Fis, in Lice district, on November 27–28, 1978. It was originally called the Ankara Democratic Association of Higher Education (ADYOD). As an armed resistance movement, it was inspired by the Hilvan resistance. The PKK's founding members included Abdullah Ocalan, nicknamed "Uncle" (Apo), Cemil Bayik, Haki Karer, Kemal Pir, Mehmet Sevgat, Mehmet Karasungur, and Kesire Yildirim, whom Ocalan would later marry. The PKK was independent minded. It accused other Leftist groups of "social chauvinism" for rejecting the possibility of a Kurdish state.[32]

The PKK was a byproduct of the revolutionary left. It was influenced by Dev Genc and other ideological groups involved in the worldwide anticolonial movement of the 1970s. The PKK's ideology was a mix of radical Marxism-Leninism and Kurdish nationalism. Its founding charter, the Proclamation of Independence of PKK, enshrined armed struggle to foster a Marxist proletarian revolution. It envisioned the PKK as the "vanguard of the global socialist movement," in which the revolution's fundamental force would be a "worker-peasant alliance."[33] The charter condemned "the repressive exploitation of the Kurds" and called for a "democratic and united Kurdistan."[34] Ocalan saw the establishment of a Kurdish state in southeast Anatolia (Turkey) as the first step toward the creation of an independent and united "Greater Kurdistan," encompassing a vast territory of Kurds with different dialects (Zaza, Kurmanji, and Surani), different Muslim denominations (Sunni, Shafii and Alevi), and people from different countries (Turkey, Iran, Iraq, and Syria).[35] Ocalan and his cohorts believed that establishing an independent, socialist Kurdish state was the only way to free Kurds from the yoke of repression. According to Kemal Pir, "We all loved life enough to die for it. Life was beautiful. However, an honorable life was the most beautiful one."[36]

The PKK assumed prominence and gained broad popular support after the Maras Massacre. In Maras, 111 Alevi Kurds were killed during a week of bloodletting between December 18 and 25, 1978. According to Seyho Demir, an eyewitness that day,

> The massacre was organised by MIT (the Turkish secret service), the Nationalist Movement Party (MHP) and the Islamists together.... As soon as I heard about the massacre, I went to Maras. In the morning I went to Maras State Hospital. There I met a nurse I knew.... When she saw me, she was surprised: "Seyho, where have you come from? They are killing everyone here. They have taken at least ten lightly-wounded people from the hospital downstairs and killed them." This was done under the control of the head physician of the Maras State Hospital. Everyone knows that such a big massacre cannot be carried out without state involvement. In the Yörükselim neighborhood they cut a pregnant woman open with a bayonet. They took out the eight-month fetus, shouting "Allah Allah" and hung it from an electricity pole with a hook. The pictures of that savagery were published in the newspapers that day.[37]

The Maras Massacre was not an isolated incident. It inaugurated a systematic campaign of violent confrontation by the State against the Kurds. Seyho Demir explained, "Just as people were attacked in Maras for being Alevi, now people's doors are being marked, their workplaces looted for being Kurdish, and campaigns to stop people from buying from Kurds are being started."[38] The PKK seized on the Maras massacre to recruit Kurds to its cause. Initially, the PKK engaged in an urban war against the regime and its security structures. Abdullah Ocalan was glorified for defending Kurds, who took pride in the PKK for standing up to the Turkish State.

As the PKK emerged, deadly violence escalated around the country, including the 1980 assassination of ex–prime minister Nihat Erim by Dev Sol. The PKK was also involved in violent activities, targeting Turkish officials for assassination. The military conducted another coup d'état on September 12, 1980. Martial law was declared. The prime minister, cabinet ministers, and opposition leaders were arrested. Tens of thousands of leftists and Kurds were also rounded up. Some disappeared. Many were subject to capital punishment. General Kenan Evren declared himself the seventh president of Turkey and prepared a new constitution. The 1982 constitution curtailed Kurdish rights even further. Evren and his cohorts followed Ataturk's example, glorifying Turkishness. Billboards across Turkey echoed Ataturk's message: "Happy is he who can call himself a Turk."[39]

*****

Abdullah Ocalan and his PKK cadres made the strategic decision to leave Turkey in 1980.[40] They were welcomed by Syrian President Hafiz al-Assad and moved the organization's headquarters to the Syrian-controlled Bekaa Valley in Lebanon. Ocalan lived in plain sight at a villa in Damascus. Syrian Foreign Minister Faruk al-Shara lauded the PKK as a "resistance movement" rather than a terrorist group.[41] Syria was not motivated by sympathy for Kurds in Turkey. Assad thought he could use the PKK to destabilize the Turkey-Syria border and, as a result, reclaim Hatay Province. Hatay-Iskenderun was part of France's Syrian territory. After Turkish politicians assumed a majority of seats in the local council election of 1938, they engineered a plebiscite severing Hatay-Iskenderum from Syria and joining Turkey.

The PKK founded the Mahsum Korkmaz Academy in the Bekaa Valley, which was under control of the Palestinian Liberation Organization (PLO) at the time. The Mahsum Korkmaz Academy offered ideological instruction and training in guerilla operations. Instructors came from the Soviet Union, Bulgaria, Cuba, and Iran. Mahsum Korkmaz also served as a base of operations for the PKK's guerrilla war against Turkey. Cross-border operations from Syria complemented PKK hit-and-run attacks against Turkish gendarmerie in Southeast Turkey.

Ocalan was a proponent of a women's liberation theology. The PKK's first congress, from September 22 to 27 of 1980, enshrined a leadership role for women in the organization. Many women served on the central committee. Women's emancipation became a symbol of the PKK's egalitarian ideals and its fight for social justice against the feudal and patriarchal Kurdish society. Hundreds of women were recruited into the PKK's armed forces. A majority of the PKK's suicide bombings were carried out by women.[42]

The PKK convened its second congress near the Jordanian border from August 20 to 25, 1982. The congress endorsed the establishment of military and political organizations as well as the continuing leadership of Abdullah Ocalan. Major decisions were taken on the return to Kurdistan, cooperation with leftist movements, and the importance of diplomatic activities. The PKK vowed to intensify its armed struggle to liberate Kurdistan. In 1984, the PKK established the People's Liberation Forces. They were replaced by the People's Liberation Army of Kurdistan (ARGR) in 1986, which became the People's Defense Force (HPG) in 2000.

The Congress also called on PKK political prisoners to maintain their protests. Turkey's penitentiaries were a locus for ideological training and radicalization, especially after the capital punishment of Sakine Cansiz, a cofounder of the organization. Martyrs were potent symbols of resistance. Mazlum Dogan, a PKK Central Committee member, protested the treatment of detainees in Diyarbakir Prison. On March 21, 1982, Newroz-Dogan lit three matches, urged people to revolt, and slit his throat. Later on May 17, PKK prisoners—Ferhat Kurtay, Eşref Anyik, Mahmut Zengin and Necmi Oner—self-immolated to protest Diyarbakir Prison conditions. Hayri Durmus, Kemal Pir, Ali Cicek, and Akif Yilmaz declared a fast on July 14 and were dead by September.

The PKK became a formidable fundraiser due to battlefield victories and persuasive public relations. In 1982, the PKK opened a new public diplomacy and recruitment front, targeting Kurds in Europe. Cultural organizations, such as the newly established Kurdish Artists Forum and other PKK front organizations, were tasked with raising revenue and lobbying for Kurdish interests. The National Liberation Front of Kurdistan (ERNK) opened diplomatic bureaus in many European countries after its establishment on March 21, 1985. These cultural associations and information centers were integral to the PKK's fundraising and recruitment efforts.[43] Europe proved to be a fertile field.

Kurdish youth were a key demographic. Many lived in city slums of northern Europe and Turkey, or in villages of Turkey's southeast. They were drawn by the romantic appeal of Kurdish guerrillas standing up to vastly superior Turkish forces.

Kurdish newspapers and publications were widely available at European kiosks. The first international Kurdish television station (Med-TV) had studios in England and Belgium. Its programs were translated and distributed in six languages. It was banned by France and Britain in 1999. Both claimed Med-TV had links to the PKK and fostered violence. Roj TV was launched in Denmark as a replacement for Med-TV in 2004. It similarly faced opposition, especially from Turkey's Foreign Ministry, which pressured Copenhagen.

Media helped raise funds for the Kurdish cause. Donations were provided by the Kurdish Diaspora in Europe through cultural associations and information centers such as the Kurdish Employers Association, the Kurdish Islamic Movement, and the Kurdish Red Crescent. These organizations also raised funds for the PKK and facilitated money transfers through subsidiary foundations in Switzerland, Britain, Sweden, Belgium, Denmark, and Cyprus.

From Dev-Genc emerged a plethora of Kurdish youth organizations such as the Patriotic Revolutionary Youth Movement (YDG-H). In 1986, more than two thousand female delegates met in Cologne, Germany, to establish the Kurdistan Patriotic Women's Association (YJKW), which became the Kurdistan Women's Freedom Movement (TAJK), and later the Kurdistan Working Women's Party (PJKK). However, European countries were growing increasingly uneasy about PKK activities on their territory. Swedish Prime Minister Olof Palme was assassinated while strolling down the central Stockholm street of Sveavagen on February 28, 1986. Based on information provided by the Turkish authorities, Swedish authorities suspected the PKK of masterminding the killing. A period of confrontation between the PKK and European governments ensued, which resulted in the PKK's criminalization. In February 1988, Germany's state police undertook a coordinated operation against the PKK. Senior Commander of the PKK Duran Kalkan and Ali Haydar Kaytan were arrested and tried in what was called the Dusseldorf Case. By November 1993, Germany banned PKK activities and closed thirty-four Kurdish cultural centers. It accused these organizations of extorting funds from Kurdish and Turkish workers. The French government took similar steps. The Kurdistan National Parliament was targeted by local security services in the Netherlands, which sought to curtail its political and fundraising activities.

*****

By PKK's third Congress in Bekaa on October 25–26, 1986, the US government estimated that the PKK had nearly 15,000 full-time guerrillas. About a third were in Turkey and the rest in Iran, Iraq, and Syria. Up to 75,000 part-time guerrillas were also in the PKK's ranks.[44] The Congress emphasized ideological purity. However, romantic notions of a Greater Kurdistan were eroding under the pressure of armed conflict. The PKK was also tarnished by its close cooperation with rogue partners and criminal regimes. In addition to its headquarters in Syria, the PKK had bases in Iran, Iraq, and Libya. Saddam Hussein gave weapons to the PKK in exchange for information on the Kurdistan Democratic Party of Masoud Barzani. Ocalan and Libya's leader, Moammar Khadafi, enjoyed close personal relations. Khadafi pledged support for the "Kurdish cause." Greek nationalists also supported the PKK to weaken Turkey, allowing PKK cadres free passage through Athens. While Greek politicians dismissed the possibility of official cooperation, they acknowledged links between the PKK and Greek private citizens. These links included cooperation with retired members of the Greek armed forces.[45]

The PKK signed an agreement of cooperation with the Armenian Secret Army for the Liberation of Armenia (ASALA) on April 6, 1980.[46] The PKK bombed the Turkish Consulate in Strasbourg, France, during a joint operation with ASALA on November 10, 1980. The PLO provided sanctuary and training to the PKK beginning in 1982. Germany's Red Army Faction (RAF) helped the PKK organize rallies in Bonn, and RAF members visited PKK bases in Turkey.

Reports leaked from Bekaa about the PKK's rigid hierarchical structure and Stalinist discipline. Ultimate authority rested with Ocalan, who cultivated a cult of personality, brutally suppressed dissent, and purged opponents. Ocalan, whose surname means "avenger" in Turkish, consolidated absolute control through a campaign of torture and execution against his closest cadres between 1980 and 1984. Defectors were allegedly assassinated in Sweden (1984 and 1985), Denmark (1985), the Netherlands (1987 and 1989), and Germany (1986, 1987 and 1988).[47] In 1986, up to sixty PKK members were executed, including five of the original central committee members. Mahsum Korkmaz, the supreme military commander, was murdered on March 28, 1986. Huseyn Yildirim, the PKK's spokesman in Brussels, broke with Ocalan in 1988. Inevitable splits and factions emerged within the PKK, intensifying factional violence.

Ocalan demanded that Kurds choose between loyalty to Turkey and support for the PKK. Brutal and swift punishment was meted out to those who refused to cooperate. The PKK targeted Kurdish elites who sided with the Turkish establishment, as well as Kurds who worked for state institutions. Between 1984 and 1987, the PKK kidnapped or killed 217 teachers. It burned hundreds of rural schools, effectively shutting down the education system.[48] Hospitals were attacked, and doctors and nurses were killed. In June 1987, the PKK slaughtered residents in the village of Pinarcik for collaborating with the regime. Two months later, it killed twenty-four residents of Kilickaya including fourteen children. Between 1995 and 1999, its "suicide guerilla teams" were responsible for twenty-one suicide terrorist attacks. Most were committed by female cadres.[49]

Financing came from a "revolutionary tax" provided by Kurdish businessmen in Turkey who were forced to pay or face the consequences. The PKK also organized protection rackets targeting Kurdish owned businesses across Europe. The PKK attacked Turkish diplomatic and commercial facilities in dozens of West European cities in 1993 and again in spring 1995. The PKK financed its operations through drug and arms smuggling, human trafficking, and extortion. It charged a fee for "visas" to visitors from Europe.[50] It bombed tourist sites and hotels and kidnapped foreign tourists, demanding ransom. In 1998, the British government maintained that the PKK was responsible for 40 percent of the heroin sold in Europe.[51] At its peak, the PKK's annual income was as high as $500 million.[52]

*****

PKK tactics were in response to systematic human rights abuses, and Turkey's brutal counterinsurgency measures. The government put several southeastern provinces under martial law and, in the late 1980s, declared a state of emergency, empowering super-governors with military and administrative powers. It invoked Article 14 of the constitution to crack down on activities that threatened the "indivisibility of the state."[53] It also invoked Article 125 of the penal code, which stipulated: "Any person who carries out any action intended to destroy the unity of the Turkish state or separate any part of the territory shall be punishable by death." Article 8 of the Law for Fighting against Terrorism defined terrorism so broadly it was used to criminalize any free discussion about Kurdish issues.[54] Army camps, police checkpoints, and military airports were established from the Semdinli Mountains in the southeast to Siirt near the border with Syria. Major military operations against the PKK were launched in 1989. With intelligence backing from the United States, 300,000 Turkish troops crossed the Iraqi border to attack 10,000 guerrillas in 1992. PKK activities peaked in 1993 when there were 4,198 reported clashes between the PKK and security forces.[55]

Over 1,500 persons affiliated with the Kurdish opposition were murdered by unidentified assailants between 1989 and 1996. Government-backed death squads killed hundreds of suspected PKK sympathizers.[56] The crackdown included mass arrests, extended periods of administrative detention, and torture. Close to 500 people disappeared between 1991 and 1997. Between 1983 and 1994, another 230 people disappeared.[57] Many died from torture while in police custody.[58] Kurdish cultural rights were denied. When thousands gathered to celebrate Newroz on March 21, 1989, the police attacked them and scores were killed. The same crackdown occurred during Newroz in 1992, when more than one hundred people were killed in the towns of Cizre, Sirnak, and Nusaybin.[59] The first daily Kurdish newspaper, *Ozgur Gundem*, was founded in May 1992. Its offices were bombed, and thirteen employees killed. The paper was published intermittently, due to arrests of its employees and other impediments imposed by the authorities.

The government's displacement policy sought to drain the swamp of support for the PKK. In the early 1990s, security forces burned between 2,000 and 4,000 villages and displaced 3 to 3.5 million Kurds. As a result, cities such as Diyarbakir, Cizre, and Nusaybin more than doubled in size.[60] Diyarbakir's unemployment rate skyrocketed to 70 percent; its poverty rate rose to 39.7 percent, and more than 10,000 shantytown homes sprung up in the city.[61] The scorched-earth policy was a military success but a tactical failure. Deprived of logistical support, the PKK fled to strongholds across the border in Iraq with Turkish troops in hot pursuit.[62] Popular support surged in response to Turkey's draconian practices.

The Village Guard System pit Kurd against Kurd.[63] The state hired and equipped sixty thousand Kurds to serve as paramilitaries. According to the authorities, the system was intended to help villagers defend themselves, but it had the opposite effect by polarizing communities and acting as a magnet for PKK operations.

Official and paramilitary groups were aligned with the Deep State—an ultranationalist amalgamation of interest groups including the army, police, government bureaucrats, and corrupt politicians who cooperate with mafia-style figures. They formed a shadow government in Turkey. The constitution empowered the National Security Council (NSC) to take whatever steps it deemed "necessary for the preservation of the State," which it called "sacred."[64] Instead of promoting the interests of individual citizens, the Deep State was preoccupied with preserving its privileges and power. Ensuring State security and the continuity of official institutions comprising the bureaucracy were paramount. According to Suleyman Demirel, a former president and seven-time prime minister, "It is a fundamental principle that there is one State. But in our country there are two."[65] The preference for uniformity and the State's failure to reconcile ethnic, religious, and cultural identities resulted in a breakdown of social cohesion and exacerbated social estrangement.

Historically, Turkey's military was the unflinching guardian of secularism, nationalism, and modernization. Officers saw their mission extending beyond the protection of Turkish territory to include warding off threats to public order, such as separatism, terrorism, and religious fundamentalism. Kurds resent the army's paternalistic approach, exemplified in a statement by the TGS: "If there is need for more democracy, we will bring it."[66] Threats, both real and imagined, were used to sustain a primacy of the military's role in public affairs and justify its expenditures. Rather than promoting security, the military was known for staging incidents to justify recrimination against the Kurdish community.

In 1996, a car crashed in the village of Susurluk. In the vehicle were Sedat Bucak, Istanbul's deputy police chief, and a leader of the ultranationalist Grey Wolves on Interpol's red bulletin list. The car was loaded with cash, weapons, and false identification cards. The incident revealed a cabal between the State, security services and the mafia to assassinate civilian opponents in return for sharing the spoils from narcotics trafficking. The "Susurluk incident" dramatized pervasive activities of the Deep State.

*****

Kurdish political parties were able to win control of municipal governments, but they had had little success at the national level. Turkey's electoral law prohibits parties from being seated in parliament unless they receive more than 10 percent of the vote nationwide. No exclusively Kurdish party has been able to pass the threshold. When hybrid coalitions comprised of leftist or other parties successfully passed the threshold, they were banned by Turkish authorities.

President Turgut Ozal became prime minister in 1983 and served as president from 1989 to 1993. He was strategic and visionary. He believed that the PKK's influence could be neutralized through increasing the role of Kurdish political parties nationally. He officially broke the taboo against using the term "Kurd," referring publicly to the people of eastern Anatolia as "Kurds." Ozal believed these reforms would moderate Kurds and make them loyal citizens. In 1991, he lifted the ban on the Kurdish language in private arenas and the possession of Kurdish materials in the home. Ozal even floated the idea of providing general amnesty for PKK fighters.

The People's Labor Party (HEP) was founded to advance Kurdish interests through the political process. It won eighteen seats in the parliamentary elections of October 1991. However, Turkish legislators were incensed when Leyla Zana insisted on speaking Kurdish during her parliamentary oath and wearing the PKK's tricolor band. Other Kurdish deputies—Hatip Dicle, Orhan Dogan, Ahmet Turk, Sirri Sakik and Mahmut Alinak—were charged as accessories to a terrorist organization. They were tried in the State Security Courts under Article 301 and sentenced to a total of 895 years. Denied political representation, Diaspora Kurds launched the Kurdistan National Parliament (KNK) or Kongra Netewiya Kurdistan, in March 1992.

Two months after Ozal's death in April 1993, the Constitutional Court banned HEP. Foreseeing the ban, Kurdish deputies resigned from HEP and established the Democracy Party (DEP). DEP was banned in June 1994. Kurdish Deputy Murat Bozlak formed the New People's Democracy Party (HADEP). HADEP took part in the general elections of December 24, 1995, but it failed to pass the required 10 percent barrier. Its successor, the Democratic People's Party (DEHAP) also failed to pass the threshold in the general elections on April 18, 1999, but it gained control of thirty-seven local councils.

Kurds were persistent in their efforts to participate in the political system but were thwarted every time. Turkey's electoral law was manipulated, preventing Kurds from reaching a critical mass and thus parliamentary representation. Their political leaders suffered arrest and prosecution. The Constitutional Court criminalized and banned political parties that sought to peacefully advance Kurdish interests. Absent political representation nationally, Kurds had to focus on delivering services through local councils. For demanding basic rights, Kurds were accused of affiliation or membership with terrorist groups and charged under the Penal Code and Anti-Terror Act. Regressive legislation was used to limit freedom of expression and association.

The PKK held its Fifth Congress from January 8 to 27, 1993. Delegates sought to moderate perceptions of the PKK. Radicalism had undermined political dialogue with the government. It also gave the government justification to oppress the Kurds. The PKK flag, a heinous symbol to Turks, was changed. The PKK had no status as a state party but signed the Geneva Convention and committed itself to international accords of war. Most importantly, the PKK declared a unilateral ceasefire on March 20, 1993. The ceasefire declaration was intended to test Ozal's commitment to equal rights and political reforms. Ocalan explained, "We never took up arms for the sake of it. All we did was to open a road for our nation to freely develop. But we had no other means of struggle to adopt: that is why we had to take up arms and have brought the struggle to this stage."[67]

"To ensure a calmer, more peaceful atmosphere," Ocalan demanded that Turkey reciprocate and cease military operations. He enumerated cultural rights, such as free press and media, use of the Kurdish language in media and education. He also demanded political rights, such as freedom of expression and association, constitutional recognition of Kurdish identity, and legalization of Kurdish organizations. Ocalan sought compensation for Kurds driven from their villages and whose property was destroyed.[68]

Ozal suffered a fatal heart attack in April 1993. Suleyman Demirel, his successor, tried to continue Ozal's reform agenda. Demirel did not challenge the Deep State, but he was still denounced by ultranationalists. The NSC dismissed the PKK's unilateral ceasefire. Prospects for dialogue dimmed when thirty-three soldiers were killed on the road between Elazig and Bingol on May 24, 1993. The soldiers were unarmed; they had just finished their military service and were on their way to being discharged.[69] Turkey recommitted to a military solution.

*****

While keeping up the pressure militarily, Turkey tried to deny PKK support through economic development. Ankara reasoned that jobs and economic security would instill gainful purpose into Kurdish youth, de-radicalizing them. Its efforts were well intended but poorly implemented.

Beginning in the early 1960s, Turkey launched the Southeastern Anatolia Development Project (GAP), a massive investment plan designed to harness the waters of the Tigris and Euphrates Rivers for the region's economic development. It built twenty-three dams, including the $2.3 billion Ataturk Dam, the ninth largest in the world.[70] The GAP Project's irrigation network was designed to service 1.7 million hectares, support seventeen hydroelectric plants, and increase agricultural production sevenfold. It also planned to triple per capita income and create 3.3 million new jobs. A six-lane highway was built between the cities of Adana, Gaziantep, and Diyarbakir. Turkey also instituted a GAP Social Action Plan emphasizing human development and social services.

GAP failed because of cronyism and flawed execution. Though tens of billions were spent, financing shortfalls and the ongoing security crisis undermined GAP's success. Both public and private investment were affected by conflict conditions with serious repercussions to the local economy. Seasonal herding and small-scale agriculture activities became almost impossible under a state of emergency. Land mines limited the area that could be productively used. Security operations also drained the national economy costing $8 billion per year. Turkey estimated the total cost of the conflict at $200 billion.[71]

*****

Tensions increased between Syria and Turkey, as GAP deprived Syria of water from the Tigris and Euphrates Rivers. Assad supported the PKK to gain leverage over Turkey's upstream water management. The PKK intensified its attacks when Turkey completed construction of the Ataturk and Bicercik dams on the Euphrates. Ankara responded with threats to cut off Syria's water supplies unless Damascus broke with the PKK. The TGS also threatened to attack PKK bases in Syria.[72]

Assad succumbed to Ankara's threats and signed the Adana Memorandum in October 1998. The Adana Memorandum required Syria to designate the PKK a terrorist organization and evict the PKK from its territory. Ocalan fled Syria on October 9, 1998. Thus began his global odyssey to Moscow, Rome, Amsterdam, Athens, and Nairobi, where he was finally apprehended by Turkish Special Forces working alongside US intelligence.

On February 16, 1999, Turkish television showed images of Turkey's most wanted fugitive—hooded, drugged, and dazed. Kurds stormed embassies, seized hostages, and burned themselves in protest across Europe. They were expressing solidarity with Ocalan, whom they revered for standing up to the state and demanding dignity and human rights for Kurds. Kurds chanted in defiance: "You cannot eclipse our sun."

Ocalan was jailed on Imrali Island in the Marmara Sea. In a surprising display of remorse, Ocalan offered to end the PKK's armed struggle in exchange for his life. "The democratic option is the only alternative to solving the Kurdish question. Separation is neither possible nor necessary. We want peace, dialogue, and free political action within the framework of a democratic Turkish state."[73] He pleaded, "Give me a chance. In three months, I will bring all of them down from the mountains."[74] A Turkish state security court convicted Ocalan of treason in June 1999. Conforming to EU prohibitions against capital punishment, his death sentence was commuted to life in prison.[75]

Notes

1.   Boston Review | John Tirman: Ataturk's Children. www.photius.com/thus/ataturk.html.
2.   *The Kurdistan Tribune*. When will the Turkish state give Kurds the secret grave of Sheik Said? Solin Hacador. kurdistantribune.com/2013/when-will-turkish-state-give-kurds . . . (accessed March 4, 2014).
3.   "Understanding The Kurdish Issue History Essay." *Understanding The Kurdish Issue History Essay*. Web. 19 May 2014.
4.   www.kurdishglobe.net/article/913986E6C6333262450A50ABB06EF93D/ . . .
5.   Boston Review | John Tirman: Ataturk's Children www.photius.com/thus/ataturk.html.
6.   ('İskân Kanunu' Law No.2510, 13 June 1934). Çağaptay, Soner (2002). "Reconfiguring the Turkish nation in the 1930s". Harvard. Retrieved 2010-08-02.
7.   Hasretyan, M. A. (1995) *Türkiye'de Kürt Sorunu (1918–1940)*, Berlin, Wêşanên, ênstîtuya Kurdî: I., p. 262.
8.   "Kurdistan House." *Kurdistan House*. Web. 20 May 2014. www.kurdistan-house.org/?p=145.
9.   "Resmi raporlarda Dersim katliamı: 13 bin kişi öldürüldü", *Radikal*, November 19, 2009. (Turkish).
10. (Gemeinnützig), Dersim-Gesellschaft Für Wiederaufbau E.v., Holweider Str.40 51065 Köln, Tel.: 02216160611, and Www.dersim-Wiederaufbau.de. *To the Attention of Press and Public "DERSĐM '38 CONFERANCE"* (n.d.): n. page. Web.

11. Hüseyin Aygün, *Dersim 1938 ve zorunlu iskân: telgraflar, dilekçeler, mektuplar*, Dipnot Yayınları, 2009, ISBN 978-975-9051-75-4.
12. Martin van Bruinessen, *Kurdish ethno-nationalism versus nation-building states: collected articles*, Isis Press, 2000, ISBN 978-975-428-177-4, p. 116.
13. "Pamukoğlu: Dersim'in emrini Atatürk verdi", *Hürriyet*, August 19, 2010. (Turkish).
14. Mustafa AKYOL. *Evropeos*. How Turkey massacred the Kurds of Dersim. November 17, 2009. greekturkish.fr.yuku.com.
15. Ibid.
16. Yonca Poyraz DOĞAN. Today's Zaman. TPM Erdoğan apologizes over Dersim massacre on behalf of Turkish state. 23 November 2011.
17. Yılmaz, Kamil. *Disengaging from Terrorism: Lessons from the Turkish Penitents*.
18. The Baghdad Pact included Britain, Iran, Iraq, and Pakistan.
19. "Country Studies." *Country Studies*. Web. 20 May 2014.countrystudies.us/turkey/15.htm.
20. Ibid.
    Oron, Yitzhak. *Middle East Record*. Jerusalem: Published for Tel Aviv U The Reuven Shiloah Research Center by Israel Program for Scientific Translations, 1961.
22. "Turkish Constitution of 1921." *Turkish_Constitution*. Web. 19 May 2014.
23. Ibid.
24. Ibid.
25. Blood and Belief: The PKK and the Kurdish Fight for Independence, by Aliza Marcus, p. 15, 2007.
26. (Yılmaz, Kamil, 30).
27. "Turkey: May Day Celebrated at Taksim Square, Istanbul for the First Time in 33 Years." *Frontlines of Revolutionary Struggle*. Web. 19 May 2014.
28. Joost Jongerden, PKK, CEU Political Science Journal. Vol. 3, No. 1 page 127–132.
29. "Mehmet Karasungur - Halil Cavgun | Partiya Karkerên Kurdistan - PKK Official Site." *Mehmet Karasungur - Halil Cavgun | Partiya Karkerên Kurdistan - PKK Official Site*. Web. 19 May 2014.
30. Ibid.
31. Ibid.
32. "European Journal of Turkish Studies." *The Kurdistan Workers Party and a New Left in Turkey: Analysis of the Revolutionary Movement in Turkey through the PKK's Memorial Text on Haki Karer*. Web. 20 May 2014.
33. Eager, Paige Whaley. *From Freedom Fighters to Terrorists: Women and Political Violence*. Aldershot, England: Ashgate, 2008.
34. Party program of the PKK adopted at the Fifth Victory Congress, January 1995.
35. Dogu Ergil. "Suicide Terrorism in Turkey." *Civil Wars*, Vol. 3, No. 1 (Spring 2000). Pgs. 37–54.
36. Ibid.
37. www.bianet.org/. . . /103813-remembering-the-maras-massacre-in-1978 (accessed March 6, 2014).

38. Ibid.
39. The author first visited Diyarbakir in February 1992.
40. Tejel, Jordi, Emily Welle, and Jane Welle. *Syria's Kurds: History, Politics and Society.* London: Routledge, 2009. Print.
41. www.fas.org/irp/world/para/docs/studies3.htm.
42. Suri, Sanjay (11 May 2005). "Torture and Oppression of Kurds in Syria". *antiwar.com.*
43. MFA - A Report on the PKK and Terrorism. www.fas.org/irp/world/para/docs/mfa-t-pkk.htm.
44. "MFA - I. Historical Background and Development." *MFA - I. Historical Background and Development.* N.p., n.d. Web. 22 July 2014.
45. "MFA - III. International Sources of Support." *MFA - III. International Sources of Support.* Web. 20 May 2014.
46. Ibid.
47. MYNET/Fact Sheet. September 6, 2005.
48. "Disarming, Demobilizing and Reintegrating the PKKby David L. Phillips." *Today's Zaman, Your Gateway to Turkish Daily News.* Web. 20 May 2014.
49. State Security Court Indictment of Abdullah Ocalan. Pg. 58.
50. "Ocalan Conducted Ruthless Offensive." *By Amberin Zaman.* Special to The Washington Post. February 1999.
51. *The Spectator.* 28 November-5 December, 1998.
52. Michael Radu. "The Rise and Fall of the PKK." *Orbis,* Vol. 45, No. 1 (Winter 2001). Pg. 47.
53. "Republic of Turkey, Ministry of Foreign Affairs - Printer Friendly Version." *Republic of Turkey, Ministry of Foreign Affairs - Printer Friendly Version.* Web. 20 May 2014.
54. Article 8 was adopted in 1991.
55. Ergil. "Suicide Terrorism in Turkey."
56. Stephen Kinzer. "The Big Change." *The New York Review of Books.* January 12, 2006.
57. Turkish Human Rights Association, *Annual Report 2004.*
58. Turkish Human Rights Association, *Annual Report 2004.*
59. "American Kurdish Information Network (AKIN)." *American Kurdish Information Network AKIN RSS.* Web. 20 May 2014.
60. Human Rights Watch. *World Report 2005.*
61. Diyarbakir Metropolitan Municipality. "Democratization in Turkey and the Kurdish Question." Report issued by Osman Baydemir, Mayor of Diyarbakir. September 1, 2005.
62. "Ocalan Conducted Ruthless Offensive." *By Amberin Zaman.* Special to The Washington Post. February 1999.
63. "PKK Attacks on Civilian Targets Sign of Weakness, Experts Say." *Today's Zaman, Your Gateway to Turkish Daily News.* Web. 20 May 2014.
64. "Republic of Turkey, Ministry of Foreign Affairs - Printer Friendly Version." *Republic of Turkey, Ministry of Foreign Affairs - Printer Friendly Version.* Web. 20 May 2014.

65. "Telling the Truth for More than 30 Years . . ." *Washington Report on Middle East Affairs*. Web. 20 May 2014.

66. Osman Baydemir, Mayor of Diyarbakir, and Diyarbakir Metropolitan Municipality. "Democratization in Turkey and the Kurdish Question." September 1, 2005.

67. Cited by Adem Uzun in "Living Freedom. Berghof Foundation. Transition Series No. 11.

68. www.serxwebun.org/arsiv/136/.

69. History of PKK in Turkey. Hürriyet Daily News. September 14, 2009. SEVİM SONGÜN.

70. Phillips.

71. National Intelligence Organization. http://www.yesil.org.terror/pkkrakam-lar.htm. April 9, 2005.

72. "Picture Id: 478646." *478646. Members of the Kurdistan Workers Party, or PKK, Attend a Rally in Lebanon's Bekaa Valley. The PKK Is a Marxist Organization Run by an Enigmatic Figure Named Abdullah Ocalan, Also Known as Apo, or Uncle Apo, Who Promises to Form an Independent Kurdistan in the Border Area of Iraq, Syria, Turkey and Iran, Has a Following of Tens of Thousands of Kurds in Turkey, Syria, and Lebanon. The PKK Runs the Ma Hsum Korkmaz Academy in the Bekaa Valley, a Guerrilla Training Base Operated Under Syrian Protection. from the Mahsum Korkmaz Academy, the PKK Carries on a Guerrilla War against Turkey. Syria's Interest in Supporting the PKK Is Not One of Kindness towards a Minority Group That Is Repressed by the Turkish Government. In Fact, Syria Uses Its Kurdish Card as Leverage against Turkey's Control of Fresh Water from Such Rivers as the Euphrates That Flow from Turkey into Syria. The New Ataturk Dam Has Given Turkey Control of the Euphrates.* N.p., n.d. Web. 30 May 2014. <http://www.natgeocreative.com/photography/478646>.

73. Abdullah Öcalan. *Declaration on the Democratic Solution of the Kurdish Question*. Published by the Kurdistan Information Centre, Mesopotamian Publishers, London. 1999). Pg. 85.

74. Metin Munir. "Kurdish leader gains support for deal that will end military struggle." *Financial Times*. June 3, 1999. Pg. 2.

75. Some Kurds believe that Öcalan is under the control of Turkish authorities, and that he is being manipulated to sustain the PKK to justify the state's efforts to subvert reforms and democratization.

4

Kurds in Syria

Consistent with the Sykes-Picot Agreement of 1916, France's World War I mandate included Syria and Lebanon. The territory of the French and British mandates was demarcated by a straight line from Jordan to Iran. After the discovery of oil in Mosul in the 1920s, the border was slightly altered, ceding territory to Britain. Syria was the largest state to emerge from the Ottoman Levant.

France divided its mandate into six entities: Greater Lebanon, Damascus, Aleppo, Alawites, Jabal Druze, and the autonomous Sanjak of Alexandretta, which is now Hatay Province in Turkey. Syria's population was about three-quarters Arab. The balance included minorities such as Kurds, Armenians, Assyrians, Yazidi, and Turks. Of these, Kurds were the largest ethnic minority in Syria. Kurds reside on a patchwork of territories, which they call Rojava. Syrian Kurdistan encompasses regions in northern Syria such as Kobani, near Jarabulus, and Afrin, whose plains extend to the Turkish border. Kurds predominate in Jazira province, Hasakah Governorate, and the cities of Qamishli and Hasakah. There are also Kurds in Syria's northeast.[1] In religious terms, most Kurds are Sunni Muslims and secular. The Kurds of Syria speak Kurmanji and Arabic. There is no contiguous landmass where Kurds are the majority

Syrian Kurds were inspired by President Woodrow Wilson's Fourteen Points, caught in the wave of nationalism after World War I. In 1920, they declared Jazira, as an autonomous Kurdish region in Syria. The Kurdish population in Jazira is from both Syria and Turkey. They speak the same dialect and share tribal identities. They have a long history of commercial and cultural contact. Many Kurds relocated to Syria from Turkey after Sheikh Said's rebellion in 1925. They were welcomed by their Kurdish brethren, blending with Syria's Kurdish community. Kurds from Turkey also fled to northeastern Syria, Aleppo, and Damascus. When Sultan al-Atrash, the Christian Druze leader, launched an Arab rebellion against the French administration, Kurds refused to join.

They feared that Syrian independence would bring an Arab nationalist government to power, which would replace officials from minority groups with Arabs from Damascus, further marginalizing them. Kurds in Syria preferred France's dominion to Arab dominance.

Kurds maintained a deep resentment toward Turkey for betraying Sheikh Said and abusing the Kurdish cause. They came together to form the pan-Kurdish Xoybun League in Beirut on October 5, 1927. In Kurmanji, "Xoybun" means "one who controls his destiny."[2] Xoybun was a secular nationalist movement whose aim was a united and independent Kurdistan. It was established by Kurdish intellectuals, including the writer Celadet Bedirxan and the philosopher Qedri Can. It was headed by Ihsan Nuri, a member of the Jalali tribe and decorated solider who fought in the Ottoman Army.[3] Xoybun captured the imagination of Kurds across Western Kurdistan. It served as the intellectual foundation of the Kurdish nationalist movement. *Hawar*, a cultural review, was read region-wide. Branches in south, north, and west Kurdistan popularized ideas of nationalism, self-determination, and self-defense. These inspired the Ararat uprising between 1927 and 1930.

Kurdish members of Syria's constituent assembly proposed autonomy in 1928. However, French authorities resisted. According to French administrators, Kurds were not entitled to autonomy because they were not concentrated in a contiguous territory. Nor were Kurds a religious minority like the Druze or Alawites. Kurds sought to build a pro-autonomy coalition, reaching out to Assyrians in Jazira, as well as Christians and Bedouins. When elections were held for a constitutional committee in December 1931, Xoybun delegates from Jazira, Jarablus, and Kurd Dagh were elected. The Kurdish leader, Osman Sabri, did not participate in elections. In 1930, he was convicted of separatism and exiled to Madagascar. He and other more militant Kurds were repeatedly arrested and spent years in jail. They became symbols of Kurdish resistance against France, and later against Arabs. Osman Sabri was arrested eighteen times and spent twelve years in jail.[4] His death in 1993 was as traumatic to Kurds in Syria as the 1979 passing of Mullah Mustafa Barzani was to Kurds in Iraq.

Kurdish and Arab nationalism arose in parallel. Syria and France negotiated a Treaty of Independence in September 1936, but implementation was overtaken by the onset of World War II. France was occupied by Nazi Germany in 1940, and her Syrian mandate was seized by the puppet Vichy government, which lasted from July 1940 to August 1944. British and Free French forces launched the Syria-Lebanon campaign in July 1941. When the envoy of General Charles De Gaulle arrived in Damascus, his mission was "to end the mandatory regime and to proclaim you free and independent."[5] Syria was recognized as the Syrian Arab Republic on September 27, 1941.

Xoybun was active during World War II, but disbanded in 1946. Two ideologies were gaining ground at the time: Communism and pan-Arab unity. Many members of Xoybun, which championed social and economic justice, joined the Communist Party. Though Kurds were a stateless people, their tribal and fraternal ties transcended national boundaries. Kurdish nationalism was a challenge to the principle of pan-Arab unity. Kurds were targeted by the Arab overlords. Jaladat Badir Khan was assassinated in 1951. General Tawfiq Nizamaldine, a Kurd and chief of the general staff of Syria's Armed Forces, was removed from his post in 1958. Other Kurds were purged from the army and police.[6]

Egyptian President Gamal Abdel Nasser established the United Arab Republic (UAR) with Syria in 1958. The UAR was envisioned as a pan-Arab socialist state, linking Egypt and Syria with the Mutawakkilite Kingdom of Yemen and other like-minded Arab leaders. Arab nationalist ideology was near its zenith in the wake of the 1956 Suez War. The UAR was founded on the belief that "All the population of the Arab countries are Arabs. Non-Arabs have to become Arabs or go away."[7]

*****

Kurds viewed the UAR with disdain. They tried to organize themselves to counter the dominance of Arab culture. Jalal Talabani was living in Damascus at the time. He helped revive the principles of Xoybun, revitalize the Kurdish nationalist movement, and link Syrian Kurds to their Kurdish brethren in Iraqi Kurdistan. The Syrian Communist Party welcomed Kurds as part of its ideological struggle with the West. However, Kurds did not want the cause of Kurdish rights to be subsumed in the broader struggle for worker's rights.

The Kurdish Democratic Party of Syria (KDPS) was founded by Osman Sabri and Daham Miro in 1956. Nur al-Din Zaza, a leading Kurdish intellectual, was elected its first president in 1957. The KDPS was a "left-wing and nationalist" alternative to the Communist Party.[8] With Jalal Talabani's encouragement, the KDPS changed its name to the Kurdistan Democratic Party of Syria. Use of the term "Kurdistan" concerned Arabs, who suspected that the KDPS wanted to divide Syria and establish a "greater Kurdistan." The KDPS was driven underground in 1960. More than five thousand

KDPS leaders were rounded up and interrogated. Many were convicted of separatism or were jailed or executed.

Kurds were systematically persecuted by the country's Arab elite. They were marked by the Mukhabarat and Syria's security services. In Amude, a mixed Kurdish and Assyrian town in Hasakah Governorate, 152 schoolchildren perished in a movie theater fire on November 13, 1960. Kurds believed that Arab agents set the fire and then stood by as the theater was engulfed in flames. Kurds mourned the tragedy. The Amude inferno inflamed ethnic tensions.[9]

*****

The UAR was struggling. Syrians resented subordination to Egypt and Nasser's condescension. Members of the Syrian Officer Corps established a military committee to revive the Baath Party of Syria, which was dissolved during the merger. Hafiz al-Assad and his compatriots in the military resented Nasser's Free Officers. They rejected Egyptian-style land reform, which threatened Syria's agricultural system. Bedouins chafed under Egypt's control. The UAR was an ill-conceived merger.

The final straw came when Nasser nationalized Syria's cotton crops, its banks, insurance companies, and heavy industries on July 23, 1961. Syria's Officer Corps disassociated from the UAR. They were supported by the Kurds. Syria's Baath Party was preferable to subjugation by the pan-Arab behemoth of Egypt and Syria. The Soviet Union supported Kurdish nationalism prior to the establishment of the UAR. But Moscow then turned against the Kurds, aligning itself with Nasser, who opposed the West.[10]

Ignoring the Soviet Union's protest, Syria formally withdrew from the UAR in September 1961. Social instability and violence ensued. To restore order, Baathists launched a military coup on March 8, 1963. Elections for Syria's First Regional Congress were held on September 5. However, the Kurds had no representation in the political process. The KDPS was banned as a political body, thereby denying Syrian Kurds a voice in the country's tumultuous transition.

Kurdish disunity contributed to their disenfranchisement. Factionalism was endemic. The Hasakah Governorate was populated by five Kurdish tribes—Dukurie, Kikie, Reshwanie, Millie, and Aschetie. Rivalries between the Reshwan and the Milli confederations dated back to the sixteenth century. The KDPS was a microcosm of tribal and ideological divisions, which limited its impact as a social movement.

Important tactical and ideological differences also divided the KDPS.[11] Led by Osman Sabri and other intellectuals, the left drew its support from ex-Communists, intellectuals, and students. It made the strategic decision to cooperate with Syria's democratic forces in the hope of advancing Kurdish national rights. The left was engaged in mass mobilization, through rallies and marches. It aligned with Mustafa Barzani, who was fighting for Kurdish autonomy in Iraq and Iran.

The right was led by Nur al-Din Zaza and Hamid Hajj Darwish, who took over when Zaza went to prison. It was supported by notables— urban merchants, landowners, professionals, and religious leaders.[12] The right refused to join the broader Kurdish national movement, focusing more narrowly on cultural rights. Rather than grass-roots mobilization, it preferred negotiations and rapprochement with Damascus.

In 1970, Mustafa Barzani invited the leaders of KDPS factions to meet in Iraqi Kurdistan. He tried unsuccessfully to reconcile them. Mustafa Barzani created the KDPS-PL (Provisional Leadership), as a Syrian branch of his Kurdistan Democratic Party (KDP). The KDPS-PL failed to gain traction and ultimately lost relevance.

*****

Damascus intensified discriminatory policies toward the Kurds. Thousands of Kurds had immigrated illegally from Turkey to the Hasakah Governorate beginning in 1945.[13] Additionally, one hundred thousand Kurds migrated to Cezire, Qamishli, and Amude between 1954 and 1962. Kurds overwhelmed civil registers in districts where they became the majority.[14]

The government conducted a population census in 1962. Kurds had to prove they lived in Syria prior to 1945 or lose their citizenship. About 120,000 Kurds in Jazira were registered as aliens and stripped of their Syrian citizenship. In addition, three hundred thousand Kurds were denied national identification cards.[15] Many Kurds did not understand the census and therefore, did not participate. They were listed as "unrecorded," including Kurds who had served in the armed forces. The census was a flawed process. It separated family members, classifying them differently. Some Kurds in the same family were identified as citizens, and others were labeled foreigners. In many places like Jarablus and Kurd Dagh, Kurds had coexisted harmoniously with Arab neighbors for centuries. Now, they were strangers in their own land.

Rendered stateless and without citizenship, Kurds were denied basic services and suffered serious repercussions. They could not secure employment, get married, or own property. They were denied school admissions, school degrees, or admission to universities. Those already enrolled in universities were prevented from receiving degrees. Aliens and unrecorded Kurds could not vote in elections, run for public office, or get jobs in the civil service. They were prevented from receiving medical care at state hospitals. Stateless Kurds lacked passports or other internationally recognized travel documents and could not leave Syria to resettle in another country. The denial of their status allowed the government to seize their property and assets, which were awarded to Arab settlers.[16] A vicious media campaign demonized the Kurds, using slogans such as "Save Arabism in Jazira" and "Fight the Kurdish Menace."[17]

Syria was placed under Emergency Law in 1963.[18] Harsh restrictions were imposed on use of the Kurdish language. While Kurds were allowed to speak Kurdish in public, they were barred from using Kurdish in official proceedings. Kurdish was even barred in private schools. Kurds were prevented from giving their children Kurdish names. Kurdish street names were changed, and village names were Arabized. Kurdish-language media and books were barred. Rules were adopted requiring businesses to use Arabic, or lose their registration.[19] The wholesale assault on Kurdish culture was an attempt to eliminate Kurdishness.

Mustafa Barzani's nationalist and pan-Kurdish movement alarmed the Syrian government. His uprising was an existential threat with regional ramifications. Syria provided material support to assist Iraq's battle. It deployed six thousand troops, armored vehicles, and warplanes.[20] Syrian forces were involved in hot pursuit of Barzani's peshmerga. Ignoring the border between Syria and Iraq, they occupied Zakho, a border crossing between Iraq and Turkey. Syria's crackdown in Jazira, which borders Iraq, was intended to prevent the Kurdish rebellion from spreading to Syria. It also coincided with the discovery of oil fields in Qamishli, a town largely populated by Kurds.

Damascus decided to set up an Arab belt as a security buffer in Jazira. Fully operational by 1973, the Arab belt was three hundred kilometers long and ten to fifteen kilometers wide. It stretched from the western town of Ras Al-Ain to Syria's border with Iraq in the East. In addition to preventing the infiltration of Mustafa Barzani's peshmerga, the government repopulated the area with Arabs to mitigate the possibility of a Kurdish insurrection. As many as 140,000 Kurds were evicted and replaced by Bedouins. Kurds were arbitrarily uprooted from traditional Kurdish lands and deported to towns in Syria's desolate southern desert.

The Kurds were too factionalized to mount a political response or launch an effective insurgency. Jalal Talabani broke with the KDP to form the PUK in 1975. Talabani's ally in Syria, Darwish, changed the name of the KDPS to the Kurdish Democratic Progressive Party in Syria. Darwish's Progressive Party divided into the Equality Party (Wekhevi) and the Kurdish National Democratic Party. Salah Badreddin rejected the PUK faction and established the Unity of the People Party (Yekitiya Gel). It was renamed the Kurdish Popular Union Party in 1980, but split again in 1991. One group called themselves Wekhevi and the other Yekiti, which splintered in 1994 to become the Kurdish Democratic United Party. The proliferation of Kurdish political parties was not so much a product of political pluralism in the Kurdish community. It was a measure of disunity, fomented by Damascus to keep the Kurds from organizing an effective opposition.

*****

The crackdown on Kurds coincided with the rise to power of Syria's Baath Party, which embodied Arab chauvinism. The Baath Party was founded in 1947 by Michel Aflaq, a Syrian teacher and radical Arab nationalist. Aflaq was a student at the Sorbonne between 1928 and 1932. He was expelled for political agitation and went to Germany, where he found common cause with the Nazi Party. Aflaq returned to Syria in 1940 and launched the Baath Party in 1947 with the slogan "Unity, Freedom, Socialism." He rallied support on university campuses for his new movement.

The Baath Party broadened its base of popular support by merging with the Arab Socialist Party in 1953. Baathists in the Syrian Army included the future Syrian leader Hafiz al-Assad, who emerged as a public figure in 1963 and ruled in various capacities until 2000. After a split between the Baathists in Syria and Iraq, Assad launched the Corrective Movement and came to power as prime minister in 1970. Baathism became an ideology. It controlled the government, intelligence agencies, armed forces, and trade unions. While overtly secular, it also used Islamism to galvanize opposition to Christians and ethnic minorities. The Baath Party applied brutal tactics to suppress any and all forms of dissent.

Syria's constitution was adopted on March 13, 1973. It included several anti-Kurdish provisions. Its preamble embraced a wider Arab revolution with the goal of establishing Syria as the leader of a pan-Arab movement. It read: "The Arab revolution is an integral part of the wider world liberation movement for freedom."[21] Article 4 made Arabic the official language of the Syrian Arab Republic. Article 8 established the Baath Party as the "leading party in the society and the state."[22] It presented the National Progressive Front as the only authorized body for political party participation, effectively outlawing all political parties but the ruling Baath and its coalition partners. Article 21 stipulated that "The educational and cultural system aims at creating a socialist nationalist Arab generation."[23] While referring to individual rights and freedoms, the constitution omitted any mention of group or communal rights.[24]

Assad did not interfere with Kurdish political parties in Syria. Weak and divided, they posed no threat to his power. However, Assad shrewdly manipulated the Kurdish movements in Turkey and Iraq to leverage Syria's regional interests. He allowed the PUK to establish a Damascus headquarters in 1975. The KDP also opened an office in 1979. He convened meetings of PUK and KDP representatives to coordinate their actions against Baghdad. Both the PUK and KDP were allowed to open field offices in Qamishli, across the Tigris River from Iraq in Syria's northeast corner.

Relations between Syria and Turkey had been tense dating back to 1938, when the League of Nations allowed Turkey to annex Hatay province, removing it from Syria's French administration. Syria and Turkey were ideological opponents during the Cold War. Turkey acted as the eastern flank of NATO. Syria, Moscow's closest Arab ally, was squarely in the Soviet camp. Damascus objected when Turkey launched the Southeastern Anatolia project in the 1980s. Its extensive network of dams, hydroelectric stations, and irrigation systems regulated water flows to Syria with adverse effects on Syria's economy. Assad's tacit support of the PKK was the greatest irritant to Syrian-Turkish relations.[25] Assad gave the PKK free reign in Syria. The PKK moved its headquarters into the Syrian-controlled Bekaa Valley of Lebanon in September 1980. Abdullah Ocalan was resident in Damascus. The government turned a blind eye to the PKK's operations, as well as its sundry business practices. Narcotics and weapons smuggling was widespread, with the complicity of Syrian authorities. Many of the PKK's rank and file, as much as 20 percent, were Kurds from Syria.

Assad was also a major player in the Israeli-Palestinian conflict. More than four hundred thousand Palestinian refugees resettled in Syria after the State of Israel was created in 1948. Palestinians refer to Israel's creation as the *Nakba*, which means "Day of the Catastrophe."[26] A Palestinian exodus followed Israel's Declaration of Independence in 1948. Arab states were too weak and divided to take effective action at the time. The rise of Arab nationalism and support for Palestinian militants were rooted in guilt for allowing the Nakba to occur. Assad was committed to destroying Israel. He had deep animosity toward the Jewish State, as well as its backers in the West, especially the United States.

Syria became a one-party state with a supremely powerful presidency. Like Saddam Hussein in Iraq, Assad cultivated a cult of personality. His portraits and statues proliferated across Syria. Assad exercised absolute and ruthless authority. Violence was a form of social control. It was also a way to deny people their dignity and make them subservient to the State. Between 1973 and 1997, Syria's military grew nearly quadrupling men under arms.[27]

Assad made membership in the Muslim Brotherhood punishable by death, following a 1980 assassination attempt by the Brotherhood. Between 1980 and 1981, hundreds of religious scholars and prominent Sunni Arab leaders were killed in Hama, a city in central Syria. In retaliation, the Muslim Brotherhood targeted police posts and government officials. They declared Hama a "liberated city" and called for an uprising by Sunni Arabs against Assad and his secular circle of Alawites. Just 20 percent of the population, Alawites dominated the country's politics and military.[28] The response by Syria's armed forces was swift and decisive, when Hama residents rebelled in February of 1982. After days of artillery attacks, Syrian tanks moved into Hama. They were accompanied by Special Forces and infantry who went house to house in search of rebels. Up to forty thousand men, women, and children were slaughtered in the carnage.[29] "Hama rules" denotes the disproportionate use of force to suppress dissent.[30]

The Hama massacre was part of a pattern. Assad would repeatedly use indiscriminate violence to suppress potential opposition. Arab Sunnis and Kurds represented the greatest challenge to Assad's hegemonic rule. On March 10, 1980, Syrian armed forces fired mortars against Jisr Alshaghoor, a Kurdish city in the Idlib Governorate in northwestern Syria with a strong Muslim Brotherhood presence. After the town was demolished, its residents were rounded up and seventy were executed.[31]

That month, another forty people were executed in Sarmadah. The village of Kinsafrah was attacked when poor rural residents demanded water and improved public services. Up to a thousand people were killed for demanding improved conditions at the Palmyra prison in June. No day was sacred. In Mashariqah, eighty-three people were killed at dawn on the morning of Eid Al-Adha, the Feast of Sacrifice. Another forty-two people were killed at the Sunday market. In Al-Raqah, purported opponents of the regime were incinerated when a secondary school was burnt to the ground.[32]

Any Kurdish assembly or cultural gathering was seen as a potential challenge to Baathist authority, and suppressed. In the so-called Jernak massacre, military intelligence murdered twenty-two Kurds in 1980. Kurdish culture was denied. Thousands of Kurds gathered in Damascus to celebrate Newroz in March 1986. Women were adorned in Kurdish festival clothing of sheer fabric ornamented with beads sequins. The women wore a "lira belt" made of connected gold coins. Brilliantly colored embroidery covered their heads. Men wore traditional baggy pants and brightly colored cummerbunds. Police arrived on the scene and ordered the Kurds to disperse, noting prohibitions against Kurdish clothing. Police opened fire, killing one person. Another three people were killed in Afrin during Newroz celebrations. Kurds were outraged by the crackdown on Newroz. Funerals typically served as rallying points for unrest. More than forty thousand Kurds gathered the next day for the funeral service in Damascus. The angry crowd was surrounded by Syrian security services. Pushing and shoving threatened to escalate into deadly violence.[33]

Elections were held for the People's Council on May 22 and 23, 1990. Assad increased the number of seats from 195 to 250, explaining the People's Council would make room for "independent" candidates who were not members of the Baath party.[34] Restructuring the Majlis was presented as a democratic reform. But the parliament functioned more as a consultative than a legislative body. It had no real oversight responsibility over the executive.

Syria's elections were a concession to reforms that were underway worldwide. Reforms occurred during the Soviet Union's perestroika. Tyrants in eastern and central Europe were being challenged by democratic forces, leading to convulsive political change. Assad was prepared to create the appearance of a "correction," but the election was a farce. Only individuals, not parties, could be candidates. There were nine thousand independent candidates, all of whom required approval by the government. The list of Baathist candidates and its Nasserite allies exceeded two-thirds of eligible seats, assuring Assad control.[35]

Sheikhs, businessmen, landlords, and professionals were elected as independents. Some Kurds were also elected. However, their participation in parliament did not change Assad's approach to Kurdish issues. The Emergency Law, in place since 1963, was used to arbitrarily detain Kurds. Article 307 of the penal code criminalized "inciting sectarian, racial, or religious strife."[36] Article 267 made advocating "cutting off any portion of Syrian land to join to another country" an offense.[37] Article 336 forbade "any gathering of more than 7 people with the aim of protesting any decision by the authorities."[38] Article 288 prevented the formation of "any political organization or social organization with an international character."[39] The ability of Kurds to organize or express their views was essentially forbidden.[40]

Up to seven thousand Kurds disappeared between 1980 and 2000.[41] Thousands of Kurds were detained and held in administrative detention. The most common form of torture involved beating the feet, causing terrible pain and crippling. Many Kurds were stricken with cancer and thyroid disease from nuclear waste dumped in Hasakah. Like the prisons in Turkey, which became a PKK fraternity club, Syria's prisons were also a locus of ideological instruction and political activism. Kurds protested prison conditions at the central prison of Hasakah. When Syrian security services stormed the prison on March 23, 1993, seventy-two prisoners were burnt to death. Of the survivors, five were executed.[42] Elsewhere, Kurds continued to suffer attacks, discrimination, and restrictions on political, social, and cultural expression. The government also restricted Kurdish land rights, in response to a severe drought beginning in 1995. Hundreds of thousands lost their livelihoods and were forced to abandon their homes in the countryside. They sought subsistence wage work in city slums, which became hotbeds of Kurdish discontent.[43]

Turkey demanded that Assad hand over Abdullah Ocalan. Ankara threatened to interrupt the flow of water from the Euphrates, a vital supply to Syria's agricultural sector. Assad betrayed Ocalan, whom he had supported for fifteen years, by signing the Adana Agreement. The accord designated the PKK a terrorist organization, banned its activities, and required Syria to interdict the flow of money, weapons, and logistical support to the organization. Ocalan departed Syria on October 9, 1998. After an international manhunt, he was captured in Nairobi on February 15, 1999. The PKK evacuated its bases in Syria, and taking advantage of the power vacuum after the 2001 Gulf War, moved its headquarters from Syria to the Qandil Mountains in Iraqi Kurdistan.

*****

Bashar al-Assad took over as president after the death of his father in the summer of 2000. Bashar was not his father's first choice. Hafiz had groomed his eldest son, Bassel al-Assad, to assume the presidency. However, Bassel died in a fiery car crash in 1994. Bashar initially seemed ill equipped for the rough and tumble of Syrian politics. He studied medicine at Damascus University before enrolling in London's Western Eye Hospital, where he studied ophthalmology. Bashar returned to Syria after Bassel's death, enrolled in the military academy, and assumed responsibility for Syria's occupation of Lebanon. Bashar was socially awkward and uncomfortable around his father's hardline security advisers. His only previous public role was as head of the Syrian Computer Society.

Bashar al-Assad launched the Damascus Spring soon after becoming president. He closed the notorious Mezzeh Prison and released political prisoners. He spoke about democracy as a vehicle for improving the welfare of Syrians. Bashar also showed a more relaxed approach to the Kurds. He withdrew some security personnel from Kurdish-populated regions. He also reached out to Kurdish figures, allowing Baath Party representatives to meet them.

Beginning with Bashar's presidency, the Kurdish Alliance—made up of the Left Party, Azadi, the Democratic United Party, and the Progressive Party—sought accommodation with Damascus. In exchange for its cooperation, the government allowed the Progressive Party to open a cultural foundation called Nur al-Din Zaza Hall, which doubled as a political party headquarters. The Kurdish Democratic Front, another block consisting of the KDPS, Wekhevi, and the National Democratic Party, occupied the middle ground. A third faction called the Coordinating Committee was made up of the Future Movement, Yekiti, and a branch of Azadi. Less trusting of Bashar, it demanded constitutional recognition of the Kurds as an ethnic minority in Syria.

The Democratic Union Party (PYD) was founded in 2003 by Syrian Kurds with ideological ties to the PKK. The PYD is essentially non-hierarchical, unlike most other Kurdish political parties in Syria. Its leadership is democratically elected, with term limits to recycle the party's politburo. Of all the political formations of Kurds in Syria, the government was hardest on the PYD. According to a PYD leader, the PYD is targeted by Syrian security because "we adopt Öcalan's ideology."[44] PYD fighters display Öcalan's picture and a red star as reminder of its Marxist origins. Echoing Öcalan's demands, the PYD's charter calls for "the constitutional recognition of Kurdish rights and 'democratic autonomy' for the Kurdish region."[45]

Syrian-Turkish relations improved greatly after the Adana Agreement. Ankara viewed the PYD as an extension of the PKK and demanded that Damascus treat it as such. Assad pressured the PYD. Damascus also constrained activities of the Kurdistan Communities Union (KCK), an umbrella organization for PKK-affiliated parties, operating in both Syria and Turkey. The KCK has membership in Turkey, Syria, and Iraq.[46] The PYD acted independently when making tactical decisions locally. However, strategic decisions were coordinated with the PKK and KCK. Hafiz al-Assad used the Kurdish issue as leverage against Turkey and Iraq. In contrast, Bashar acted at the behest of Ankara and Baghdad. Kurds hoped that Bashar would be more compliant, but they were deeply disappointed.

*****

The Qamishli football club hosted a match with Deir al-Zour on March 12, 2004.[47] The stadium was packed with Kurdish supporters. Sunni Arab supporters of Deir Ezzor were also present. With the Iraq War in full swing, Arabs from Deir Ezzor chanted slogans in support of Saddam Hussein. The Kurds chanted "Long Live Kurdistan" and declared their admiration for George W. Bush. Violent clashes broke out in the stands. Police used tear gas and water cannon to calm the crowd, firing warning shots into the air. Nine Kurdish youth were killed before the match even started.[48]

The next day, Kurds gathered for the funeral. Syrian police viewed the procession of mourners as an illegal demonstration and fired live ammunition into the crowd, killing eight people. Protests spread to Cezira, Aleppo, and Damascus. The enormity of protests throughout Rojava was unprecedented. Thirty-two were killed, hundreds wounded, and two thousand arrested over a five-day period that Kurds called The Great Uprising.[49]

Kurds in Amude destroyed statues of Hafiz al-Assad and displayed posters of Öcalan. Protesters also removed Syrian flags from government buildings, trampled and burned them, and replaced them with the flag of Kurdistan. They stormed the central bank and city hall. The courthouse, police station, and Baath Party headquarters were set on fire. The military draft office and police vehicles were torched. The police made a determined stand to protect a huge state-owned fertilizer storage facility. Street battles continued into the night, spreading the next day to Afrin.[50]

The whole affair was broadcast on Roj TV, a Kurdish network based in Copenhagen. Its reports fueled further unrest in Syria as well as Europe. Kurds in Turkey and Iraqi Kurdistan also rallied in support. Social media also served as a tool for mass mobilization. The uprising spread to Switzerland and Belgium, where Kurds occupied Syrian embassies. Kurds tried to storm the Syrian Embassy in London but were repelled. They spray-painted the building with the tricolor Kurdistan flag.[51]

Syrian security services launched reprisals. A heavy contingent of troops was deployed to Jazira. Political leaders from the PYD were targeted. The Mukhabarat identified Kurdish students participating in the protests, and they were expelled from university. Kurdish businesses were burned and ransacked. Bashar sent his brother, Mallas, and the defense minister to Qamishli. However, talks failed to quell the violence.[52]

The uprising marked a watershed moment for the Syrian opposition. Regime opponents—Arab Sunnis, Assyrians, Christians, and tribal sheiks—showed solidarity with their Kurdish brothers. *Asabiyya*, which means "group solidarity," is the primary organizing principle of Syrian society, reflecting kinship, tribe, village, ethnicity, and religious sect. On March 16, 2004, Kurdish parties and Arabs in Qamishli signed a joint declaration calling for an end to the violence. The Damascus Declaration set a precedent for cooperation between opponents of Baath regime.

Notes

1. "The Rojava Report." *The Rojava Report*. N.p., n.d. Web. 27 May 2014. <http://rojavareport.wordpress.com/>.
2. Cited by Jawad Mella. "The Colonial Policy of the Syrian Baath Party in Western Kurdistan." Western Kurdistan Association. London 2006. Pg. 155.
3. Bletch Chirguh, *La Question Kurde: ses origines et ses causes*, Le Caire, Impimerie Paul Barbey, 1930, front cover, *IHSAN NOURI PACHA Généralissime des forces nationales Kurdes*.
4. 1066236, Charity Number:. *WESTERN KURDISTAN ASSOCIATION Komela Rojava Kurdistan* (n.d.): n. pag. Web.
5. Rogan, Eugene L. *The Arabs: A History*. New York: Basic, 2009. Print.

6. Jawad Mella. "The Colonial Policy of the Syrian Baath Party in Western Kurdistan." Western Kurdistan Association. London 2006. Pg. 24.

7. Cited by Jawad Mella. "The Colonial Policy of the Syrian Baath Party in Western Kurdistan." Western Kurdistan Association. London 2006. Pg. 27.

8. McMurray, David A., and Amanda Ufheil-Somers. *The Arab Revolts: Dispatches on Militant Democracy in the Middle East.* Bloomington: Indiana Univ, 2013. Print.

9. http://www.al-monitor.com/pulse/originals/2013/04/kurdish-clashes-syria-pyd-kdp-pkk-ocalan-barzani.html##ixzz31tlZoaCd (Accessed May 16, 2014).

10. Ginat, Rami. *Syria and the Doctrine of Arab Neutralism: From Independence to Dependence.* Portland, Or.: Sussex Academic, 2005. Print.

11. "Kurds in Syria." *Kurds in Syria.* N.p., n.d. Web. 27 May 2014. <https://www.triposo.com/poi/T__059fa3ac4321>.

12. Romano, David. "Review: Syria's Kurds: History, Politics and Society." *International Journal of Middle East Studies* 43.1 (2011): 183–85. Web.

13. Kurdish immigration was exacerbated by the influx of 400,000 Palestinians after Israel declared independence in 1948.

14. "Theme Showcase." *Theme Showcase.* N.p., n.d. Web. 27 May 2014. <http://theme.wordpress.com/credits/civiroglu.net/>.

15. *Syrian Arab Republic.* London: Board, 1975. Web.

16. Kurdwatch Is A Project Of The, European Center For Kurdish Studies, Emser Straße 26, and 12051 Berlin. *KURDWATCH • Report 5* (n.d.): n. pag. Web.

17. Jordi Tejel, Pg. 52.

18. "World Directory of Minorities and Indigenous Peoples." *Minority Rights Group International : Syria : Kurds.* N.p., n.d. Web. 29 May 2014. <http://www.minorityrights.org/5270/syria/kurds.html#sthash.vWU4GrD7.dpuf>.

19. Ibid.

20. "Kurdistan at the Tri-Border Area between Iraq, Syria, and Turkey." *Jerusalem Center For Public Affairs.* N.p., n.d. Web. 27 May 2014. <http://jcpa.org/article/the-future-of-kurdistan-between-turkey-the-iraq-war-and-the-syrian-revolt/>.

21. Robbers, Gerhard (2007). Encyclopedia of World Constitutions. Facts on File library of world history (in English). New York: Facts On File.

22. Ibid.

23. Ibid.

24. Ibid.

25. Primoz Manfreda."Turkish-Syrian Relations: From confrontation to partnership and back." http://middleeast.about.com/od/syria/a/Turkish-Syrian-Relations-Overview.htm (Accessed May 16, 2014).

26. "May, 2010 - One Democratic State." *May, 2010 - One Democratic State.* N.p., n.d. Web. 27 May 2014. <https://sites.google.com/site/onedemocraticstatesite/archives/previous-headlines-from-this-site/may-2010>.

27. "Some Lessons in Barbarism." *The Hindu.* N.p., n.d. Web. 29 May 2014. <http://www.thehindu.com/todays-paper/tp-opinion/some-lessons-in-barbarism/article2996424.ece>.

28. "1982 Syria Massacre Still Haunts Mideast." *Newsmax.* N.p., n.d. Web. 29 May 2014. <http://www.newsmax.com/Newsfront/syria-hama-massacre-egypt/2011/02/02/id/384785#ixzz320vb1pFD>.

29. Rodrigues, Jason. "1982: Syria's President Hafez Al-Assad Crushes Rebellion in Hama." *Theguardian.com.* Guardian News and Media, 01 Aug. 2011. Web. 26 May 2014. <http://www.theguardian.com/theguardian/from-the-archive-blog/2011/aug/01/hama-syria-massacre-1982-archive>.

30. "Hama Rules - What Are Hama Rules? - Syrian Massacre of Muslim Brotherhood." *About.com Middle East Issues.* N.p., n.d. Web. 27 May 2014. <http://middleeast.about.com/od/syria/f/hama-rules.htm>.

31. Reporter, Daily Mail. "Syrian Government Vows Bloody Retaliation against Town Where Police Were Killed." *Mail Online.* Associated Newspapers, n.d. Web. 27 May 2014. <http://www.dailymail.co.uk/news/article-2000286/Syria-Government-vows-bloody-retaliation-Jisr-al-Shughour.html>.

32. "The Hama Massacre in Syria:." *Politicsie RSS.* N.p., n.d. Web. 29 May 2014. <http://www.politics.ie/forum/foreign-affairs/28177-hama-massacre-syria.html>.

33. "World Directory of Minorities and Indigenous Peoples." *Minority Rights Group International: Syria : Kurds.* N.p., n.d. Web. 29 May 2014. <http://www.minorityrights.org/5270/syria/kurds.html#sthash.vWU4GrD7.dpuf>.

34. "The World Factbook." *CIA -.* N.p., n.d. Web. 27 May 2014. <http://www.emprendedor.com/factbook/fields/2101.html>.

35. "Syria's Parliamentary Elections | Middle East Research and Information Project." *Syria's Parliamentary Elections | Middle East Research and Information Project.* N.p., n.d. Web. 29 May 2014. <http://www.merip.org/mer/mer174/syrias-parliamentary-elections>.

36. Syria. *Group Denial R I G H T S* (n.d.): n. pag. Web. <http://www.hrw.org/sites/default/files/reports/syria1109webwcover_0.pdf> Accessed May 17, 2014).

37. Ibid.

38. Ibid.

39. Ibid.

40. Ibid.

41. Cited by Jawad Mella. "The Colonial Policy of the Syrian Baath Party in Western Kurdistan." Western Kurdistan Association. London 2006. Pg. 331.

42. Cited by Jawad Mella. "The Colonial Policy of the Syrian Baath Party in Western Kurdistan." Western Kurdistan Association. London 2006. Pg. 331.

43. http://www.minorityrights.org/5270/syria/kurds.html#sthash.vWU4GrD7.dpuf.

44. Human Rights Watch, *Group Denial: Repression of Kurdish Political and Cultural Rights in Syria* (New York, November 2009), p. 43.

45. "THE MAIN KURDISH POLITICAL PARTIES IN IRAN, IRAQ, SYRIA, AND TURKEY: A RESEARCH GUIDE." *GLORIA Center.* N.p., n.d. Web. 29 May 2014. <http://www.gloria-center.org/2013/08/the-main-kurdish-political-parties-in-iran-iraq-syria-and-turkey-a-research-guide/>.

46. Ibid.

47. "Syria Kurds Commemorate Kurdish Uprising of 2004 | ARA News." *ARA News*. N.p., n.d. Web. 27 May 2014. <http://aranews.net/2014/03/residents-of-syria-s-qamishli-commemorate-kurdish-uprising-of-2004/>.
48. Ibid.
49. "The Evolution of Kurdish Politics in Syria | Middle East Research and Information Project." *The Evolution of Kurdish Politics in Syria | Middle East Research and Information Project*. N.p., n.d. Web. 29 May 2014. <http://www.merip.org/mero/mero083111?ip_login_no_cache=80d496e766fff3bf997ff4cb2f9358e3>.
50. Kurdwatch Is A Project Of The, European Center For Kurdish Studies, Emser Straße 26, and 12051 Berlin. *KURDWATCH • Report 4* (n.d.): n. pag. Web.
51. Jawad Mella. "The Colonial Policy of the Syrian Baath Party in Western Kurdistan." Western Kurdistan Association. London 2006. Pg. 55.
52. "Clashes Break Out Between Kurdish Groups In Syria - Al-Monitor: The Pulse of the Middle East." *Al-Monitor*. N.p., n.d. Web. 29 May 2014. <http://www.al-monitor.com/pulse/originals/2013/04/kurdish-clashes-syria-pyd-kdp-pkk-ocalan-barzani.html>.

5

Kurds in Iran

Iranian Kurdistan, otherwise known as Eastern Kurdistan, spans a rugged mountainous terrain southeast of Mount Ararat and the Zagros mountains in northwestern Iran. At least ten million Kurds live in Iran, exceeding the total combined Kurdish population in Iraq and Syria.[1] Iranian Kurds are dispersed in parts of Kermanshah, Ilam, West Azerbaijan, and Kordestan provinces on Iran's border with Iraq and Turkey. The City of Mahabad is the political capital of Iranian Kurdistan, and a locus of Kurdish nationalism. It lies south of Lake Urmia in a narrow valley 1,300 meters above sea level.[2] Nearly two hundred thousand people, predominantly Kurds, live in Mahabad.[3]

Other ethnic groups also live in these areas. Lurs are the dominant minority in Ilam Province, and Azerbaijanis in West Azerbaijan Province. Between 40 to 50 percent of Iran's population is non-Persian. About two-thirds of Kurds in Iran are Sunnis, and 27 percent are Shiites. Shiite Kurds reside mostly in Kermanshah, the largest Kurdish city, and Illam.[4]

The Kurdish region has abundant water supplies, which are exploited to benefit other parts of Iran.[5] The region is oil rich. It also has abundant mineral supplies, including copper, chrome, iron, and coal.[6] Kurds were never compensated for resources taken. Furthermore, they were marginalized by a policy that prevented Kurds from using their natural resources to meet local needs. Economic subjugation occurred during the Pahlavi period and continued after the Iranian Revolution of 1979. A new constitution came into effect on December 3, 1979. Linguistic and religious plurality was acknowledged, but Farsi and Shia Islam remained the official language and religion. While Article 15 of Iran's 1979 constitution promises uniform development and cultural rights to all Iranian citizens, Kurdish areas were denied investment and lag behind.

Kurds have a strong oral tradition of bards, folklore, and music, which the government tried to control. Kurds reject state-sponsored education in Farsi, which limits educational access and contributes to "extremely high levels of illiteracy."[7] The supreme leader, Ayatollah Ali Khamenei, oversees the "armed forces and appoints the Expediency Council, leaders of judiciary, and the heads of state media."[8] His power is unchecked.

Regional events fueled the pan-Kurdish struggle for self-rule, such as the PKK rebellion in Turkey and Iraq's 1974 autonomy deal. As in other countries, the Iranian regime viewed Kurdish national aspirations as a security threat. Iranian Kurds were targeted. They were also collateral damage in regional conflicts. Border areas were attacked by artillery and heavily mined during the Iran-Iraq War (1980–88). Violent conflict precipitated the mass exodus of farmers and herders to urban centers. Denied their traditional livelihoods, many Kurds turned to smuggling and black-market activities.[9]

Iranian Kurdistan is one of the poorest regions in Iran, ranking high on the poverty index. It ranks low on development goals such as average income, literacy, and life expectancy. Kurdish unemployment is around 50 percent. The lack of opportunity pushes youth to leave their traditional lands for work in urban areas.[10] Iranian Kurds have accumulated frustration from decades of marginalization, discrimination, and disenfranchisement.[11]

*****

The first Iranian constitution was adopted in 1906. It included democratic attributes such as the separation of powers and majoritarian rule. Though it stressed equality, it did not acknowledge diversity or protect minority rights.[12] In response to preferences for Persians, the Kurdish separatist movement began in 1918.

Jaafar Sultan took control of the Hewraman region north of Halabja and declared independence. Jafar's revolt was joined by other tribal leaders. Simko, chief of the Shikak tribe, seized control of lands west of Lake Urmia.[13] Hama Rashid, another prominent tribal leader, also joined the fray. Reza Khan, who would become the first Pahlavi monarch, counterattacked in 1922 and defeated Simko. The campaign included forced deportation, exiling, and seizing Kurdish lands. Jafar's state existed until 1925. His resistance was crushed in 1929. Reza Shah systematically arrested Kurdish chiefs and deported them into exile. He confiscated Kurdish lands, establishing garrisons throughout Iranian Kurdistan. After overthrowing the Qajar dynasty,[14] Reza Shah Pahlavi was anointed the new monarch of the Imperial State of Persia on December 12, 1925. He focused on modernizing and nationalizing Iran while suppressing ethnic and religious diversity.

Though Iran declared neutrality during World War II, Allied Powers suspected the Shah of collaborating with the Nazis and invaded in 1941. The Iranian Army quickly collapsed, and Reza Shah Pahlavi was forced to abdicate. As the state security structures disintegrated, Kurds assumed responsibility for local administration. Kurdish peshmerga, raided weapons depots and well-armed, provided local security. Hama Rashid, a tribal chief from Bana Begzada controlled Baneh-Sardasht and Mariwan in Western Iran. The state could not effectively challenge Rashid, so it made him a "semiofficial governor, paid him a salary, and charged him with maintaining order in the region."[15] The Iranian government also supported another Kurdish leader, Mahmud Agha. The two were pitted against each other. Mahmud Agha received assistance from Iran and gained complete control of Kurdish areas in 1945.[16] Kurdish separatism was fueled by a policy of centralization and homogenization, expressed through the denial of Kurdish cultural rights and freedom of expression.

The Soviet Union refused to relinquish occupied territory in Northwest Iran after World War II. Acting under Moscow's influence, the Kurdistan Democratic Party of Iran (KDPI) cooperated with Mustafa Barzani to declare the Kurdish Mahabad Republic in 1946. It was headed by Qazi Muhammed, a respected religious and political leader. Mustafa Barzani led Mahabad's military.

The Mahabad Republic encompassed a small, independent territory in what is today the Iranian province of West Azerbaijan. The vast majority of Iranian Kurdistan fell outside this area in the Anglo-American zone of influence. The West viewed the Mahabad Republic as a puppet state of the Soviet Union. The Iranian central government, backed by the United States and Great Britain, occupied the Mahabad Republic when Soviet forces withdrew in December 1946. Qazi Mohammed was executed, and more than a thousand Kurds were killed in 1947. The Mahabad Republic lasted for less than one year.

*****

A myriad of Kurdish groups participated in the Kurdish movement for statehood. Komala Zhe Kaf was a secret organization consisting of "fifteen local citizens . . . who swore an oath never to betray the

Kurdish nation and to work for self-government."[17] It recruited Qazi Mohammad, who would break off and form a rival group. Komala Zh-e Kaff, also known as the Organization of Revolutionary Toilers of Iranian Kurdistan. It was founded by Kurdish delegates from Iran, Iraq, and Turkey during a conference in 1944 at Mt. Dalanpur, where the three countries are contiguous. This Komala would later become KDPI. A third group with a similar name, Komala-y Zehmat Keshan, was founded in 1967. Komala Zahmat Keshan adopted a Communist bent and became the Kurdish branch of Iran's Communist Party in the 1980s. It believed in a Marxist proletarian revolution, targeting feudal landlords and the elite Pahlavi regime.

The Kurdish Democratic Party of Iran (KDPI) emerged as an offshoot of Komala zhe Kaf in 1945.[18] KDPI would become a socialist political party, dedicated to the self-determination of Kurds and the struggle against imperialism. More moderate than Komala, KDPI sought "autonomy for Iranian Kurdistan within the framework of a democratic Iran." In the late 1940s and early 1950s, KDPI found common cause with Iran's Tudeh Communist Party in opposing Shah Pahlavi's rule.[19] The KDPI orchestrated a series of tribal uprisings in 1967 and 1968, which were suppressed by government forces.

Komala and KDPI were ideologically divided and political rivals. Komala rejected KDPI for being bourgeois and moderate. It called the KDPI a "class enemy," and criticized KDPI as a surrogate of the Tudeh Party and for its close coordination with Soviet Union, which it believed had betrayed socialist ideals. Disputes between Komala and KDPI turned violent, with frequent clashes in the 1980s. Despite their different tactics and ideology, Komala and KDPI shared a distrust of Islamic fundamentalism.

The Pahlavi dynasty ruled Iran as a constitutional monarchy between 1925 and its overthrow on February 11, 1979.[20] Kurds supported the Iranian revolution and the rise to power of Ayatollah Ruhollah Khomeini. In exchange for supporting abolition of the monarchy and the creation of an Islamic state, Kurds were promised control over local government, resources, and economic decision-making. They were guaranteed use of both Farsi and Kurdish in education. Kurds were also promised a role drafting Iran's new constitution. The deal was never implemented. When Khomeini delayed, KDPI members insisted that the central government implement autonomy before Kurds make any concessions. They adopted the slogan "No referendum. Self-determination first."[21]

Kurds backed Shiekh Ezzaddin Hoseini, a cleric from Mahabad who wanted a secular state. Khomeini supported an alternative leader, Ahmad Moftizadeh from Sanandaj. Unlike Hoseini, Moftizadeh was also a Sunni Kurd who supported the creation of an Islamic Republic. Later, the majority of Kurds would feel betrayed by Khomeini. The coalition of secular, religious, theocratic, leftist, democratic, and ethnic groups broke up as Khomeini institutionalized religious rule.

The KDPI tried to placate Khomeini by emphasizing the Muslim character of Kurds and abandoning demands for independence. However, Khomeini questioned the loyalty of Kurds, most of whom are Sunni. Pan-Kurdish ambitions also stirred suspicions about the Kurds acting on behalf of foreign powers.

Khomeini convened an Assembly of Experts in July to draft a new constitution. The Assembly included seventy-three persons, including fifty-five clerics, almost all of whom were members of Khomeini's Islamic Republic Party. Kurds were barred from participating. Even Dr. Abdul Rahman Ghassemlou, the elected representative of Iranian Kurdistan, was denied a seat at the table.

The constitution was approved by 98 percent of voters in a referendum on December 2 and 3, 1979.[22] The new constitution enshrined the principle of Islamic jurisprudence (Velayat-e faqih), which guaranteed clerics a leading role in government and as head of state. Khomeini consolidated his power as Supreme Leader of the Islamic Republic of Iran. In addition to the Iranian Revolutionary Guard Corps (IRGC), Khomeini controlled the Revolutionary Council, revolutionary tribunals, and local revolutionary committees. Khomeini's clerical cronies dominated pseudo-governing bodies.

The constitution established Shia primacy, while ignoring demands for regional autonomy by the Kurds. Article 15 states that the "Official language and writing script (of Iran) . . . is Persian . . . [and] . . . the use of regional and tribal languages in the press and mass media, as well as for teaching of their literature in schools, is allowed in addition to Persian." According to Article 16, "Since the language of the Qur'an and Islamic texts . . . is Arabic it must be taught . . . in school from elementary grades until the end of high school."[23] No provisions were made for use of minority languages, including Kurdish. Khomeini rejected the fundamental concept of minority rights during a speech in December 1979. He asserted that ethnic minority rights contradicted Islamic doctrines. Kurdish cultural rights were forbidden. Khomeini accused foreign powers of stirring nationalism among minorities in order to undermine the unity of Iran and coherence of the broader Muslim community.

Kurds refused to participate in the referendum of March 1979, which established the Islamic Republic of Iran. Excluded from the process of drafting Iran's new constitution, they boycotted the vote authorizing the charter. Their boycott was viewed as betrayal by Shia clerics in the Guardian Council and as a personal affront by the increasingly autocratic Khomeini.

Kurds took up arms in mid-March 1979. Two hundred thousand IRGC attacked Kurds in Paveh, Sanandaj, and Saqqez in August. A month later, Mahabad and Sardasht also fell. Kurdish peshmerga withdrew from the cities to encampments in the countryside and surrounding mountains. The KDPI dispatched a delegation to Tehran, to propose a ceasefire and a Five-Point Peace Plan. The proposal was rejected by Khomeini's representatives, who insisted that the peshmerga disarm as a precondition for negotiations.[24] Khomeini declared a holy war against the Kurds on August 19, 1979. He referred to them as "children of Satan" and the "enemies of God." By 1982, some ten thousand Kurds had been killed and two hundred thousand displaced during the counterinsurgency.[25] Thousands were executed after summary trials. By 1983, the Iranian government had reasserted its authority across Iranian Kurdistan.

*****

The Iran-Iraq War, which raged between 1980 and 1988, ran parallel to Khomeini's conflict with the Kurds. Baghdad and Tehran shared a common concern. Both suspected that Kurds were trying to weaken the central governments and position themselves for greater autonomy. "Greater Kurdistan" was a threat to both regimes.

During Saddam Hussein's Anfal Campaign, Iraq established a security belt along the Iran-Iraq border. Saddam sought to prevent Iranian Kurds from penetrating Iraq and joining the battle on behalf of Iran. He also wanted to prevent Iraqi Kurds from establishing local administration, as a step toward self-rule. Halabja is a Kurdish city about ten kilometers from the border with Iran.[26] The remote and rugged terrain was a stronghold of Komala and the Patriotic Union of Kurdistan (PUK). Kurds largely ignored the rugged and remote international boundary separating Iraq and Iran.

Use of chemical weapons against Kurdish communities in Halabja were consistent with Iraq's use of WMD against Iranian forces elsewhere along the Iran-Iraq border and at different times during the war. However, the attack on Halabja came after the Iran-Iraq War had ended. It served no strategic purpose. The chemical weapons attack was a signal to Kurds, rather than a military maneuver against Iran.

Tehran opened negotiations with Iranian Kurds after concluding its peace with Baghdad in 1988. Negotiations were not held in good faith. On July 13, 1989, the KDPI's exiled leader, Abdul Rahman Ghassemlou, was assassinated by Iranian agents in Vienna.[27] The killing occurred during a break in negotiations with Iranian officials. Ghassemlou's successor, Sadeq Sharafkandi, was assassinated in Berlin by Iranian agents while attending the Socialist International Congress in 1992.[28] A senior leader of Komala was also assassinated in Larnaca, Cyprus. The campaign of political assassinations intensified during the 1990s, with Kurdish leaders targeted in Western Iran. In December 1996, Mulla Mohammed Rabiei, a prominent Sunni cleric and prayer leader in the Al-Shafe'i mosque in Kermanshah, was murdered.[29] Three days of intense rioting ensued.

Political assassinations motivated Komala to continue its guerilla campaign against the Iranian regime. Komala operated from two camps in Iraqi Kurdistan. Komala's Executive Committee, Clandestine Organization Center, Military Training Center, Radio Broadcasting, print publications, and health center were based in Suleimani.[30] Komala leaders were under constant threat, risking political assassination in Iraqi Kurdistan or wherever they went in the world. Komala's rank and file were targeted by the Mujahadin-e Khalq, which sought to overthrow the Iranian regime while acting as a Pretorian Guard for Saddam Hussein. Under pressure from all sides, Komala and KDPI announced a ceasefire in 1996. Henceforth, Kurds emphasized political participation and democracy as the most effective way to realize their goals.[31]

*****

Mohammad Khatami spoke elegantly about Kurdish culture during Iran's presidential elections of 1997. His poetic appeals won support from many Kurdish voters. After winning the presidency, he appointed Abdollah Ramezanzadeh as the first Kurdish governor of the province of Iranian Kurdistan. Kurds were also given positions in his cabinet and as senior advisers. Kurds in the Majlis formed a Kurdish Caucus of parliamentarians from Iranian Kurdistan and Kermanshah provinces.

Discussions were initiated about Kurdish-language instruction and curriculum reform at Sanandaj University. Kurds were also allowed to set up civic organizations, including a Kurdish Human Rights Association, to monitor conditions and advocate on behalf of the Kurdish cause.

Inclusion was symbolic and progress illusory. Real power resided with the supreme leader, who was virulently anti-Kurdish. Iranian Kurds fought for their rights in Iran, demanding a federal democratic republic. However, the struggle for Kurdish rights was increasingly transnational. Reflecting Kurdish kinship ideology, an especially strong fraternity existed between Kurds in Iran and Turkey. When Abdullah Ocalan was arrested in February 1999, tens of thousands of Iranian Kurds took to the streets of Mahabad, Sanandaj, and Urmia. The Iranian government cracked down, killing at least twenty people.

Kurds were further riled by the murder of Shivan Qaderi, a Kurdish activist, in July 1999. He was killed along with two other Kurdish human-rights defenders. After torturing Qaderi, security forces tied his body to the back of their Toyota land cruiser and dragged it through the streets of Mahabad. Photos of Qaderi's bloodied and battered body were widely circulated on Roj TV and Kurdish media.[32]

Though the KDPI's armed struggle ended in late 1996, the Free Life Party (PJAK) soon emerged as the vanguard of armed struggle for rights in Iranian Kurdistan. PJAK was spurred by the arrest of Abdullah Ocalan in 1999 and propelled by the US invasion of Iraq in 2003. With its base in Western Iran on the border of Turkey and Iran, PJAK was aligned with the PKK. They shared ideology, leadership, and logistics. Both PJAK and the PKK were members of the Group of Communities in Kurdistan (KCK), a pan-Kurdish organization including Kurds in Turkey, Iran, Iraq, and Syria. According to Osman Ocalan, the brother Abdullah Ocalan, PKK forces in Iran numbered 1,500.[33]

Iraq's Transitional Administrative Law, adopted on March 8, 2004, inspired Iranian Kurds with a sense of possibility. They too wanted a federal state—or independence. Iran's security forces cracked down on PJAK'S expanded operations. Helicopter gunships attacked demonstrators in Saqqez on August 4, 2005. The attack killed thirteen people and wounded more than two hundred.[34]

Conflict was exacerbated by the 2005 election of Mahmoud Ahmadinejad as Iran's President. Escalating conflict in Iranian Kurdistan fused with the PKK's struggle in Turkey and developments in Iraqi Kurdistan. The Kurdish pro-democracy movement assumed a regional character. America's hidden hand was allegedly behind events.

Notes

1. "Unrepresented Nations and Peoples Organization." *UNPO: Iranian Kurdistan.* N.p., n.d. Web. 23 June 2014. <http://www.unpo.org/members/7882#sthash.sABMMHIq.dpuf>.
2. Laizer, S. J. Martyrs, Traitors, and Patriots: Kurdistan after the Gulf War. London: Zed, 1996. Print.
3. "Census of the Islamic Republic of Iran, 1385 (2006)" (Excel). Islamic Republic of Iran.
4. UNPO.
5. Gunter, Michael M. *Historical Dictionary of the Kurds.* Lanham, MD: Scarecrow, 2004. Print.
6. Gunter, Michael M. *Historical Dictionary of the Kurds.* Lanham, MD: Scarecrow, 2004. Print.
7. UNPO.
8. Ibid.
9. Yildiz, Kerim, and Tanyel B. Tayşi. *The Kurds in Iran: The Past, Present and Future.* London: Pluto, 2007. Print.
10. "Iranian Kurdistan: A Simmering Cauldron." *International Relations And Security Network.* N.p., n.d. Web. 27 June 2014. <http://www.isn.ethz.ch/Digital-Library/Articles/Detail/?ots591=4888caa0-b3db-1461-98b9-e20e7b9c13d4&lng=en&id=53697>.
11. Ibid.
12. "Iran's 1906 Constitution." *Foundation for Iranian Studies.* N.p., n.d. Web. 27 June 2014. <http://fis-iran.org/en/resources/legaldoc/iranconstitution>.
13. Sami Moubayed, Sami. "Roots of Kurdish Struggle Run Deep." *Asia Times Online.* N.p., 3 Nov. 2007. Web. 27 June 2014. <http://www.atimes.com/atimes/Middle_East/IK03Ak01.html>.
14. Yildiz, Kerim, and Tanyel B. Tayşi. *The Kurds in Iran: The Past, Present and Future.* London: Pluto, 2007. Print.
15. Jwaideh, Wadie. *The Kurdish National Movement: Its Origins and Development.* Syracuse, NY: Syracuse UP, 2006. Print.
16. Ibid.
17. "Mahabad – the First Independent Kurdish Republic - The Kurdistan Tribune." *The Kurdistan Tribune.* N.p., n.d. Web. 16 June 2014. <http://kurdistantribune.com/2011/mahabad-first-independent-kurdish-republic/>.
18. "22. Iran/Kurds (1943–present)." *Political Science.* N.p., n.d. Web. 16 June 2014. <http://uca.edu/politicalscience/dadm-project/middle-eastnorth-africapersian-gulf-region/irankurds-1943-present/>.
19. "About the Middle East Report | Middle East Research and Information Project." About the Middle East Report | Middle East Research and Information Project. N.p., n.d. Web. 15 June 2014. <http://www.merip.org/mer/mer141/major-kurdish-organizations-iran%2028>.
20. "Brief History of the Kurdish Struggle." Brief History of the Kurdish Struggle. N.p., n.d. Web. 15 June 2014. <http://www.mtholyoke.edu/~jlshupe/history.html>.
21. Entessar, Nader. Kurdish Politics in the Middle East. Lanham: Lexington, 2010. 42.

22. *Iran: Country Study Guide*. Washington, D.C.: International Business Publications, USA, 2006. Print.
23. "Iran Chamber Society: The Constitution of Islamic Republic of Iran." *Iran Chamber Society: The Constitution of Islamic Republic of Iran*. N.p., n.d. Web. 16 June 2014. <http://www.iranchamber.com/government/laws/constitution_ch11.php>.
24. Ibid, 42–43.
25. Kreyenbroek, Philip G., and Stefan Sperl. *The Kurds: A Contemporary Overview*. London: Routledge, 1992. Print.
26. Atroushi, Alex. "A Glance at the Position of the Town of Halabja." *Kdp.se*. N.p., 11 Mar. 1994. Web. 16 June 2014. <http://www.kdp.se/halabja.html>.
27. "PDKI – The Life & Death of Dr. A. R. Ghassemlou." *PDKI – The Life & Death of Dr. A. R. Ghassemlou*. N.p., n.d. Web. 23 July 2014. <http://www.pdk-iran.org/english/doc/kasemlu.htm>.
28. Kinzer, Stephen. "Iran Kurdish Leader Among 4 Killed in Berlin." *The New York Times*. The New York Times, 18 Sept. 1992. Web. 23 July 2014. <http://www.nytimes.com/1992/09/19/world/iran-kurdish-leader-among-4-killed-in-berlin.html>.
29. Russell, Jesse. *Iranian Kurdistan*. S.l.: Book On Demand, 2013. Web.
30. Research Directorate, Immigration and Refugee Board, Canada. 1 May 1998. (Accessed June 9, 2014).
31. "Komala Party." Komala Party. N.p., n.d. Web. 15 June 2014. <http://komalainternational.org/komala-party>.
32. Fathi, Nazila. "Unrest in Iran's Kurdish Region Has Left 17 Dead; Hundreds Have Been Wounded." *The New York Times*. The New York Times, 13 Aug. 2005. Web. 10 June 2014. <http://www.nytimes.com/2005/08/14/international/middleeast/14kurds.html?_r=0>.
33. GlobalSecurity.org (accessed June 10, 2014).
34. As reported by Radio Sedaye Iran and National Iranian TV (NITV).

Part Three

Progress

6

Self-Rule in Iraq

Iraqi Kurdistan was devastated by Saddam Hussein's brutal crackdown at the end of the Gulf War. The Iraqi Army caused enormous devastation before withdrawing to the Green Line just south of the thirty-sixth parallel in August 1992. Iraqi Kurdistan suffered a stifling double embargo after the Gulf War. The Iraqi government blockaded Iraqi Kurdistan at the Green Line. UN sanctions were imposed on all of Iraq, including Iraqi Kurdistan. Peshmerga provided security and maintained public order, but Iraqi Kurdistan faced an administrative vacuum. Iraq's blockade of food, fuel, and electricity imposed great hardship on the Kurds. Their primary access to the world was via the Habur Gate connecting Iraq and Turkey. Trucks with smuggled goods stretched for miles on either side of the Harbur.

The Iraqi Kurdistan Front consisted of the Kurdistan Democratic Party (KDP), the Patriotic Union of Kurdistan (PUK), and six other groups of Kurds. It was established to meet the people's basic needs. Iraqi Kurds went to the polls on May 19, 1992, to elect the Kurdistan Regional Government (KRG) and the Kurdistan National Assembly. The tally was a virtual draw between the KDP and PUK. The KDP received 45 percent of the vote, while the PUK received 44 percent. Only the KDP and PUK passed the 7 percent threshold necessary to gain seats in the legislature. The KDP and PUK created a unity government, allocating an even number of seats between them. Demonstrating their commitment to the rule of law, the unity government was announced during a television broadcast with a judge sitting between Jalal Talabani and Masoud Barzani to explain the legalities of government formation.

Despite their bitter experience of abuse in Iraq, most Kurds thought they could secure their rights through the creation of a democratic and federal Republic in Iraq. The Kurdistan National Assembly agreed to abide by all Iraqi laws, except those that contradicted international standards of human rights. Despite conditions of normalcy, Kurds had a false sense of security. They managed their own affairs, while

Iraqi armed forces manned checkpoints just down the road. None-theless, Iraqi Kurds made the most of their opportunity for self-rule. Kurds increasingly developed a sense of national identity. Those born after 1992 had no experience with Iraqi administration. The Kurdish flag was flown at the same height as the Iraqi flag. Newroz was freely celebrated. Youth spoke Kurdish, not Arabic. Kurdish universities were established, offering instruction in Kurdish. Iraqi Kurdistan developed a dynamic print and television media. Statues of Mustafa Barzani and other Kurdish heroes were built, replacing images of Saddam Hussein.

Kurdish authorities also gained international legitimacy. When Masoud Barzani and Jalal Talabani made their first joint trip to Wash-ington in 1990, State Department officials met them at a coffee shop in Foggy Bottom. After the Gulf War, they were received officially. The KRG established liaison offices in Washington and other Western capitals. Today, Barzani and Talabani are welcomed like heads of state, with the full red-carpet treatment.

*****

Iraqi Kurdistan gained political and cultural rights, but its economy floundered. Economic hardship caused by the embargoes stoked ten-sions between the KDP and the PUK. A civil war between the PUK and KDP broke out in 1994, leading to the collapse of their power-sharing agreement. Oil revenues, tax collection, and territorial disputes were flash-points. More than two thousand Kurds were killed before the KDP and PUK agreed to a cease-fire in late 1994.[1] As victims of Saddam, Iraqi Kurds had enormous goodwill from the international community. Friends of the Iraqi Kurds were deeply disappointed that Kurds fought over petty differences and profiteering. Inter-Kurdish conflict also created an opening for external actors to advance their agendas by manipulating the Kurds. Turkey, Iran, and Iraq all tried to take advantage of the conflict and shape events.

Turkish armed forces established permanent bases on the border with Iraqi Kurdistan. When the PKK moved to Qandil, the hamlet was transformed into a small town with electricity generators, water storage, a field hospital, and large warehouses of lethal and non-lethal supplies. The PKK also maintained a network of border camps as forward staging areas for hit-and-run operations across the border in Turkey. Masoud Barzani relied on Turkey to smuggle oil and for supplies. Under pres-sure from Ankara, KDP peshmerga joined Turkish forces in an assault on Qandil in October 1992. Many PKK were killed or taken prisoner; three thousand KDP peshmerga died.

Iran used the Iraqi Kurds to destabilize Baghdad. The Iranian Revolutionary Guard Corps (IRGC) supported the KDP to stage attacks against the PUK from Iranian territory. The Kurds conspired with a renegade faction of the Iraqi army in a plot to assassinate Saddam Hussein in 1995, after failed CIA attempts in the early '90s. The CIA's Robert Baer learned that the plot was compromised and canceled it. But nobody told the PUK, which managed to destroy three Iraqi Army divisions and take five thousand prisoners before realizing that the operation was called off.

Iraq took advantage of conflict between the KDP and PUK to reassert its influence in Iraqi Kurdistan. When a KDP-PUK cease-fire collapsed in mid-1996, Talabani entered into an alliance with Iran. IRGC attacked the Kurdish Democratic Party of Iran in Iraqi Kurdistan on July 28, 1996. Knowing that an attack was imminent, the PUK informed residents of Ainkawa, a Christian district in Erbil that housed many UN personnel. Faced with the prospect of military confrontation with both Iran and the PUK, Barzani turned to Baghdad for assistance.

Saddam deployed thirty thousand troops against the PUK in Erbil on August 31. Iraqi forces took seven hundred PUK members prisoner and executed them. The CIA-sponsored Salahuddin headquarters of the Iraqi National Congress (INC), a dissident group led by Ahmed Chalabi, was overrun. INC members were taken prisoner and killed. US military transport planes undertook an emergency evacuation of seven hundred INC members and six thousand Iraqi Kurds to Guam.

President Bill Clinton initiated Operation Desert Strike, in response to Saddam's aggression that September. Clinton launched cruise missiles against Iraq's air defense systems, moved an aircraft carrier group to the Persian Gulf, and extended the southern no-fly zone north to the thirty-third parallel. Meanwhile, violent conflict intensified between the KDP and PUK. The KDP seized Erbil and Suleimani on September 9, 1996. The PUK launched a counteroffensive a few weeks later with Iran's assistance, recapturing Suleimani.

The Washington Peace Agreement between the KDP and PUK was signed on September 17, 1998. It ended the fighting, dividing Iraqi Kurdistan between the KDP in the Northwest and the PUK in the Southeast. The Washington Agreement established revenue sharing between the KDP and PUK. A date for elections was set for the following summer. In accordance with UNSC Resolution 688, the agreement also required both sides to bar Iraqi troops from Iraqi Kurdistan and deny sanctuary to the PKK. The United States threatened to use force against any incursion by the Iraqi armed forces. Secretary of State, Madeleine Albright said the "renewed spirit of reconciliation between Mr. Barzani and Mr. Talabani, exemplified in their joint meeting and joint statement today, will make it easier for the United States and others to help their people."[2]

The Washington Agreement fully restored the UN Oil for Food Program. UN Security Council Resolution 986, adopted on April 14, 1995, mandated the UN to manage Iraq's oil sales. The KRG was designated to receive 13 percent of the country's total revenue. The program was a windfall. The KRG received $4.6 billion via the Oil for Food Program between 1997 and 2001.[3]

The incursion of Iraqi armed forces into Iraqi Kurdistan served as a reminder of Iraq's fragile peace. At a moment's notice, Saddam had the capability to overrun Iraqi Kurdistan and the Shiite South. Iraq halted its cooperation with United Nations Special Commission's disarmament work and was threatening to end all cooperation with UN weapons inspectors. It rejected the UN Security Council's demand for periodic inspections of Iraq's compliance with UN Resolutions. Faced with Saddam's defiance and threats, President Bill Clinton signed the Iraqi Liberation Act on October 31, 1998, pledging US military assistance to the KDP, PUK, and other Iraqi opposition groups.[4] US officials started thinking beyond containment about regime change.

*****

In response to the terrorist attacks of September 11, 2001, President George W. Bush adopted a Doctrine of Preemption, affirming the right to attack potential foes before they could attack the United States. Bush believed that eliminating Saddam Hussein and transforming Iraq into a model democracy for the Middle East would undermine the Baathists in Syria, pressure the mullahs in Iran, enhance Israel's security, and serve US energy interests. Iraqi Kurds shared this vision and worked closely with the Bush administration for regime change.[5]

The US launched Operation Iraqi Freedom on March 19, 2003. US forces dashed across the desert, broke through Saddam's vaunted "ring of fire," and entered Baghdad.[6] With a few Iraqi bystanders, they toppled the iconic statue of Saddam Hussein in Firdos Square on April 9, 2003. US troops had no instructions for phase-four stability operations.

They stepped aside when the decapitation of the regime led to looting and civil strife. Instead of praise for liberating Iraq, the self-described "occupation" eroded America's standing with Iraqis. Problems were anticipated by the US government's Future of Iraq Project. But warnings were ignored by ideologues who promised a "cake-walk" and that the cost of the Iraq War would quickly be recovered from Iraqi oil sales.

Ambassador L. Paul Bremmer III was appointed to head the Coalition Provisional Authority (CPA).[7] He governed like a viceroy. Arab Sunnis were incensed when Bremmer issued a decree to "dis-establish" the Baath Party on May 16, 2003.[8] De-Baathification emphasized guilt through association, deeply polarizing Iraqi society. Overnight, 120,000 Iraqis were dismissed from their jobs. The Baath leadership was indisputably responsible for atrocities and genocide, but not all party members were war criminals. Many Iraqis joined the Baath Party because they had no choice. Membership was a prerequisite to education and employment opportunities. A second order, Dissolution of Entities, eliminated Iraqi's military and its secret intelligence service (Mukhabarat): Bremer disbanded the Iraqi armed forces on May 23, refusing to pay the salaries and pensions of all military personnel. The decision to disband the army turned four hundred thousand Iraqis and their families into antagonists. It also eliminated an institution that could have played a critical role in maintaining security during the transitional period after Saddam.

Bremer's plan to transfer governance responsibilities to Iraqis also fell flat. He appointed the Iraqi Governing Council, dominated by exiles. Iraqis rejected it as a puppet of the United States. Bremmer named a committee of Iraqis to work with State Department lawyers and develop Iraq's constitution. However, Iraqis insisted that the constitution could only be drafted by a democratically elected body. Bremmer also abandoned plans to conduct a census or create voting districts. Iraqis rejected the CPA's proposal for indirect elections.

Kurds played a leading role in drafting the Transitional Administrative Law (TAL), which was adopted on March 8, 2004. TAL served as an interim constitution for Iraq, enshrining democracy, federalism, and a bill of rights. According to the preamble, "The people of Iraq, striving to reclaim their freedom, which was usurped by the previous tyrannical regime, rejecting violence and coercion in all their forms, and particularly when used as instruments of governance, have determined that they shall hereafter remain a free people governed under the rule of law." The TAL established Arabic and Kurdish as the official languages of Iraq. As requested by the Kurds, the TAL declared: "The federal system shall be based upon geographic and historical realities and the separation of powers, and not upon origin, race, ethnicity, nationality, or confession."[9]

The TAL included provisions to address disputed internal boundaries. Article 58, paragraphs A and B stated that the government "shall act expeditiously to take measures to remedy the injustice caused by the previous regime's practices in altering the demographic character of certain regions, including Kirkuk"—specifically, by making "recommendations to the National Assembly on remedying unjust changes" in administrative boundaries. According to Paragraph C, "The permanent resolution of disputed territories, including Kirkuk, shall be deferred until after these measures are completed, a fair and transparent census has been conducted, and the permanent constitution has been ratified. This resolution shall be consistent with the principle of justice, taking into account the will of the people of those territories."[10]

It also provided a timeline to draft and adopt a permanent constitution. It called for National Assembly elections by January 31, 2005 (Article 2). The National Assembly would draft a permanent constitution by August 15, and the Iraqi voters would vote in a referendum to approve the constitution by October 15 (Article 61). The permanent constitution would be approved by a majority of voters. A "no" vote by two-thirds in three provinces would veto the constitution. The super-majority provision effectively gave the Kurds a veto over the permanent constitution. They were a well-organized majority in the provinces of Dohuk, Erbil, and Suleimani. It also gave substantial leverage to Arab Sunnis, who are a majority in the provinces of Nineveh, Anbar, and Salahuddin.

The TAL uniquely recognized the KRG as the legitimate government of the Kurds, and enshrined the existence of the KRG within the new federal state. The TAL declared that Iraq's natural resources belonged to the people of Iraq and future development of natural resources, especially oil, required consultation between the central government and local governorates. It affirmed the principle that revenue from the exploitation of natural resources should be redistributed to the regions based on the region's proportion of the population and that revenue sharing would be calculated with "due regard for areas that were unjustly deprived of these revenues by the previous regime."[11]

Other Iraqis complained that the process of drafting the TAL lacked transparency. They said it favored the Kurds. Ayatollah Ali al-Sistani, the leading Shiite cleric in Iraq, feared that the two-thirds provision in

Article 61 gave a veto to the Kurds and Arab Sunnis. Sistani also wanted Islamic law more deeply embedded in the TAL. Though the TAL established Islam as Iraq's official religion, it described Islam as "a source" of legislation rather than the exclusive basis of law. Iraqi Kurds were patient during the period that followed Saddam's toppling. They had a ten-year head start on other Iraqis developing democratic institutions and civil society. International security guarantees nurtured progress in Iraqi Kurdistan. Kurds owed their opportunity to the United States and Britain, which instituted "Operation Northern Watch," a no-fly zone in 1997. Kurds were flexible when Bremmer requested their support of a unified and democratic Iraq. However, red lines would become apparent in negotiations over Iraq's permanent constitution.

*****

The overwhelming majority of Kurds dream of independence. Despite all the fraternal talk about "Iraqi brothers," Kurds are distrustful of Baghdad. Given their history of betrayal and abuse, Kurds learned to moderate their expectations. Establishing Iraq as a federal, democratic republic was the most reasonable way to protect and promote their rights. In July 2003, a group of Kurdish intellectuals in Suleimani launched the Kurdistan Referendum Movement (KRM). The KRM spread to several cities in Kurdistan, as well as to Kirkuk and Mosul. Delegates organized a petition demanding their right to an official referendum on their future political status.[12] The petition garnered 1,732,535 signatures. It was presented to the UN Office of Electoral Assistance on December 22, 2004.[13]

An unofficial independence referendum was organized in January 30, 2005. Voters were given two options: (1) to stay as part of Iraq, or (2) to be independent. A total of 1,998,061 people participated in the referendum, which was held in all Kurdish areas of Northern Iraq, including Kirkuk, Khanaqin, and Kurdish areas in Nineveh province. Kurds living in Baghdad and other Arab municipalities were not included. The pro-independence vote garnered 98.8 percent support. 1,973412 voted for independence.[14] 19,560 voted for Kurdistan to remain as part of Iraq.

The referendum was conducted in parallel to Iraqi parliamentary elections and Iraqi Kurdistan legislative elections on January 31, 2005. Kurdistan's elections were intended to resolve conflict between the KDP and PUK. However, the outcome exacerbated tensions. The PUK received a plurality of votes, but the KDP won a plurality of council seats. The KDP won forty seats and the PUK thirty-eight seats. Other seats were distributed between the Kurdistan Islamic Union and the Kurdistan Communist Party, as well ethnic minority parties such as Turkmen Democratic Movement, the Assyrian Democratic Movement, and the Chaldean Cultural Society. Masoud Barzani assumed the Kurdistan Region Presidency (KRP) through a secret ballot over the PUK's objections. Nechirvan Barzani, his nephew, would become the Prime Minister. Bickering continued over ministerial posts.

Iraqis voted for 275-member National Assembly, established by the TAL, as well as eighteen provincial councils.[15] The United Iraqi Alliance, included Ahmed Chalabi and was endorsed by Sistani. It received 48 percent of the vote.[16] The Democratic Patriotic Alliance of Kurdistan, including the two main Kurdish political parties and nine smaller Kurdish parties, made a strong showing with 26 percent.[17] Kurds voted in large numbers; they were highly motivated to show their voting power. The Iraqi List of interim Prime Minister Ayad Allawi won 14 percent. A vast majority of Arab Sunnis either boycotted the ballot or were too intimidated to vote, threatening the election's legitimacy. Leadership positions were divided between Shiites, Sunnis, and Kurds. Ibrahim al-Jaffari from the Shia Dawa Party became prime minister. Hajim al-Hassani became speaker of the parliament. Kurds occupied important positions in the Iraqi government. Jalal Talabani became the first Kurdish president in Iraq. Hoshyar Zebari continued to serve as foreign minister. Barham Salih became deputy prime minister, and six Kurds occupied other key cabinet posts.

Holding elections was itself an accomplishment. Militants threatened to "wash the streets in blood."[18] The Iraqi Islamic Party and the Association of Muslim Scholars refused to field candidates. Due to security concerns, seven thousand candidates did not reveal their identities until days before the election. Iraq's borders were sealed, and a no-fly zone imposed. Vehicles were banned from Baghdad, which was locked down under curfew. More than fifteen thousand US troops were deployed to protect polling stations. Despite the extraordinary security measures, a hundred attacks killed forty-four Iraqis on election day.

Bush stated, "The terrorists and those who benefited from the tyranny of Saddam Hussein know that free elections will expose the emptiness of their vision for Iraq. That is why they will stop at nothing to prevent or disrupt this election. As hope and freedom spread, the appeal of terror and hate will fade."[19] In this context of intense sectarian violence and bloodshed, the National Assembly designated a Constitutional Drafting Committee to begin the contentious process of drafting a charter for the "new Iraq." The Iraqi Transitional Government was created on May 3, 2005, and replaced by the first permanent government on May 20, 2006.

*****

The draft of Iraq's permanent constitution mirrored many of the TAL's provisions. Iraq's constitution clearly defined the vertical separation of powers between the presidency, parliament, and legislature, while subordinating the military and security services to civilian authority. It also included provisions for horizontal power sharing between the central government and Iraq's eighteen governorates. The federal government was given exclusive power over foreign policy, national defense, and fiscal policy. Control of customs, electrical power, environmental policy, health, and education were shared with regional authorities. All powers not exclusively granted to the federal government were retained by the regions, and priority was given to regional law in case of conflict between the federal government and regional governments. The constitution was strong on cultural rights, promoting the use of local languages in education and administration.

However, the Constitutional Drafting Committee reached an impasse toward the end of its work. Conflict over the role of Islam and sectarian differences threatened to derail the process. To satisfy demands of different Iraqi constituencies, the drafters made changes to the charter in critical areas such as disputed internal boundaries, control of the energy sector, and procedures for amending the constitution in the future. As usual, US officials asked the Kurds to modify their bottom line and accommodate others.

The Kurds wanted the committee to issue a final draft of the constitution, which would be put to an up or down vote. However, US officials wanted to make sure that Arab Sunnis had ownership of the document. The Constitution Drafting Committee brokered a compromise: the first parliament elected after the constitution was adopted would establish a Constitutional Review Committee to consider amendments. In the event of changes, another referendum would be required.

The Kurds accepted that Iraq's existing energy resources belonged to all Iraqis. However, they wanted to control future exploration and production (E&P) of oil and gas in Iraqi Kurdistan. Other Iraqis rejected the Kurds' future energy claims. Rather than resolve this matter, the constitution was ambiguous. Article 109 maintained,

> The federal government with the producing governorates and regional governments shall undertake the management of oil and gas extracted from current fields provided that it distributes oil and gas revenues in a fair manner in proportion to the population distribution in all parts of the country with a set allotment for a set time for the damaged regions that were unjustly deprived by the former regime and the regions that were damaged later on, and in a way that assures balanced development in different areas of the country, and this will be regulated by law.

Regarding future E&P, "The federal government with the producing regional and governorate governments shall together formulate the necessary strategic policies to develop the oil and gas wealth in a way that achieves the highest benefit to the Iraqi people. . . ."[20]

For Kurds, Kirkuk is their Jerusalem, integral to national aspirations. No Kurdish politician could negotiate away the historic claims of Kurds to Kirkuk. Other Iraqis balked at assigning Kirkuk to the Kurds. Arabs and Turkmen also laid claim. Moreover, Kirkuk's oil wealth would give Iraqi Kurdistan the economic base for independence.[21] The committee punted, adopting Article 140: "Article 58 of the TAL shall extend and continue to the executive authority elected in accordance with this constitution, provided that it accomplishes completely (normalization, census, and referendums in Kirkuk and other disputed territories to determine the will of their citizens) by a date not to exceed December 31, 2007."[22]

Political violence surged as Iraqis debated the constitution. The Bush administration pressured the Iraq Islamic Party to endorse the constitution. Without Arab Sunni participation, there could be no deal. And without a constitution, there could be no exit strategy to America's occupation. If the process of constitution making failed, Iraq would experience even more intense violence. A referendum on the constitution was conducted on October 15, 2007. Nine point eight million Iraqis, or 63 percent of registered voters, cast ballots.[23] Seventy-eight percent backed the charter and 21 percent opposed it.[24] It was approved with strong support by voters in the Kurdistan Region of Iraq. However, more than two-thirds of the voters in Anbar and Salahaddin provinces rejected it. In addition, 55 percent of voters in Nineveh province voted "no." However, this number did not meet the two-thirds threshold in a third province necessary to scuttle the constitution.

Iraq's constitution was by far the most democratic charter in the Middle East. It was a major step toward establishing the rule of law. "The Iraqis are making inspiring progress toward building a democracy," Bush said, "By any standard or precedent of history, Iraq has made incredible political progress, from tyranny to liberation to national elections to the ratification of a constitution in the space of two and a half years."[25] Bush heralded the process of drafting and authorizing the constitution, praising Iraqis for resolving their differences through negotiations rather than physical confrontation.

*****

Meanwhile, Iraqi Kurds were drafting their own constitution governing affairs in the Kurdistan Region of Iraq. In a transparent process, they prepared the draft for public debate.

The Kurdish constitution defined relations between the Kurdistan Region of Iraq, as a federal region within Iraq, and the central government. It affirmed the territory of Iraqi Kurdistan, addressing the issue of disputed internal boundaries. Article 2 consists of three parts:

> First, Iraqi Kurdistan consists of Dohuk Governorate in its present administrative borders, and the governorates of Kirkuk, Sulaymaniyah, and Erbil; the districts Aqrah, Shaykhan, Sinjar, Tall 'Afar, Tall Kayf, Qara Qush, and the counties Zummar, Ba'shiqah, and Aski Kalak in Niniveh Governorate; the districts Khanaqin and Mandali in Diyala Governorate; and the districts Badrah and the county Jasan in Wasit Governorate in their administrative borders before 1968. Second, The administrative border of the Kurdistan Region is based on Article 140 of the federal constitution. Third, In the case that the areas cut off from Kurdistan are returned through the application of Article 140 of the federal constitution, the inhabitants of these areas enjoy the equal rights and obligations and safeguards provided to the people of Kurdistan in this constitution.[26]

The Kurdish constitution distinguished Iraqi Kurdistan from the Iraqi state by establishing a presidency, armed forces, and citizenship guidelines (Article 6). It asserted that Iraqi Kurdistan voluntarily entered into a federal union and, as an equal party, has the right to secede from Iraq if the covenant's terms were violated:

> The people of Iraqi Kurdistan have the right to self-determination, and under this right they are free to determine their politics and free to achieve their economic, social, and cultural development. They have chosen the free union with Iraq, as people, territory, and

sovereignty as long as it is committed to the federal constitution and the parliamentary, federal, democratic, pluralistic system respectful of the human rights of the individual and the society. It will reconsider its view on the determination of the future political delineation and political position in the following cases: First - Violation of the sanctity of the federal constitution, including a retreat from the commitment to the federal system, or the basic principles of democracy and constitutional rights of the individual and the society. Second - A policy of ethnic discrimination and change of the demographic reality in Kurdistan, or work to maintain their previous implications and consequences thus retreating from the constitutional obligations contained in Article 140 of the federal constitution (Article 8).

It gave Iraqi Kurdistan its own flag, to be flown "next to the flag of the Federal Republic of Iraq," as well as its own national anthem, cultural, and national holidays (Article 12). It assigned responsibility for security to the peshmerga (Article 13). It also established the economic foundation of a state by laying claim to energy resources developed after August 15, 2005:

The government of Kurdistan, together with the federal government, administers the oil and gas fields on the territory of Iraqi Kurdistan that have been commercially exploited before 15 August 2005 for the distribution of the derived resources in a fair way according to the principles set in Article 112 of the federal constitution [and] the government of Kurdistan draws up the necessary strategic policies to develop the oil and gas wealth together with the federal government so they can be approved by the parliament of Iraqi Kurdistan.

Further, "The government of the Kurdistan Region is in possession of all the domains regarding the oil and gas fields that have not been explored or producing commercially before August 15, 2005 in terms of exploration, extraction and management, manufacturing, sales, marketing and export, and others" (Article 113).

Baghdad viewed the Kurdish constitution as tantamount to secession.[27] As a parallel document to the Iraqi constitution, it provided a roadmap for Iraqi Kurdistan's independence. Adoption of the Kurdish constitution was suspended but not cancelled. Iraqi Kurds could always revive the Kurdish constitution if Iraq became mired in conflict and collapsed from sectarian strife.

*****

The Iraqi insurgency started immediately after the US invasion of Iraq in 2003. Insurgents targeted US forces and Iraqi security, which they viewed as accomplices to occupation. Arab Sunnis blamed the United States for invading and occupying Iraq. They were enraged by Washington's transfer of power to the Shiite-dominated Iraqi government. By 2007, Arab Sunni insurgents were infiltrated by foreign fighters and al-Qaeda elements. Their aversion to the United States was matched only by their hatred of Shiites.

The Al-Askari Mosque in Samarra was built in AD 944 and is one of the holiest sites of Shia Islam. Its spectacular gold dome was bombed on February 22, 2006. Immediately after the Samarra bombing, thirty Sunni mosques were attacked.[28] Within a month, the corpses of six hundred Arab Sunnis were found on the streets of Baghdad.[29] Iraqis turned to extremist sectarian groups for protection because US and Iraqi forces could not provide their security. In February 2006, the US National Intelligence Estimate characterized conditions in Iraq as a "civil war."[30] The possibility of an Iraq that can govern, defend, and sustain itself grew increasingly remote.

US domestic opposition to the Iraq war was growing. The 2006 midterm election was a referendum on the war. Repudiating Bush's policies, voters handed control of the US Senate and House of Representatives to the Democratic Party. When House Speaker-elect Nancy Pelosi visited wounded Iraq War veterans at Bethesda Naval Medical Center, she was visibly moved and vowed to bring "the war to an end."[31] According to Pelosi, "The biggest ethical issue facing our country for the past three and half years is the war in Iraq."[32]

The Bush administration doubled down on its war strategy. Bush announced "the surge" in his State of the Union speech on January 10, 2007: "America will change our strategy to help the Iraqis carry out their campaign to put down sectarian violence and bring security to the people of Baghdad. This will require increasing American force levels. So I've committed more than 20,000 additional American troops to Iraq. The vast majority of them—five brigades—will be deployed to Baghdad."[33] Bush also extended the tour of troops, including four thousand marines in Anbar Province. Surge brigades started arriving in February 2007, bringing the total number of brigades in country from fifteen to twenty.

More than numbers, the surge embodied a new approach. It was designed to help Iraqis protect themselves collectively, isolate extremists, and create space for a new political process. It focused on regions, and let Iraqis lead. Rather than emphasize killing insurgents, the new counterinsurgency strategy (COIN) emphasized winning hearts and minds of Iraqis. COIN reduced the role of forward operating bases.

Instead, US troops sought to protect the local population and prevent civilian casualties. COIN emphasized cooperation with Iraqis to help them clear and secure neighborhoods, create conditions for reconstruction, economic revitalization, and political participation. US forces abandoned violent "cordon and search" operations. Joint security stations with Iraqi forces worked to build relationships with Iraqi communities. The focus on protecting and building contacts with the Iraqi population garnered gains in actionable intelligence, which led to more targeted and strategic military operations.

The Sons of Iraq were formed by Arab Sunni tribal leaders to counter al-Qaeda and Sunni extremists. The movement was also known as the Anbar Awakening. While the United States provided weapons and money, the Sons of Iraq did not fight on behalf of either US or Iraqi armed forces. They stood up to defend themselves from al-Qaeda and Shia militias.

General David Petraeus, commander of the Multi-National Force in Iraq, credited the surge with tamping down sectarian violence and reducing attacks against US forces. He told Congress on September 10, 2007: "The military objectives of the surge are, in large measure, being met."[34] Petraeus heralded strides against al-Qaeda in Iraq, as well as Shia militia extremists. He credited the surge, with which he was closely identified, for minimizing both the number of Iraqi civilian deaths and US fatalities.

The surge's positive impact is debatable. It did not diminish displacement. In October 2006, the UN high commissioner for refugees and the Iraqi government estimated that more than 370,000 Iraqis had been displaced since the Samarra bombing in February.[35] At that time, the total number of Iraqi refugees was about 1.6 million. Displacement continued unabated.[36] By 2008, the UNHCR estimated that 4.7 million persons were displaced, about 16 percent of the total population.[37]

Petraeus claimed that the surge contributed to reduced fatalities of Iraqis. An independent military commission led by General James L. Jones suggested that the decrease in violent incidents may have occurred because areas were purged of either Shias or Sunnis. In August 2007, the International Organization for Migration and the Iraqi Red Crescent Organization reported that Iraqis were vacating sectarian conflict zones.

Petraeus also maintained that the surge reduced the number of attacks against coalition forces in Anbar province. However, the surge had little to do with fewer attacks. It was simply the result of a split between nationalist insurgent groups and al-Qaeda in Iraq. The Iraqi Accord Front, which compromised Sunni Arabs, ended its boycott of the Iraq Parliament on December 2, 2007. Two months later, Iraq's parliament adopted legislation allowing the return to public life of Baath party members. Petraeus testified that the surge tamped down Shia extremism. This was, in fact, the result of a split between moderates and extremists in Moqtadar al-Sadr's Mahdi Army. The Badr Brigade, a rival Shiite militia, also gained strength, curtailing the Mahdi Army's operations. Shia pilgrims were slaughtered in Karbala on August 29, 2007, prompting Sadr to declare a six-month cease-fire. These events coincided with the surge, but the surge itself cannot be credited. Shiites were increasingly engaged in Iraqi politics. They found ways of advancing the Shia agenda via governance, rather than simply through violence.

The surge should be seen in context. Petraeus modeled COIN and the surge on his experience in Mosul where he commanded the 101st Airborne and coalition forces from April 2003 to February 2004. Petraeus was celebrated for his accomplishments in Mosul. His power-point presentations told a story of success: insurgents killed, police trained, roads repaired, and millions of dollars distributed for local development projects. However, his accomplishments—especially in Mosul—do not stand up under scrutiny.

General Muhammad Khayri al-Barhawi, a former Special Forces officer, was appointed Mosul's police chief by Petraeus. During Barhawi's term $41 million to procure weapons for the police disappeared. About 190,000 AK-47 assault rifles and pistols were lost and left open for the taking.[38] Two months after Petraeus left Mosul, Barhawi led an operation against insurgents in Mosul. About 8 percent of the city's 4,000 policemen deserted. Insurgents seized, radios, communication equipment, police uniforms, and a fleet of fifty police cars. Mosul was overrun by insurgents on November 11, 2004. According to General Carter Ham, who succeeded Petraeus in Mosul, the police force had been fully infiltrated by insurgents. General Stanley A. McChrystal, head of Special Operations Task Force in Iraq, indicated that Mosul was a hub for al-Qaeda in Mesopotamia and its notorious leader Abu Musab Zarqawi who founded al-Tawhid wal-Jihad.

While losing Mosul, Petraeus also alienated the Kurds. Rather than coordinating security, he forcibly disarmed the peshmerga and evicted them from Mosul. Petraeus favored Arab Sunnis despite Mosul's ethnically diverse composition of Kurds, Turkmen, and Arabs. Petraeus reflected on lesson learnt: "Not to align too closely with one ethnic group, political party, tribe, religious group or social element."[39]

Training and expansion of the Iraqi Army, which Petraeus oversaw was also a fiasco. The Iraqi Army was notoriously incapable and corrupt. A sum of $1.2 billion earmarked for weapons procurement was embezzled. As in Mosul, Petraeus favored Arab Sunnis. His work with the Iraqi Army angered the Kurds, who felt that training and sophisticated equipment provided by the United States to Iraqis would someday be turned on them, or used in sectarian conflict.[40]

*****

Article 140 of Iraq's constitution envisioned a referendum on the status of Kirkuk by December 31, 2007. The deadline was missed, which exacerbated other core Kurdish concerns including ownership of natural resources, control of oil revenues, the role of the peshmerga, and the status of disputed territories. Baghdad rejected Kurdish claims to Kifri, Khanaqin, and Baladrooz in Diyala province, Tooz in Salaheddin province, Badrah in Wasit province, Akra, Shekhan, al-Shikhan, al-Mamadniya, Tel Kaif, Tall Affar, and Sinjar in Ninevah province. Of these, oil-rich Khanaqin was the most dangerous flashpoint.

In 2006, the Khanaqin city council issued a proclamation calling for secession from Diyala Province. Zarqawi declared a caliphate in Diyala. In 2007, Diyala became a battleground between al-Qaeda, the Sons of Iraq, and Shia militias. Zaraqawi tried to provoke conflict between Kurds and the Iraqi armed forces. There were a number of attacks including a suicide bombing in a restaurant near Kirkuk frequented by Kurdish and Arab officials.[41]

In April 2008, Prime Minister Nouri al-Maliki dispatched Iraq's 5th Army Division to Khanaqin. They arrived without warning and ordered the 34th Peshmerga Brigade to evacuate. There was a standoff, but no shots were fired. In July, the Iraqi Army launched an anti-al-Qaeda operation, "Omens of Prosperity." Kurds insisted there were no al-Qaeda elements in Khanaqin. They maintained that the operation was part of an "Arabization" project designed to create facts on the ground, marginalizing Kurdish claims through the presence of Iraqi forces. According to Masoud Barzani, "It is surprising that the Iraqi army is trying to send forces to this area on the pretext of fighting terrorism and that they have not tried to coordinate with the Kurdistan Regional Government."[42] In August, Khanaqin was occupied by the 1st Iraqi Army Division. Iraqi security tried to close the offices of Kurdish political parties, which were defended by peshmerga. A shoot-out ensued when Iraqi police arrested a Kurdish intelligence officer.

Maliki was picking a fight with the Kurds to shore up his support in advance of provincial elections the next year. This confrontational approach not only risked breaking an alliance between Shia and Kurds that dated back to the period of Iraqi opposition. It also risked armed conflict between the central government and the KRG. General Raymond T. Odierno adopted a strategy for security cooperation to facilitate communication and prevent confrontation. Checkpoints manned by Kurdish, Iraqi, and US forces were set up in Nineveh and Diyala provinces.

Odierno was in a rush to help Iraqis resolve their differences. Bush announced the withdrawal of U.S. forces by the end of 2011. Soon after assuming the presidency, Barack Obama reduced US troop levels from over 160,000 during the surge to 130,000. As a candidate, Obama opposed the surge and pledged to complete Bush's withdrawal plan. He was even prepared to abandon plans for a residual force if the Status of Forces Agreement did not include immunity for US personnel.

*****

Nouri al-Malaki of the Dawa Party became prime minister in 2006. Maliki's ascent was promoted by the CIA and coordinated by Qasem Soleimani, the commander of Iran's Quds Force. Soleimani brokered the deal between Shiite and Kurdish leaders allowing Maliki to form a cabinet.[43] Though he came to power as a weak and compromised premier, Maliki asserted his nationalist bona fides by confronting the Mahdi Army in Basra and Baghdad. He also took on Sunni insurgents in Anbar and Kurds in Khanaqin. The killing of Zarqawi was announced soon after Maliki took office. Maliki said, "Today, Zarqawi has been terminated. Every time a Zarqawi appears we will kill him. We will continue confronting whoever follows his path."[44] Maliki presided over the execution of Saddam Hussein on the first day of Muslim Eid al-Adha feast, the festival of sacrifice. The year-long boycott of parliament by Sunni members ended in 2008. Maliki brokered a cease-fire with Sadr's Mahdi Army and consolidated his power over rival Shiite factions.

Maliki and Bush spoke weekly via videoconference. At the same time, Maliki catered to the Arab street by criticizing US forces for murdering Iraqi civilians and disrespecting citizens' rights. His criticism of Israel's actions in Lebanon and cozy relations with Iran did not sit well in Washington. Maliki's unconstitutional consolidation of executive powers was also a major concern to the Obama administration. Maliki was named commander in chief. He created the Baghdad Brigade, reporting directly to him, and increased the powers of the General Secretariat. Obama was wary of Maliki's authoritarian tendencies and strident condemnation of the United States. According to Hoshyar Zebari, Maliki and Obama met "once or twice" since Obama assumed the presidency.[45]

Maliki made an official trip to the White House on July 22, 2009. It was Maliki's first visit to Washington since 2006. Obama said, "We will continue to provide training and support for Iraqi security forces that are capable and nonsectarian. We'll move forward with our strategy to responsibly remove all American combat brigades from Iraq by the end of next August, and to fulfill our commitment to remove all American troops from Iraq by the end of 2011." Obama was focused on calibrating his exit strategy from Iraq. "Recently, we took an important step forward by transferring control of all Iraqi cities and towns to Iraq's security forces. This transition was part of our security agreement, and should send an unmistakable signal that we will keep our commitments with the sovereign Iraqi government. As I said before, we seek no bases in Iraq, nor do we make any claim on Iraq's territory or resources."[46] Well versed in Iraqi affairs, Vice President Joe Biden conveyed a sterner message. He warned that the US commitment to Iraq could end if the country descended deeper into ethnic and sectarian violence.

Iraqi National elections were scheduled for January 15, 2010. They were, however, postponed after Iraq's Supreme Court found the electoral law unconstitutional. The decision was a victory for Arabs and Turkmen, who claimed that the voter roll in Kirkuk Governorate had been manipulated by the KRG.

The electoral management body planned to use voter rolls from 2004. The KRG objected. Kirkuk's demography had changed as Kurds returned to their homes. The Political Council for National Security proposed merging electoral rolls from 2004 and 2009. The KRG also rejected this option. The United Nations Mission in Iraq offered a temporary solution, using the 2009 voter rolls with plans to revise them in the future. Kurdish members of parliament walked out of the meeting in protest. After intense haggling, Arabs agreed to use the 2009 voter rolls while establishing a committee to consider "dubious" ballots.

Kurds also protested new arrangements for proportional representation. The size of the national assembly was increased from 275 to

325 seats, but Kurds received only three additional seats through the expansion. Barzani demanded more seats and threatened to boycott the election. The Kurdistan Alliance presented a single Kurdish list including the Gorran Movement, which surprisingly won a quarter of the seats in Iraqi Kurdistan's legislative election on July 25, 2009. Gorran was established by Nawshirwan Mustafa, a former PUK Politbureau member and Talabani's deputy for thirty years starting in 1976. Mustafa knew the inner working of the PUK and KRG. He appealed to Kurds disaffected by alleged corruption, cronyism, and nepotism. Gorran means "change" in Kurdish.

Tensions surrounding the elections increased further when hundreds of candidates with alleged links to the Baath Party were barred from running. Rather than serving as a conflict resolution device, the 2010 elections were deeply polarizing. Iraq was gripped by waves of pre-electoral violence.

The national election was finally held on March 7, 2010. Ayad Allawi's Al-Iraqiya, the only party to cut across sectarian and ethnic lines, won ninety-one seats. Maliki's State of Law Coalition came in a close second with eighty-nine seats. The Iraqi National Alliance, a coalition of Shia Islamist parties and the Supreme Council for Islamic Revolution in Iraq, gained seventy seats. The Kurdistan Alliance came in fourth with forty-three seats.

The parties jockeyed for leadership and cabinet posts in a coalition government. The State of Law Coalition and the Iraqi National Alliance combined to form a block with 159 seats. They were, however, four seats short of the majority required to form a government. The Kurds had always played the role as kingmaker in the politics of post-Saddam Iraq. Their block was critical to a governing majority.

The new parliament convened on June 14. The National Iraqi Alliance nominated Adil Abdul-Mahdi to be prime minister, but Maliki had no intention of stepping down. The Kurdistan Block without Gorran participated in a series of meetings in Erbil and Baghdad. Masoud Barzani took the initiative to help Arab Shia and Sunnis overcome their differences on government formation. The so-called Barzani process culminated in the Erbil Agreement of November 11, 2010. It established nineteen principles for Iraqi governance, including measures to address core Kurdish concerns.[47] Mirroring power-sharing principles in the 1980 Taif Accords that ended Lebanon's civil war, the Iraqi presidency was allocated to a Kurd, the prime minister's post was awarded to a Shia, and a Sunni would serve as speaker of the house.

Allawi rejected provisions in the Erbil Agreement such as the implementation of Article 140, reserving the presidency for a Kurd, and using central government funding for the peshmerga. When Maliki accepted all nineteen principles, the Kurdistan block threw its support behind the Rule of Law Coalition. Doing so reunited the National Alliance, restoring Shia-Kurd cooperation in Iraqi politics.[48] After nine months of gridlock, Maliki became prime minister on December 21, 2010. He was also named acting interior minister, acting defense minister, and acting national security minister. Iraqiya won the most seats, but Allawi was given control of a toothless new agency, the National Council for Higher Policies. The Obama administration breathed a sigh of relief. Maliki's second mandate augured stability, which was essential with US troops preparing to withdraw the following year.

*****

The Agreement Between the United States of America and the Republic of Iraq On the Withdrawal of United States Forces from Iraq and the Organization of Their Activities during Their Temporary Presence in Iraq, otherwise known as the Status of Forces Agreement (SOFA) was signed by Bush and Maliki on Bush's fourth and final trip to Baghdad on December 14, 2008. The SOFA followed months of wrangling. Negotiations took into consideration opposition from Sadr, as well as the concerns of Sistani, who opposed the SOFA on the grounds that it violated Iraqi sovereignty.

The SOFA established a phased withdrawal of US combat forces, starting with their departure from Iraqi cities by June 30, 2009. It prevented the detention of Iraqis by US forces for more than twenty-four hours without criminal charges. It required a warrant for US personnel to enter Iraqi homes. Some US contractors would be subject to Iraqi criminal law; others would retain their immunity in special cases. Bush heralded the SOFA at the signing ceremony: "The Security Agreement addresses our presence, activities, and withdrawal from Iraq. Two years ago, this day seemed unlikely—but the success of the surge and the courage of the Iraqi people set the conditions for these two agreements to be negotiated and approved by the Iraqi parliament."[49]

The Obama administration sought to extend the SOFA, as the deadline loomed for the full and final withdrawal of US troops on December 31, 2011. Secretary of Defense Robert M. Gates wanted a residual force to be used in counterterrorism operations and to provide ongoing training to the Iraqi Armed Forces. Gates expected to see "perhaps several tens of thousands of American troops" in the residual force.[50] But negotiations to extend the SOFA broke down over the issue of immunity for US troops and contractors. The Obama administration abandoned negotiations; Obama fulfilled his promise of a full and final end to US military involvement in Iraq.

The ceremonial retiring of the US flag in Iraq occurred on December 16. 2011. With presidential elections in 2012, Obama wanted the American people to see US forces home for Christmas. Heartwarming images of US service men and women returning from Iraq were celebrated by the American public. The United States was weary of the grinding war in Iraq that cost $ 2.2 trillion dollar resulted in 4,486 American deaths according to the US Department of Defense.[51] The withdrawal created a power vacuum in Iraq. It also limited the leverage of the United States to shape events going forward.[52]

*****

Iraq quickly degenerated into conflict and chaos. Maliki purged hundreds of former Shia and Sunni members of the Baath party from Iraq's security services on October 21, 2011. Sunni Arabs exercised Article 119 of the Iraqi constitution to call for the creation of semi-autonomous federal regions in Salahuddin Province on October 27 and Diyala Province on December 12. Shia residents of Salahuddin and Diyala strongly objected. Maliki's security forces harassed leaders of the Salahuddin and Diyala provincial councils in an attempt to disrupt plans for a referendum.[53]

Key power-sharing elements of the Erbil Agreement were never implemented. Sunni Vice President Tariq al-Hashemi explained, "People in the central and southern areas" are demanding federalism "because they are unwilling to accept further injustice, corruption and bad management from the central government."[54] Maliki was accused of violating the constitution and seizing power from other branches of government. He brought security forces under his direct personal control, rather than awarding security positions to other groups.[55] The government launched a systematic campaign to marginalize prominent Sunnis. Iraqi forces and tanks surrounded Hashemi's home in the Green Zone. Two bodyguards were beaten, and fifty-three of Hashemi's employees were arrested. The Ministry of Interior broadcast confessions from Hashemi's bodyguards alleging that the vice president was operating death squads and other terrorist activities. Hashemi fled to Suleimani, where he was welcomed by Jalal Talabani, and given residence at Talabani's guest house.[56]

Article 78 of the Iraqi constitution allows the prime minister to dismiss ministers with the "consent" of parliament, Maliki sought a no-confidence vote for Sunni Deputy Prime Minister Saleh al-Mutlaq, who called him a "dictator" during a CNN interview. Mutlaq said he was threatened by Maliki: "We're coming for you, you and all of your people."[57] Mutlaq was spared because the Kurds boycotted the impeachment, preventing a quorum in the parliament. An arrest warrant was issued for Sunni Finance Minister Rafa al-Issawi. It was never carried out, after residents in Fallujah, Issawi's hometown, threatened violence.[58] Security forces detained thousands without charges. Angry crowds gathered in towns across the Sunni heartland. Protesters in Ramadi raised black jihadi flags. A Sunni member of parliament, Ahmed al-Alwani, called Maliki an "apparatchik who became the boss."[59] He accused Maliki of working for Iran, referring to him as a "Safavid." Alwani maintained, "Al Qaeda was here all along, lying low. And now they control Fallujah."[60]

In the spring of 2012, the Kurdistan block and Sadr's allies proposed a parliamentary vote of no confidence in Maliki.[61] In July 2012, the Ministry of Defense announced the Tigris Operations Command to take over the military and police in Diyala, Tamim, and Salahuddin. Masoud Barzani was extremely critical, likening Maliki's move to the Khanaqin crisis of 2010 and Chemical Ali's Northern Command in the 1980s. The United States and Turkey endorsed Barzani's initiative for a national conference to peacefully resolve disputes.

Barzani and Talabani discussed the crisis. Appointed on March 7, 2012, Nechirvan Barzani had a reputation for effective and steely-eyed leadership. Nechirvan previously served as prime minister in two successive cabinets from 1999 to 2009. Relations between Turkey and the KRG had warmed. Nechirvan Barzani brought KRG-Turkey relations back from their low point in 2003.

Erdogan visited the White House in June 2005. He criticized the "failure" of the United States to evict PKK fighters and urged the US to take action "eradicating the major thorn."[62] Turkey adamantly opposed Article 140, which required a popular referendum on Kirkuk's status by December 31, 2007. It viewed the Kirkuk referendum as a step toward the realization of statehood for Iraqi Kurdistan. Many Kurds look longingly across the border at their brethren in Northern Iraq. Kurds in Turkey and other countries want what Iraqi Kurds have.

During the summer of 2007, more than 150,000 Turkish troops massed on the Iraqi border threatening a cross-border operation to break the back of the PKK. The buildup was also intended to send a signal of Turkey's concern about Kirkuk. Erdogan appealed to the Bush administration, "We cannot do it alone. All countries must cooperate."[63] Masoud Barzani had no appetite for war with the PKK. Since 1992, Iraqi Kurds unsuccessfully engaged the PKK militarily on three occasions, twice in consort with Turkish troops.

Turkey started to redefine its relations with Iraqi Kurdistan after the KRG passed the Oil and Gas Law of the Kurdistan Region in 2007. Ankara initiated discreet discussions with Erbil on energy cooperation. Iraq's reserves are estimated 143 billion barrels (bbl) of oil and could grow to 200 bbl. Iraq is currently the fifth largest oil producer worldwide.[64] Its natural gas reserves are put at 127 trillion cubic feet (Tcf), making it the twelfth largest in the world.[65] Iraqi Kurdistan currently has about 12 bbl of oil and 22 TcF of gas, but these quantities are expected to increase. Moreover, they do not include reserves in Kirkuk, disputed between Baghdad and the KRG. Oil reserves in eight northern provinces to which Kurds make total or partial claims is 22.5 percent of Iraq's total.[66] The largest known reserves are the Shaikan field with up to 3.3 billion barrels and Bardarash with 1.2 billion barrels. The Khor Mor and Chemchemal gas fields have a combined reserve of 10 Tcf. Taq Taq and Tawke are the newest fields to come online.[67]

Baghdad maintained that all E&P arrangements entered into by the KRG are unconstitutional and invalid. It demanded that the KRG suspend E&P until the adoption of a hydrocarbon law and revenue sharing law. Baghdad's obstructionism did not dissuade Ashti Hawrami, the KRG Minister of Natural Resources, from entering into E&P deals with Turkish, European, Canadian, American, Chinese, Indian, Russian, Emirati, and other companies, including oil giants like ExxonMobil, Chevron, Gazprom Neft, and Total of France.

Norways's DNO, the first international company to drill in Iraqi Kurdistan, and the Anglo-Turkish Genel Energy have leading position in the Tawke field estimated at 771 million barrels, and Taq Taq at 647 million barrels.[68] Baghdad complained to Washington about the deal between Turkey and the KRG. The Obama administration sided with Maliki, discouraging ExxonMobil from its deal with the KRG. However, its entreaties were ignored. Washington warned that oil sales would bolster Kurdistan's independence. The deal also risked setting a precedent. More than 60 percent of Iraq's oil reserves are in southern

Iraq. If Basra and other southern provinces sought greater autonomy, it would critically weaken the central government.

The KRG completed construction of a new pipeline in 2013. The first section included a twenty-inch diameter pipeline from Taq Taq to Khurmala, with the capacity to transport two hundred thousand barrels/day. In January 2014, high quality, heavy crude oil from the Tawke field was delivered via the new pipeline to storage facilities in the Mediterranean port of Ceyhan in Turkey.[69] Turkey also started work on multi-billion-dollar oil and gas pipelines linking Iraqi Kurdistan to world markets. At peak capacity, pipelines will transport two million barrels per day of oil and at least ten billion cubic meters of gas annually.

Oil from the first pipeline was stored in Ceyhan. However, sales were put on hold so Erbil and Baghdad could negotiate their differences.[70] The KRG invited independent monitoring of the meters, with participation by Iraqi auditors. Ashti Hawrami pledged to send 83 percent to the central government. Baghdad balked, indicating that the arrangement was illegal.[71] Iraqi Oil Minister Abdul Kareem Luaibi accused the KRG of selling "smuggled" Iraqi oil, and threated legal actions against both the KRG and the Turkish government. Baghdad retaliated. It blocked the KRG's 17 percent share of the annual budget. It threatened to blacklist Turkish companies working with the KRG from doing business in Iraq and banned two airlines flying between Europe and Erbil. Nechirvan Barzani noted, "We went to Baghdad for talks, but they shocked us by cutting Kurdistan's salaries. We can pay out the salaries without Baghdad, and we have done it so far."[72] Masoud Barzani blasted Baghdad, calling its actions "a declaration of war against the people of Kurdistan."[73]

On May 2, 2014, the sale of oil from Iraqi Kurdistan stored in Ceyhan commenced without Baghdad's consent. According to Nechirvan Barzani, "The oil we export we will sell at an international price. If Turkey wants to buy it, we will sell it to Turkey, or else we will sell it to other countries." Two days after finalizing the deal with Turkey, Ashti Hawrami signed a deal with Tehran to build two pipelines between Iraqi Kurdistan and Iran. The KRG agreed to send crude oil to Iran, in exchange for receiving three to four million liters of refined oil and natural gas.[74]

Turkey and the KRG became strategic partners. Turkish firms sold $13 billion in goods to consumers in Iraqi Kurdistan in 2013. Its construction companies signed contracts for more than $30 billion. Energy cooperation is expanding. Turkey's prime minister Recep Tayyip

Erdogan invited Barzani to Diyarbakir on November 16, 2013. Erdogan described Barzani's visit as a "historic" step to further solidifying the relations between Turkey and the KRG.[75] The two stood side by side discussing peace in "Kurdistan."

Notes

1. N.p., n.d. Web. 29 May 2014. <https://www.fas.org/irp/news/1998/09/98091707_nlt.html>.
2. Ibid.
3. Ibid.
4. http://www.gpo.gov/fdsys/pkg/PLAW-105publ338/pdf/PLAW-105publ338.pdf (Accessed May 13, 2014).
5. This section draws on "Losing Iraq: Inside the Post-War Reconstruction Fiasco." Westview Press, 2005.
6. Graham, Bob. "SADDAM'S RING OF FIRE." - *The Mail on Sunday (London, England)*. N.p., 23 Mar. 2003. Web. 22 May 2014.
7. Sissons, Miranda, and Bdulrazzaq Al-Saiedi. "A Bitter Legacy: Lessons of De-Baathification in Iraq." *Http://ictj.org*. Ictj, Mar. 2013. Web. 22 May 2014. <http://ictj.org/sites/default/files/ICTJ-Report-Iraq-De-Baathification-2013-ENG.pdf>.
8. Ibid.
9. "Coalition Provisional Authority." *Iraq's Transitional Administrative Law ('Provisional Constitution') of March 8, 2004*. N.p., n.d. Web. 22 May 2014. <http://www.cesnur.org/2004/iraq_tal.htm>.
10. Ibid.
11. Ibid.
12. "Google Translate Google +1 Button Twitter Button Facebook Button Cable Reference Id: #06KIRKUK124." "All of Them, Those in Power, and Those Who Want the Power, Would Pamper Us, If We Agreed to Overlook Their Crookedness by Wilfully Restricting Our Activities." — "Refus Global", Paul-Émile Borduas." *Cable Reference Id: #06KIRKUK124*. N.p., n.d. Web. 26 May 2014. <http://www.cablegatesearch.net/cable.php?id=06KIRKUK124>.
13. Ibid.
14. Press Release, Kurdistan Referendum Movement - International Committee. London, 8 February 2005. http://www.aliraqi.org/forums/showthread.php?t=100978 (accessed May 6, 2014).
15. *COUNTRY OF ORIGIN INFORMATION REPORT IRAQ* (n.d.): n. pag. Home Office, Apr. 2006. Web. 22 May 2014. <http://www.justice.gov/eoir/vll/country/uk_cntry_assess/2006/iraq0406.pdf>.
16. Ibid.
17. Ibid.
18. "Iraq Update January 28 & 29." *The Agonist*. N.p., n.d. Web. 22 May 2014. <http://agonist.org/963-905/>.
19. http://www.cnn.com/2005/WORLD/meast/01/29/iraq.main/index.html?eref=sitesearch.

20. "Full Text of Iraqi Constitution." *Washington Post.* The Washington Post, 12 Oct. 2005. Web. 22 May 2014. <http://www.washingtonpost.com/wp-dyn/content/article/2005/10/12/AR2005101201450.html>.

21. Talabany, Nouri. "WINTER 2007 • VOLUME XIV: NUMBER 1." *Who Owns Kirkuk? The Kurdish Case.* N.p., n.d. Web. 22 May 2014. <http://www.meforum.org/1075/who-owns-kirkuk-the-kurdish-case>.

22. Washington Post.

23. "Iraq Draft Constitution Approved, Officials Say." *Msnbc.com.* N.p., n.d. Web. 26 May 2014. <http://www.nbcnews.com/id/9803257/ns/world_news-mideast_n_africa/t/iraq-draft-constitution-approved-officials-say/#.U2lQMldPr3A>.

24. Ibid

25. Ibid.

26. "Draft of Constitution." *Kurdish Democratic Party Electoral Establishment.* N.p., n.d. Web. 26 May 2014. <http://www.electkdp.org/english/laws/197-constitution-of-kurdistan-region--iraq.html>.

27. http://kurds_history.enacademic.com/341/Kurdistan_Regional_Government.

28. Burke, Jason (2011), *The 9/11 Wars* (London: Allen lane) Pg. 240.

29. Kilcullen, David (2009),*The Accidental Guerrilla: Fighting Small Wars in the Midst of a Big One* (Oxford: Oxford University Press) Pg. 120.

30. "Elements of 'civil war' in Iraq". *BBC News.* 2007-02-02.

31. Nancy Pelosi (2006-11-17). "Bringing the War to an End is my Highest Priority as Speaker". The Huffington Post.

32. Nancy Pelosi (2006-11-17). "Bringing the War to an End is my Highest Priority as Speaker". The Huffington Post.

33. President George W. Bush (January 10, 2007). "President's Address to the Nation". Office of the Press Secretary.

34. Weiner, Eric, and Scott Neuman. "Military Goals of 'Surge' Largely Met, Petraeus Says." *NPR.* NPR, n.d. Web. 22 May 2014. <http://www.npr.org/templates/story/story.php?storyId=14288514>.

35. "UNHCR worried about effect of dire security situation on Iraq's displaced." *UNHCR News.* N.p., n.d. Web. 22 May 2014. <http://www.unhcr.org/news/NEWS/452fa9954.html.

36. Ibid.

37. "Iraq's Displaced: Where to Turn?." *The Brookings Institution.* N.p., n.d. Web. 22 May 2014. <http://www.brookings.edu/research/articles/2008/12/10-iraq-cohen#_ftn3>.

38. "A Word or Two about Petraeus." *A Word or Two about Petraeus.* N.p., n.d. Web. 25 May 2014. <http://www.dailykos.com/story/2007/09/15/385863/-A-Word-or-Two-about-Petraeus>.

39. Gareth Porter. "How Petraeus Created the Myth of His Success." Truthout. 27 November 2012. http://truth-out.org/news/item/12997-how-petraeus-created-the-myth-of-his-success (Accessed May 9, 2014).

40. Patrick Cockburn. "Two Big Skeletons in Petraeus's Closet." *Counterpunch.* September 10, 2007. http://www.counterpunch.org/2007/09/10/two-big-skeletons-in-petraeus-rsquo-s-closet/ (Accessed May 9, 2015).

41. http://www.understandingwar.org/region/diyala-%D8%AF%D9%8A%D8%A7%D9%84%D9%89#sthash.37to1S0K.dpuf (Accessed May 9, 2014).

42. http://www.americanprogress.org/issues/military/news/2008/08/29/4794/standoff-in-khanaqin/ (Accessed May 9, 2014).

43. Filkins, Dexter. "The Shadow Commander" The New Yorker, 30 September 2013.

44. "World Reaction: 'This Is An Important Day'". Sky News. 8 June 2006. Retrieved January 17, 2011.

45. Washington Post. Wednesday, July 22, 2009 http://www.washingtonpost.com/wp-dyn/content/article/2009/07/22/AR2009072200174.html (Accessed May 9, 2014)

46. THE WHITE HOUSE. Office of the Press Secretary. Remarks by President Obama and Prime Minister Nouri Al Maliki in Joint Press Availability. July 22, 2009.

47. *www.kurdishglobe.net/article/.../Erbil-Agreement-content-disclosed.html* (accessed May 10, 2014).

48. http://www.ekurd.net/mismas/articles/misc2010/8/state4137.htm (Accessed May 10, 2014).

49. White House: Statement by the President on Agreements with Iraq.

50. *New York Times*: Trying to Redefine Role of U.S. Military in Iraq (Accessed May 11, 2014).

51. "Brown University." *Estimated Cost of Iraq War Is 190,000 Lives and $2.2 Trillion.* N.p., n.d. Web. 25 May 2014. <http://news.brown.edu/pressreleases/2013/03/warcosts>.

52. http://www.understandingwar.org/backgrounder/iraqs-recurring-political-crisis#sthash.8j77flKw.dpuf (Accessed May 11, 2014).

53. http://www.understandingwar.org/backgrounder/iraqs-recurring-political-crisis#sthash.8j77flKw.dpuf.

54. http://www.crisisgroup.org/en/regions/middle-east-north-africa/iraq-iran-gulf/iraq/126-deja-vu-all-over-again-iraqs-escalating-political-crisis.aspx (accessed May 11, 2014).

55. http://www.crisisgroup.org/en/regions/middle-east-north-africa/iraq-iran-gulf/iraq/126-deja-vu-all-over-again-iraqs-escalating-political-crisis.aspx (accessed May 11, 2014).

56. Shashank Joshi. The Daily Telegraph. December 21, 2011. http://www.telegraph.co.uk/news/worldnews/middleeast/iraq/8971030/Nouri-al-Maliki-is-pulling-Iraq-apart.html (Accessed May 11, 2014).

57. "Iraq's Recurring Political Crisis." *Institute for the Study of War*. N.p., n.d. Web. 26 May 2014. <https://www.understandingwar.org/backgrounder/iraqs-recurring-political-crisis>.

58. Ibid.

59. Dexter Filkins. "What We Left Behind." *The New Yorker.* April 28, 2014.

60. Dexter Filkins. "What We Left Behind." *The New Yorker.* April 28, 2014.

61. http://www.upi.com/Business_News/Energy-Resources/2014/02/28/Iraq-This-is-war-say-Kurds-in-oil-fight-with-Baghdad/UPI-71281393609878/#ixzz30hkNgaUv (Accessed May 4, 2014).

62. *Turkish Daily News*. June 6, 2005.

63. Recep Tayyip Erdogan at the Council on Foreign Relations.

64. "U.S. Energy Information Administration - EIA - Independent Statistics and Analysis." *Iraq*. N.p., n.d. Web. 26 May 2014. <http://www.eia.gov/countries/cab.cfm?fips=IZ>.

65. "U.S. Energy Information Administration - EIA - Independent Statistics and Analysis." *Iraq*. N.p., n.d. Web. 26 May 2014. <http://www.eia.gov/countries/cab.cfm?fips=IZ>.

66. 2006 Revenue Watch Institute.

67. "U.S. Energy Information Administration - EIA - Independent Statistics and Analysis." *Iraq*. N.p., n.d. Web. 26 May 2014. <http://www.eia.gov/countries/cab.cfm?fips=IZ>.

68. http://www.insightturkey.com/northern-iraqs-oil-chessboard-energy-politics-and-power/posts/282.

69. "Kurdistan." *Genelenergy*. N.p., n.d. Web. 10 May 2014. <http://www.genelenergy.com/.../kurdistan-region-of-iraq.aspx.>.

70. Humeyra Pamuk and Orhan Coskun. "Turkey, Iraqi Kurdistan clinch major energy pipeline deals." Reuters. November 6, 2013.

71. http://uk.reuters.com/article/2013/11/06/uk-turkey-iraq-kurdistan-idUKBRE9A50HN20131106.

72. Turkish Daily News. "Kurdish oil export to world 'starts in May,' Arbil and Ankara declare." May 4, 2014. http://www.hurriyetdailynews.com/kurdish-oil-export-to-world-starts-in-may-arbil-and-ankara-declare.aspx?pageID=238&nID=65715&NewsCatID=348 (accessed May 4, 2014).

73. UPI. Iraq: 'This is war,' say Kurds in oil fight with Baghdad Feb. 28, 2014. http://www.upi.com/Business_News/Energy-Resources/2014/02/28/Iraq-This-is-war-say-Kurds-in-oil-fight-with-Baghdad/UPI-71281393609878/#ixzz30hkbkvEa (accessed May 4, 2014).

74. "Iran, Iraqi Kurdistan Sign Energy Deal." *Iran, Iraqi Kurdistan Sign Energy Deal*. N.p., n.d. Web. 26 May 2014. <http://www.ecasb.com/en/news/27268>.

75. "President Barzani on Historic Visit to Diyarbakir." *President Barzani on Historic Visit to Diyarbakir*. N.p., n.d. Web. 26 May 2014. <http://www.krp.org/english/articledisplay.aspx?id=8gFTSPTTKp8=>.

7

The Imrali Peace Process

The Justice and Development Party (AKP) received 34.28 percent of the vote in the national election of November 2002, winning over two-thirds of parliamentary seats.[1] *Ak* means "white" in Turkish. AKP ran on a platform of change and clean government. Its landslide victory represented a seminal shift in Turkish politics. The AKP was established in 2001 as a center-right, social conservative party.[2] AKP'S founders were members of the Islamist Virtue Party, which was banned by Turkey's constitutional court for violating secularist principles of the constitution. Abdullah Gul, former speaker of parliament and politician; Bulent Arinc; and Ankara's mayor, Melih Gokeck, were leading personalities from the Virtue Party who established the AKP.[3] Other founders, Speaker of Parliament Cemil Cicek and Parliamentarian Abdulkadir Aksu, came from the Motherland Party of Turgut Ozal. Recep Tayyip Erdogan was the charismatic driving force behind the AKP.

Erdogan was born in the Kasimpasa neighborhood, a tough, poverty-stricken area of Istanbul. Erdogan studied at Imam Hatip School, which offers courses on Islamism. His role in politics started when he organized an Islamic youth group. Erdogan declared himself a "servant of sharia" during his successful 1994 mayoral campaign in Istanbul.[4] As Istanbul's mayor, Erdogan won praise for administrative efficiency, but his Islamic tendencies were also clear. He used his post to ban alcohol from restaurants, stirring fears that he would challenge Turkey's secular principles. His wife wore a headscarf as a symbol of her Islamic faith. Since the times of Ataturk, Turkey had been devoutly secular and had banned headscarves.[5]

In 1999, Erdogan was imprisoned for ten months for "inciting hatred based on religious differences."[6] Erdogan was prosecuted for a poem he read at a political rally in Siirt:

> Our minarets are our bayonets,
> Our domes are our helmets,

Our mosques are our barracks, . . .
My reference is Islam.

Erdogan reinvented himself after getting out of jail. Though Erdogan is a devout Muslim, he advanced his political ambitions by distancing himself from radical Islam, condemning corruption, and embracing moderate, democratic positions. He rhetorically abandoned his Islamist ideology, embracing socially "conservative democracy."[7]

Secularists doubted Erdogan's sincerity. Turkey's chief prosecutor petitioned the Turkish Constitutional Court to close the AKP just ten days before national elections on November 3, 2002.[8] The prosecutor asserted that Erdogan should be banned from holding elected office based on his conviction for Islamist sedition. Erdogan maintained that he was committed to secular governance. He claimed, "We are not an Islamic party, and we also refuse labels such as Muslim-democrat."[9] Turkey's elite believed that Erdogan had a hidden agenda to establish an Islamic state. Erdogan pronounced, "Democracy is like a streetcar. When you come to your stop, you get off."[10]

After the AKP's landslide victory, Erdogan stepped aside, allowing Abdullah Gul to become prime minister for four months.[11] Erdogan continued to tack to the center, backing Turkey's bid to join the European Union. Greek Prime Minister Costas Simitis was the first foreign leader to call and congratulate him. Within days of the AKP's landslide victory, Erdogan went to Greece for his first overseas trip. During his trip to Athens, Erdogan reaffirmed Turkey's EU bid and endorsed the UN's plan to settle the longstanding Greek-Turkish impasse over Cyprus.

Erdogan also reached out to the United States, assuaging concerns about his Islamist agenda. US Undersecretary of State Marc Grossman said, "Turkish people have a right to choose who will be their leaders, and we look forward to working with the new Turkish government."[12]

*****

Erdogan went to Washington for a meeting with President George W. Bush on December 11, 2002. The White House meeting was implicit recognition that Erdogan, who held no elected office, was the undisputed leader of Turkey's governing party. The Bush administration was eager to secure Turkey's support for its plan to oust Saddam Hussein. Bush also wanted to gain Turkey's support for his Global War on Terror (GWOT). The Bush administration viewed Turkey as counterweight against Islamic extremism. Bush embraced Turkey's participation in the GWOT, heralding its "moderate Islam."

Turkey proved itself a loyal ally in Afghanistan. Article 5 of the North Atlantic Charter states that an armed attack against one NATO member shall be considered an attack against them all. After 9/11, Turkey opened its airspace for flights in support of Operation Enduring Freedom and allowed the use of Incirlik air base as a staging ground. Turkey also assumed command of the International Security Assistance Force (ISAF) in Afghanistan.[13]

While supporting NATO operations in Afghanistan, Erdogan strongly opposed US plans to attack Iraq. He warned of instability, refugee flows, and the break up of Iraq. He feared that Kurds in Turkey would demand the same freedom as Kurds in Iraqi Kurdistan. Erdogan also worried about the effect of war on Turkey's economy. He protested the war, warning that the removal of Saddam would bring to power a Shiite regime with strong ties to Iran. The Bush administration took Turkey's concerns on board, pledging a unified Iraq with territorial integrity. It guaranteed that Kirkuk's energy resources would remain under the central government's control. It promised equal treatment of all major ethnic groups, including Turkey's ethnic brethren, the Turkmen. Despite these assurances, Erdogan insisted that no decision could be made about Turkey's participation without authorization from parliament.

On March 1, 2003, the Turkish Grand National Assembly (TGNA) refused to allow the passage of US troops through Turkey to Iraq. The AKP had nearly two-thirds of the seats in parliament, but the measure failed by three votes. Turks opposed the invasion of Iraq. They believed that chaotic conditions in Iraq allowed the PKK to find safe haven. The Turkish General Staff (TGS) could not reach consensus and issue a statement endorsing the passage of US troops through Turkish territory, which revealed its opposition. Kurdish deputies in the TGNA also opposed military action. They feared it would involve Turkish troops, undermining the interests of Iraqi Kurds and putting pressure on the PKK. The Bush administration's failure to act against the PKK further fueled anti-Americanism in Turkey. Many Turks believe that the United States has a hidden agenda to establish a greater Kurdistan. According to Turkish officials, up to three thousand PKK members operated from sixty-five bases in Iraqi Kurdistan with their headquarters in the Qandil Mountains, fifty kilometers from the Turkish border.[14] Erdogan insisted, "No country can tolerate the presence of a terrorist organization just across its border that threatens its stability and territorial integrity."[15]

The United States started angling for a new vote in the TGNA. However, Erdogan insisted that the AKP could only consider it after he was sworn in as prime minister. Less than a week after winning a by-election in the province of Siirt, the parliament passed a constitutional amendment allowing Erdogan to replace Abdullah Gul as prime minister. He was sworn in on March 14, 2003. The United States launched major combat operations against Iraq on March 19. During that day, the TGNA finally voted to permit over-flight by US warplanes. Even after the vote, the TGS tried to attach a condition by demanding a written guarantee that Turkish troops would be allowed to occupy Northern Iraq. US officials were incensed. The Iraq War had started with the 4th Infantry Division waiting offshore to enter Iraq via Turkey.

US officials were concerned that Turkey would act independently and invade Iraq. Seizing Iraqi Kurdistan would give Turkey control of the Kirkuk oil fields, thereby undermining Kurdish aspirations for nationhood. Turkish troops would protect Iraqi Turkmen. To prevent Turkey's unilateral action, the Bush administration promised that Turkish troops could establish a twenty-kilometer buffer zone along its border inside Iraqi Kurdistan. It also guaranteed Turkey a meaningful role in determining Iraq's future governance.

The "Ankara process," which involved negotiations between Turkey, the United States, and Iraqi Kurdish representatives, was overtaken by events. US troops raced across the desert from Basra, demolished the Republic Guards defending Baghdad, and seized the Iraqi capital. The 4th Infantry Division never made it into battle. The absence of a northern front forced the United States to focus all its operations in the south, stretching supply lines and making US forces more vulnerable to attack. Rather than a joint US-Turkish force in the North, Turkish Special Forces infiltrated Iraqi Kurdistan to undermine any possible move of Iraqi Kurds for independence. They plotted the assassination of Kirkuk's governor, a Kurd, so he could be replaced by his Turkmen deputy. Turkish Special Forces were arrested, hooded, and returned to Turkey. The government did not disclose the reason for their arrest, intensifying feelings of humiliation and anti-Americanism. US protection of the KRG fueled suspicions of a hidden agenda to create a Kurdish state, which were exacerbated by the arrest and humiliating treatment of Turkish Special Forces.

*****

The EU Copenhagen Summit was convened on December 13, 2002. The meeting started just forty-eight hours after Erdogan's visit to the White House. Washington strongly backed Turkey's bid to join the EU. At the Copenhagen Summit, the EU outlined the political and economic conditions that prospective members had to satisfy before formal accession talks could begin. Known as the "Copenhagen criteria," these conditions included economic reforms and the presence of stable institutions guaranteeing democracy, human rights, and the rule of law. Erdogan strongly supported Turkey's EU aspirations, claiming: "[Turkey will] expand the reach of the EU and demonstrate that a genuine harmony is possible between civilizations."[16]

To advance the goal of EU membership, Erdogan vigorously pursued legislative and constitutional reforms that liberalized the political system and relaxed restrictions on freedom of the press, association, and expression. The government abolished the death penalty, revised the penal code, reinforced the rights of women, reduced restrictions on minority language and broadcasts, ended random searches without a court order, and implemented a policy of zero tolerance toward torture. It adopted measures to dismantle state security courts, enhance independence of the judiciary, and reform the prison system. It amended the anti-terror statutes as well as the Penal Code and the Codes of Criminal and Administrative Procedure. Turkey signed and ratified protocols 6 and 13 of the European Convention on Human Rights.

The AKP also took steps to tackle the thorny task of subordinating Turkey's powerful military to civilian authority. In May 2004, a constitutional amendment terminated special off-budget accounts that were used to finance the pet projects of commanders. Military courts were barred from prosecuting civilians in peacetime. The NSC was enlarged, giving civilians the majority of seats. A provision was removed that required that the NSC secretary general be a four-star general, and the NSC rotation was used to expedite the retirement of hardline military men. The NSC's specific powers were also curtailed by, for example, denying it carte blanche to investigate civilians. Measures were adopted preventing the military from convening meetings and curtailing their frequency. The NSC became a consultative body under control of the elected government. Reforms helped protect Erdogan from attacks by the Deep State.

New regulations were adopted allowing forty-five minutes per week of Kurdish-language broadcasts on TRT Ses, a state-sponsored Kurdish

TV channel."[17] Kurdish language was permitted in private schools. The Homecoming Law was adopted in August 2003. It offered incentives to Kurds who laid down their arms. A Back to Village Program promised grants to returnees so they could rebuild their homes, farms, and livestock. In June 2004, an appeals court ordered the release of Leyla Zana and three other Kurdish parliamentarians who had languished in jail for over a decade. Reforms affecting Kurds were intended to broaden domestic support among Kurds and curry favor in Western capitals.

Erdogan recognized that the PKK problem could not be solved through military means alone. During a visit to Diyarbakir in August 2005, he said, "A great and powerful nation must have the confidence to face itself, recognize the mistakes and sins of its past, and march confidently into the future . . . ready to consult anyone. . . . Turkey will not retreat from the point we have reached. We will not step back from our process of democratization."[18] He further commented, "[Kurdishness] is a sub-identity. We must not confuse sub-identity with supra-identity. They must all be viewed as a whole, as citizens of the Republic of Turkey." Judges ordered the release of some PKK members and reduced the sentences of others. Turkish media described Erdogan's approach as a "discreet and limited amnesty" aimed at "healing the wounds by our twenty years of trauma."[19] The PKK hoped the release signaled the AKP's readiness to negotiate a formal amnesty arrangement, allowing the PKK to "come down from the mountains without losing face."[20]

Despite Turkey's progress, the EU deferred a decision on starting membership negotiations at the Copenhagen summit. Luxembourg's Prime Minister Jean-Claude Juncker added insult to injury by stating, "A country in which torture is still a common practice cannot have a seat at the table of the European Union."[21] His derogatory comments convinced many Turks that the EU was shifting the goalposts. They felt that Europeans simply did not want Turkey in their Christian club.

*****

The EU finally initiated membership negotiations with Turkey in 2005. EU membership remains a daunting challenge. There are sixty thousand pages of regulations governing candidacy, and no guarantee of membership even if Turkey makes decisive progress. Turkey's refusal to implement a customs union agreement with Cyprus, an EU member, compounds the challenge of membership. So does the fact that EU membership requires approval by all members, some of whom make their decision subject to popular referendum.

The European Council prepares annual progress reports on Turkey's candidacy. In August 2005, Erdogan visited Diyarbakir. He stated, "The Kurdish problem is my problem. [It] will be solved with the deepening of democracy."[22] In 2005, however, the council criticized Turkey's halting progress on Kurdish issues. The amount of time allocated to Kurdish-language television broadcasts was limited. Though Kurdish was allowed in private schools, few students could afford the tuition. Turkey also failed to reform laws stifling free speech. Moreover, it adopted news laws limiting freedom of expression. Adopted in October 2005, Article 150 of the Criminal Code imposed penalties for insulting state institutions. In 2005, the Turkish novelist Orhan Pamuk stated that, "Thirty thousand Kurds and a million Armenians were killed in these lands but nobody dares to talk about it."[23] He was charged with "insulting Turkishness" under Article 301 of the Penal Code.[24]

The security situation remained a problem. Diyarbakir, Batman, Sirnak, Mardin, Siirt, Hakari, Bingol, and Tunceli were called "critical provinces."[25] They were governed under a special administrative law giving the armed forces extraordinary authority, allowing it to commit abuses with impunity. The village guard system remained largely intact. The Semdinli affair echoed the Susurluk incident, highlighting the lack of accountability for security personnel.

In November 2005, a bomb was thrown from the window of a white Dogan car window, killing the owner of the Hope bookstore in Semdinli, Hakkari province. A crowd pursued the vehicle and apprehended the bombers, who turned out to be security officers. In the car, which belonged to the gendarmerie, they found an identification badge from the Ministry of Internal Affairs, several AK-47 rifles, and a list of other Kurdish targets. The bombing was one of twenty incidents that occurred in Hakkari. All were staged to look like acts of PKK terrorism. A parliamentary committee was established to investigate, but at least one member received death threats. Concerns about military interference were sparked when it was revealed that General Yasar Buyukanit tampered with the judiciary to exonerate the Semdinli bomber. Highlighting the military's impunity and its role in undermining the rule of law, the Semdinli prosecutor was removed from his post, and his license to practice law was revoked.

Despite the lofty goals of the Back to Village Program, there was limited progress reintegrating former fighters and returning displaced persons to their homes. Only 1,873 persons were reintegrated during the first six months of the program, in part because the Back to Village Program failed to create amenable conditions for return.[26] Basic infrastructure, such as electricity and telephone service along with heath and education services, remained inadequate. Only 5,239 of 104,734 persons eligible for compensation applied and, of those, only 1,190 received any payment.[27]

Europeans warned that Turkey's EU membership would signify the end of Europe. French voters rejected ratification of the European constitution on May 28, 2005. Dutch voters acted similarly just three days later. The French and Dutch referenda, which killed the constitution, were, in part, a reaction to Turkey's candidacy. To salvage Turkey's prospects, German Chancellor Angela Merkel and French President Nicolas Sarkozy called for a "special partnership" short of full membership. Erdogan was incensed and demanded equal treatment.[28]

Despite Europe's chauvinism towards Turkey, a 2005 popular opinion poll found that 77.4 percent of Turkish respondents favored EU membership. Kurds, too, overwhelmingly preferred to be a part of Europe than a landlocked "greater Kurdistan." Of Kurds, 83.3 percent responded affirmatively when asked about EU membership.[29] The vast majority of Turkish citizens still believe in the transformative effect that joining the EU will have on living standards and political freedoms.[30]

*****

Abdullah Ocalan's arrest and incarceration created an unprecedented opportunity. At its 6th Party Congress, which transpired just days after Ocalan's arrest, the PKK announced a unilateral ceasefire and plans to withdraw forces from Turkey. It dropped its demands for an independent Kurdistan, in lieu of meaningful political and cultural rights for Kurds in Turkey.[31]

Turkey was one of the first countries to send condolences after the attacks of September 11. In exchange for its assistance to ISAF and cooperation with Bush's GWOT, it asked the United States to include the PKK on the State Department's list of Foreign Terrorist Organizations (FTOs). The United States agreed to list the PKK as an FTO. In quick succession, Canada and the United Kingdom classified the PKK as a terror group. The EU then added it to the terror list in May 2002. During that spring, the PKK formally disbanded and became the Kurdistan Freedom and Democracy Congress (KADEK). KADEK dissolved in 2003 after the State Department also classified it as an FTO. A year later, it was reestablished under a new name, the Kurdistan Society Congress (Kongra-Gel/KGK), which the United States and EU also designated as an FTO. Interpol issued "red bulletins" for 134 leaders of the PKK, further limiting their freedom of movement. The PKK's fundraising faltered in the absence of military operations.[32]

Even after arrest, Ocalan remained the organization's undisputed head and leader. Ocalan was a powerful figure, issuing instructions through his lawyers and via European-based media outlets from his jail cell. However, other factions emerged. The Democratic Society Party (DTP) was founded in 2005 as an extension of the PKK. TGNA deputies and DTP operatives followed Ocalan's instructions. Led by co-chairs Ahmet Turk and Aysel Tugluk, the DTP won control of sixty-nine municipal governments in local elections that year. Its offshoot, the Kurdish Communities Union (KCK) was established as an umbrella organization for emancipation activities. It, too, was an instrument for advancing the agenda of Ocalan. In response to Erdogan's demand that DTP parliamentarians renounced the PKK, an MP explained that neither he nor his colleagues supported violence, but "Every Kurd has a family member involved with the PKK. How can I condemn my own children?"[33]

Hardliners dominated the Kurdish Diaspora, like all Diaspora communities who live apart from local conditions. Kurds in Europe maintained that violence was the only response to abuses by the Turkish state. The Diaspora was tied to PKK fighters in Qandil. The Qandil faction was well armed and led by Osman Ocalan and Murat Karalyan. Its field commanders were involved with the insurgency for many years. According to Karayilan, "use of arms fulfilled its duty in the 1990s by putting the Kurdish question on the agenda."[34] Angered that the government would not respond to its overtures, the PKK ended its self-declared ceasefire in June 2004.

*****

Various public opinion polls indicated that Kurds do not want a separate state. The overwhelming majority of Kurds in Turkey believe that they can advance their goals through living in peace with Turks and through the political process. Kurds were never conquered, so they prefer redress through governance reforms rather than dissolution of the republic. Kurds shared the land and history with other peoples in Turkey during the Seljuk, Ottoman, and Republican periods. They oppose government policies that exclude and marginalize them. Despite abuses, most are committed to work for reform within the system. Ahmet Turk maintains, "All Kurds want status and the right to self-determination. This means different things to different Kurds. Every Kurd dreams of independence, but we must consider the possibilities." The KCK proposed "democratic autonomy," which Ahmet Turk describes as a strategy for conflict resolution "promoting solidarity and dialogue among the peoples of Turkey."[35] The KCK definition of democratic autonomy is actually a surrogate for statehood. There is a Turkish expression: "Show death; people will welcome malaria."[36]

The proposal for democratic autonomy sparked a debate among Kurds on what system of governance could best uphold Kurdish interests. They considered the range of associational arrangements to address center-periphery and majority-minority conflicts. Kurds embrace vertical separation of powers involving national and subnational arrangements. A debate is underway about the merits of confederation, federation, asymmetric federalism, or provisions for regional or cultural autonomy.

Kurds reject Turkey as a unitary state. A unitary state is governed by a single unit, the central government, that exercises final authority. Subnational units may exist in a unitary state, but they only have powers that are allocated by the central government. In a unitary state, subnational units are created and abolished, and their powers may be broadened and narrowed unilaterally by the central government. A unitary state can delegate power through devolution to local government. However, the central government can take back what it gives by revoking or amending devolved powers.

In a federal system, the central government usually has paramount power, retaining responsibility for defense, foreign policy, and fiscal affairs. In federal states, sovereignty is shared between the central government and subnational units. Federalism is non-centralized, which means that units at each level have final authority and can be self-governing in different areas. Citizens have rights secured by both the central government and subnational authorities. States constituting the federation have an existence and functions that cannot be unilaterally changed by the central government. Federalism can be symmetrical or asymmetrical. Symmetrical federalism allocates the same powers to all subnational units. In asymmetrical arrangements, regions vary in their power and status.

Autonomy is an effective system to protect and promote group rights, devolving authority in the areas of governance, economy, and culture. Democratic autonomy would involve a local executive, legislature, judiciary, and the administration of justice, including local police drawn from the communities they serve. Economic power sharing includes decisions affecting the development of natural resources, taxes, and revenue, trade, employment, hiring practices, and land ownership. Cultural autonomy typically encompasses minority language use and local control of education. Cultural autonomy also includes cultural rights such as the display of the PKK tricolor flag, its seal, and emblems, as well as unfettered celebration of Newroz and other cultural festivals.

Cimsit Firat, a Diyarbakir-based businessman and founder of an opposition group, presents an alternative view. He insists on independence for North Kurdistan while rejecting political violence unless in self-defense. He envisions a Greater Kurdistan encompassing all territories where Kurds live in Turkey, Iraq, Iran, and Syria. According to Firat, "The PKK was a state project." He maintains that the organization was created by the Deep State after the 1980 military coup to oppose leftists and coopt the intellectual Kurdish national movement. "Before the PKK, Kurdish nationalism was a strong movement demanding territory. The PKK cooperated with the Deep State to kill real Kurdish nationalists." He maintains, "Kurds need a national movement bigger than the PKK."[37]

PKK cadres defended their struggle for national liberation in the 1990s as a form of self-defense. Young recruits flocked to join the organization because it stood against the state's abuses and was a source of pride to downtrodden Kurds. A year after the unilateral ceasefire announcement in 1999, the People's Liberation Army of Kurdistan was renamed the People's Defense Forces. It maintained armed struggle through "passive self-defense." Increasingly frustrated with the government's unwillingness to negotiate and repeated closures of Kurdish political parties, the PKK abandoned its ceasefire and resumed "active self-defense."[38]

The Turkish Armed Forces responded by intensifying military repression. The PKK met the challenge with a series of attacks on the security services and symbols of the regime. In addition to armed struggle, Kurds pursued their goals through the ballot box, mobilizing for national parliamentary and local elections in 2007.

*****

On April 24, 2007, Erdogan announced that the AKP would nominate Abdullah Gul as its candidate for president. Deeply unsettled by the prospect of an Islamist as president, the secular elite mobilized against Gul's candidacy. In April and May, millions rallied against Gul in Istanbul and Izmir. The CHP and MHP mounted legal challenges. The military issued a warning on its website, which the AKP called an "E-coup."[39] Erdogan suspended his nomination of Gul and called for early elections on July 22, 2007.

The AK Party won 46.6 percent of the votes, a considerable increase in electoral support since its inception.[40] It controlled 341 of the 550 available parliamentary seats. AKP's margin was fueled by support in the South and Southeast. DTP members participated in the general elections by filing as independent candidates in an attempt to overcome the threshold. This tactic allowed the DTP to win twenty-two seats in parliament. However, its vote total was less than expected. AKP made inroads into traditional strongholds of Kurdish political parties. In the Kurdish region of Bingol, AKP won 71 percent of the popular vote.[41] The DTP mistakenly addressed voters in Kurmanji, instead of Zaza, which is spoken locally. It did the same in Bitlis. The AKP was rewarded for spending lavishly on roads, schools, and different social services. Kurds credited AKP for legislative reforms that enabled greater cultural rights including Kurdish language broadcasts and educational instruction. The AKP's conservative values and grassroots outreach through local organizations also appealed to Kurdish voters who increasingly rejected ethnic politics.

Kurds had become increasingly disaffected with the PKK. Its constant criticism of the Turkish state fell on deaf ears. Many Kurds were simply exhausted after two decades of violent conflict and felt the AKP was a better alternative. According to a DTP parliamentarian, "By voting for the AKP and DTP, both Turks and Kurds demonstrated that they are against their respective militaries."[42] Another factor was the pattern of closures targeting Kurdish political parties. Kurds feared that the DTP would also be banned and did not want to waste their vote. Moreover, the AKP's success was a result of its performance and policies. It helped rescue Turkey from economic recession and triple-digit inflation. It was inclusive, placing many ethnic Kurds in government jobs.

Erdogan addressed supporters from the balcony of AKP headquarters on election night, casting himself as the champion of all Turks as well as Muslims worldwide. "Sarajevo won today as much as Istanbul. Beirut won as much as Izmir. Damascus won as much as Ankara.

Ramallah, Nablus, Jenin, the West Bank, [and] Jerusalem won as much as Diyarbakir."[43] Emboldened by his popular support, Erdogan tried to redefine the meaning of secularism. In a visit to Cairo a couple of months later, Erdogan posited that secularism does not require the renunciation of religion.[44]

Gul's nomination was renewed. He was finally elected president in a third round with 339 votes in the 530-seat parliament on August 28, 2007. The army's bullying backfired, antagonizing Turks and further increasing support among Kurds for the AKP. In his inaugural address to parliament, Gul maintained: "Turkey is a secular democracy. These are basic values of our republic, and I will defend and strengthen these values."[45]

Erdogan's attempt to redefine the definition of secularism, while establishing himself as a leader of the broader Muslim community, was deeply disturbing to the secular elite and Turkish armed forces. Gul's ascent to the presidency, an office once held by Mustafa Kemal Ataturk, was abhorrent. Mehmet Ali Birand, a highly acclaimed columnist, proclaimed: "With a first lady in a head scarf, a taboo is finished in Turkey."[46]

The headscarf was one of the most emotionally charged and divisive issues in Turkey. The ban was introduced by Ataturk and enshrined through measures secularizing the state in the 1924 Turkish constitution. It applied to any woman working on public premises, including parliamentarians, lawyers, and teachers. The AKP insisted that the ban was discriminatory, keeping observant women out of work in the public sector. President Ahmet Necdet Sezer refused entry to the wives of AKP members at a ball celebrating Turkish independence in October 2006. He maintained that their presence in a headscarf at such an occasion would "compromise" secular principles of Ataturk.[47] General Yasar Buyukanit and other top generals boycotted Gul's swearing-in ceremony. They also violated a longstanding tradition by skipping Gul's first official reception. He posted a statement on the military's website warning against "furtive plans that aim to undo modern advances and ruin the Turkish republic's secular and democratic structure."[48] Buyukanit waited more than two weeks before finally congratulating Gul on his election.

Erdogan fulfilled his campaign promise to lift the ban on headscarves in public institutions. The TGNA adopted an amendment on February 7, 2008, allowing women to wear the headscarf in Turkish universities. The MHP joined the AKP in sponsoring the bill, which passed by a vote of 403 to 107. Deeply humiliated, the TGS mobilized the Constitutional Court, which agreed to review the constitutionality of liberalizing the headscarf ban. On April 1, 2008, the Constitutional Court also agreed to take up a case closing the AKP. The AKP was charged with undermining secularist principles by allowing women to wear a headscarf at universities and other public institutions. The case included a ban on seventy-one high-level AKP officials from engaging in politics for five years, including Gul and Erdogan. According to Article 69 of the Constitution, if seven of the Constitutional Court's eleven members ruled that the AKP violated the separation of religion from the state, the AKP could be banned or deprived of financial assistance from the State.[49]

The headscarf issue galvanized opposition to the AKP. Thousands rallied outside the parliament to protest the amendment. The State Educational Board vowed to oppose implementation. On June 5, 2008, the Constitutional Court rejected the amendment for violating the constitution. Its decision was not subject to appeal.[50] The closure case failed, but barely. Only six of the judges ruled in favor of closing the AKP. However, ten out of eleven judges agreed that the AKP had become "a center for anti-secular activities." Its ruling led to a loss of state funding for the party.[51] Erdogan called the ruling "a step against the national will." As a harbinger of future conflict between the AKP and the staunchly secular judiciary, Erdogan warned: "This injustice committed against the nation will not be accepted. A judicial position, which uses its power in the name of the people, cannot go against the will of the nation. The national will cannot be ignored. Those who are imposing the closure trial will also experience its embarrassment."[52]

Kurds were disappointed that the AKP used its electoral mandate to address the headscarf issue, rather than focus on Kurdish rights. They decried the AKP's double standard. The AKP vehemently objected when the Constitutional Court questioned its legitimacy. However, the AKP was silent when Abdurrahman Yalcinkaya, chief prosecutor of the Supreme Court of Appeals, filed charges on November 16, 2007, alleging ties between the DTP and the PKK and banning 219 of the party's leading members.[53]

*****

The DTP's first action after elections in July 2007 was a call for greater access to Ocalan at Imrali. It demanded improved prison conditions for Ocalan, including fresh supplies of toothpaste. When the AKP ignored its appeal, DTP parliamentarians abstained from the third round of voting to confirm Gul as president. Despite tensions between the AKP and DTP, Gul addressed the Kurdish problem during his inaugural speech. He heralded diversity as Turkey's strength, called for greater cultural rights of minorities, including official use of minority languages, and underscored the need for greater individual rights in the new constitution. Gul's first domestic trip as president was to the Southeast where he appealed for Kurdish rights.

With its electoral mandate, the AKP-led government undertook to draft a new "civilian constitution." It was envisioned as Turkey's first constitution written entirely by civilians and vetted by civil society. The initial draft sought to harmonize Turkey's approach to ethnic and religious issues with the standards set by the European Convention on Human Rights. It eliminated provisions in the 1982 constitution allowing suspension of human rights during martial law, which threatened "the indivisible integrity of the state."[54]

Turkish society was buzzing with discussion about constitutional reform. Without a supermajority of 376 seats, Erdogan would have to compromise in order to gain enough support. Even if the TGNA passed constitutional reform, the Constitutional Court could oppose it. The process of drafting the constitution was done in secret. It was widely known that Erdogan wanted to use constitutional reform as a way of enhancing his powers, changing Turkey from a parliamentary system to a presidential one. Then, like the rotation between Dmitri Medvedev and Vladimir Putin in Russia, Erdogan would switch jobs assuming the newly empowered post of president. The government would control the State and manage all the levers of power. By stripping the system of checks and balances, especially through control of the judiciary, the State could dictate all matters to both the bureaucracy and the people. The AKP claimed that constitutional reform would advance human rights. To the AKP, however, individual freedom meant freedom of religious expression.[55]

Though the AKP's resounding electoral victory was based on support from Kurdish voters, it continued a policy of repression toward the Kurds. The PKK resumed its sensational violence in order to reassert its importance to the political scene. The PKK ambushed and killed thirteen elite special commandos in Sirnak on October 7, 2007. In response, there was a popular outcry for a major cross-border operation and air strikes on Qandil. After Sirnak, Erdogan took a pugilistic approach to the PKK, emboldened by an agreement with the United States to provide live video feeds from drones and satellites that could track movement along the rugged border between Iraq and Turkey. Turkey also increased its cooperation with the governments of Syria and Iran, launching coordinated attacks against PJAK, the PKK's sister organization in Iranian Kurdistan. Erdogan addressed the TGNA in March 2008: "Our security forces will do whatever is necessary regardless of whether it involves women and children." He was also unforgiving on Kurdish issues. "There is no Kurdish question if you do not think about it."[56]

*****

Erdogan was making plans to address Kurdish issues. In January 2009, he inaugurated twenty-four-hour Kurdish language broadcasts on state-owned TRT-6 television with remarks in Kurdish. The broadcast had not subtitles. TRT officials indicated there would be no censorship or time limit on news broadcasts. Given Turkey's denial of Kurdish language and identity for so many years, the prime minister's remarks had a huge impact on the psychology of Turks. Gul promised "good things" were on the way during an interview on March 11, 2009.[57] The PKK responded by announcing a ceasefire on April 13, 2009.

The government declared its "Democracy Initiative" on August 15, 2009. The Democracy Initiative started as the Kurdish Opening and was also referred to as the Unity and Fraternity Project. Interior Minister Beşir Atalay stated the initiative sought to end terrorism in Turkey through democratization, and respect for human rights. According to Erdogan, "We will issue circulars in the short term, pass laws in the medium term, and make constitutional amendments in the long term and take required steps."[58] Building on Erdogan's 2005 address in Diyarbakır, the path to peace was described in a fifty-five-page roadmap with main headings of language, education, and the media. The document also addressed political participation, criminal justice, and amnesty.[59] The AKP pamphlet explained,

> We are exhibiting a courageous and determined intention to put an end to endless argument, deaths and pain. We are willing and sincere. . . . [W]e want . . . to put an end to the deaths of young people . . . to make sure that the sons we send off to serve in the army with heartfelt celebrations do not come back home in bemedaled coffins . . . that mothers do not weep. . . . [W]e want every citizen . . . to feel like a first-class citizen and to work for our country.[60]

It highlighted the benefits of a potential peace dividend. The pamphlet addressed the economic costs to the conflicts, estimated to be at least $300 billion. The 2008 global economic recession had a big impact on the interconnected economies of G-20 countries. Addressing the PKK problem would also create conditions to expand economic cooperation with Iraq in the fields of security, energy and economy.

The democracy initiative would also revitalize Turkey's faltering aspirations to join the EU. In its February 2008 Accession Partnership evaluation, the EU stated that Turkey should "develop a comprehensive approach to reducing regional disparities, and in particular to improving the situation in southeast Turkey, with a view to enhancing economic, social and cultural opportunities for all Turkish citizens, including those of Kurdish origin."[61]

In addition, the democracy initiative was motivated by domestic political considerations. The DTP had proven itself as a formidable force by winning control of ninety-nine municipal councils in local elections on March 29, 2009. The DTP held twenty-two seats in the TGNA. The AKP's support declined from its hiatus in the 2007 general elections. It received 39 percent of the vote, 3 percent less than in the local elections of 2004. The CHP, which recorded 23 percent, and MHP with 16 percent, opposed constitutional reform, maintaining its ultimate goal was "dividing" Turkey. The military was also opposed. On August 25, 2009, the TGS issued a statement insisting that the democracy opening was not a concession to the PKK, nor did it reflect a wavering in its commitment to preserving Turkey as a unitary state. The AKP remained the dominant party, but Erdogan needed the DTP's support for constitutional reform.

Abdullah Ocalan presented his roadmap for peace to the government in August 2009, which was not released publicly until the following year. He envisioned a three-stage process: ceasefire, constitutional reform, and normalization. At the end of the process, the PKK would be legalized and transformed into a political party. Its members would receive unconditional amnesty.

The Government organized an experiment based on Article 221 of the Turkish Penal Code, the Active Repentance Law. It allowed the repatriation of thirty-four Kurds from Iraqi Kurdistan on October 19, 2009. The group included eight PKK members and twenty-six Kurds from the Makhmour refugee camp, which was a haven for PKK sympathizers. Their repatriation turned into a fiasco. The group crossed into Turkey on August 25, 2009. Instead of a discreet process, the PKK members arrived in battle dress. They received a hero's welcome by thousands of Kurdish supporters who were bussed to the Habur border crossing by the DTP. The incident underscored the difficulties of amnesty. It also poisoned many Turks against the democracy opening.

A number of factors derailed the Democracy Initiative. The Constitutional Court banned the DTP on December 11, 2009. Its decision indicated that the DTP was "a center of activities against the unity of the state and the nation." DTP members were "in contact and solidarity" with the PKK. They "supported the armed attacks" of the PKK. The DTP co-chairs, Ahmet Turk and Aysel Tugluk, were stripped of their parliamentary immunity. In addition, thirty-six other DTP members were barred from politics for five years. Kurdish mayors were handcuffed and lined up for the cameras in December 2009. More than three thousand KCK members were arrested and charged with "terrorism."[62]

Just as the Democracy Initiative was at an impasse, constitutional reform was also languishing. The AKP lacked a super-majority to approve constitutional amendments. It called a vote, gaining 336 votes in the 550-seat parliament. The tally was not enough to approve reforms, but it was sufficient to require a referendum. Fifty-eight percent of voters approved reforms on September 12, 2010. Reforms addressed the structure of the constitutional court, allowed individuals the right of appeal to the constitutional court, created an ombudsman's office, empowered civilian courts to convict members of the military, and increased the Supreme Board of Judges and Prosecutors from seven to twenty-two members. The referendum focused on the judiciary, which had oversight of the government. Erdogan reformed the judiciary, then later seized control of it. Reforms also advanced the rights of women and workers, as well privacy laws. Kurds boycotted the vote. None of the amendments addressed their unique concerns.

*****

Beginning in 2010, Ocalan was allowed to meet with his lawyers. They were flown to Imrali in military helicopters. He was also visited by parliamentarians from the Peace and Democracy Party (BDP), which replaced the DTP. Representatives from Turkish National Intelligence Agency (MIT) and the PKK were conducting secret meetings in Oslo. The Oslo process was facilitated by Norway, and coordinated by the United Kingdom. First contact between Turkish officials and the PKK occurred in 2006, followed by indirect meetings to explore the proto-cols for future dialogue. The first face-to-face meeting was held at the end of 2008. The Turkish delegation was led by Emre Taner, who was then head of MIT. He was succeeded by Hakan Fidan in April 2010, who was joined by Deputy Undersecretary Afet Gunes. The PKK was represented by Sabit Ok, a high-ranking member of the PKK; Mustafa Karasu, a military leader and former member of the PKK presidential council; and Zubeyir Aydar, who chaired the KCK parliament in Brussels. Progress was made during five meetings.

The Oslo process was supposed to be secret. However, a fifty-minute tape of discussions was leaked to Dicle News Service and broadcast on September 12, 2011. Erdogan accused the PKK of leaking the tape. "If Turkey's intelligence agency had held secret talks with the PKK, it was not right to leak these talks as documents."[63] The PKK grew tired of "talks about talks." Leaking details about the Oslo process may have been intended to move the dialogue to Imrali, under Ocalan's direct control. It exposed the government in a bid to expedite negotiations.

In any event, the Oslo process was designed to set the agenda for direct negotiations between the Turkish State and Ocalan. Zubeyir Aydar called for direct contact with Ocalan. "He is the president of our movement and our principal negotiator. The doors of Imrali prison must be open. The government cannot negotiate with us and keep Ocalan in jail."[64] Murat Karayilan explained that meetings in Oslo and Imrali "were developed in parallel in a complementary manner."[65] He too called for Ocalan's release. Legalizing the PKK and allowing it to function like a political party would allow its leaders—Ocalan, Karalyan, Cemil Bayik—to freely participate in politics.

However, Erdogan was wary of direct contact with Ocalan and the BDP, which won thirty-six parliamentary seats in the general elections of June 12, 2011. Footage surfaced showing BDP members embracing and kissing PKK fighters in a remote area near Semdinli. "Why would we talk to people who have close relations with the terrorist organiza-tion?" asked Erdogan. "What will the mothers of soldiers who were killed in PKK attacks think of me when they see me sitting at the same desk with those people? Sorry, but tears in a martyr's eyes are much more precious."[66] Erdogan demanded the PKK declare a ceasefire. "First of all, the terror organization needs to put down arms. As long as they do not, neither this process can advance nor will military operations end."[67]

The opposition criticized the government for "deception," condemn-ing talks with the PKK. A state prosecutor opened an investigation, subpoenaing Hakan Fidan. Erdogan protested, "It is an outright lie that my MIT chief had given any promises in Oslo. No record has been kept in writing there. They just verbally discussed matters." Erdogan took responsibility: "I am the one who sent our MIT chief to Imrali and Oslo. Why? There is a fight against a terror organization. We have to be successful in this fight." According to Erdogan, "The judiciary attempted to cross the line, and wanted to intervene in the business of the executive. . . . If they're going to summon Fidan to questioning, that's a summons to me."[68]

The Imrali process stalled. The government suspended its contact with Ocalan and blocked his contact with lawyers and BDP members on June 27, 2011. The Oslo process was also suspended, with its cover blown. The arrest of up to three thousand KCK members on terror-related charges, including many BDP operatives, also undermined confidence. KCK members were charged with membership in an illegal organization under Article 314 of the Turkish Penal Code. Karayilan observed, "The KCK operation was one of the main reasons why the negotiations ended without a positive result."[69] The Uludere incident of December 28, 2011, in which thirty-four villagers were mistaken as PKK militants and killed in an air strike, further eroded confidence.

*****

Erdogan accused military officers of plotting a coup through a secret conspiracy called Ergenekon. The investigation targeted active duty and retired officers, elements of the police, paramilitary groups, organized crime, journalists, judges, the secular elite, and their allies in the judiciary. Ergenekon plotters were allegedly trying to overthrow the government through a series of assassinations and bombings to foment unrest.

The Ergenekon investigation started in June 2007, when two retired police officers were found with explosives. The hard drives on their computers allegedly included details of a conspiracy against Islamism and the AKP. In 2008, eighty-six individuals were arrested, including retired senior military officers. In 2009, police uncovered an alleged military plot to eliminate the AKP and Fetullah Gulen, a Muslim preacher, who supported Erdogan. Chief of the General Staff İlker Basbug and other active military officers were implicated. Erdogan cast the investigation as a victory for civilian democracy over dark ultranationalist forces. However, by 2010 the Ergenekon investigation had turned into a witch-hunt aimed at eradicating political opponents and silencing critics of the government. Many journalists were arrested under Article 288, which forbids influencing a trial, for simply reporting on the investigation.[70] Fear and self-censorship were widespread. In 2011, the entire TGS resigned in protest. By 2012, thousands were under investigation and hundreds in detention.

Erdogan tightened his grip on power.[71] The AKP steadily increased its popular support. It received 34.28 percent in 2002, 46.58 percent in 2007, and 49.90 percent of the votes in 2011.[72] Despite the steady upward trend, AKP seats in the parliament went down after each electoral victory—from 363 seats in 2002, to 341 in 2007, and 326 in 2011. Violent conflict with the PKK intensified after the 2011 elections. Resurgent violence was more intense than any time since Ocalan's capture in 1999.

The AKP faced a fork in the road. It could intensify pressure on the PKK, seeking a military solution to the conflict. Alternatively, a strong State under AKP control could make concessions required for peace. Under pressure from the European Court of Justice, the AKP abolished Special Terror Courts that were used to prosecute KCK members. Cases were referred to the Heavy Criminal Court where they took longer, but which conformed more closely to international human rights standards. Special Courts were abolished as part of a broad campaign against prosecutors and members of the judiciary investigating corruption by Erdogan, his family, and inner circle. Judicial "reform" was intended to head off moves against the government, rather than demonstrate a commitment to rule of law.

The AKP's consolidation of power accentuated Erdogan's hegemonic tendencies, undermining checks and balances and putting Turkey on the path to authoritarian single party rule. According to Ahmet Turk, "We can never trust the State. Erdogan talks about peace, while calling the PKK terrorists." Talks are intended to disarm the PKK and bring fighters down from the mountains. They are not about rights and local government.

In June 2014, the AKP adopted a "democracy package," otherwise known as the Framework Agreement. The law was intended to keep negotiations going with the PKK, by preventing prosecution of MIT. The word "Kurd" or "Kurdish" was not mentioned in any of its six sections, fueling concerns about Erdogan's sincerity. According to a KCK leader, "There are so many democracy packages, but so little democracy."[73]

Notes

1. Carkoglu*, By Ali. *TURKEY'S NOVEMBER 2002 ELECTIONS: A NEW BEGINNING?* (n.d.): n. pag. *A New Beginning.* GloriaCenter, 22 Dec. 2002. Web. 27 May 2014. <http://www.gloria-center.org/meria/2002/12/carkoglu.pdf>.

2. Duran, Burhanettin (2008). "The Justice and Development Party's 'new politics': Steering toward conservative democracy, a revised Islamic agenda or management of new crises". *Secular and Islamic politics in Turkey*: 80 ff

3. Kinzer, Stephen. "Under Close Scrutiny, Turkey's Pro-Islam Party Has a Makeover." *The New York Times.* The New York Times, 25 Feb. 1998. Web. 11 Sept. 2014. <http://www.nytimes.com/1998/02/26/world/under-close-scrutiny-turkey-s-pro-islam-party-has-a-makeover.html>.

4. "Research and Writing." *Will Turkey Have an Islamist President?* N.p., n.d. Web. 27 May 2014. <http://www.meforum.org/1637/will-turkey-have-an-islamist-president>.

5. "Turkey lifts decades-old ban on headscarves." - *Europe.* N.p., n.d. Web. 24 May 2014. <http://www.aljazeera.com/news/europe/2013/10/turkey-lifts-decades-old-ban-headscarves-201310814177943704.html>.

6. "Why Are Turks So Angry? | World Policy Institute." *Why Are Turks So Angry? | World Policy Institute.* N.p., n.d. Web. 27 May 2014. <http://www.worldpolicy.org/blog/2013/06/11/why-are-turks-so-angry>.

7. Ibid.

8. "World Socialist Web Site." *Turkey: Coup Plot Arrests Deepen Political Crisis* -. N.p., n.d. Web. 11 Sept. 2014. <https://www.wsws.org/en/articles/2008/07/turk-j07.html>.

9. Taşpınar, Ömer (April 2012). *Turkey: The New Model?.* Brookings Institute.

10. Sontag. "The Erdogan Experiment."

11. Tepe, Sultan. "Turkey's AKP: A Model "Muslim-Democratic" Party?"*Journal of Democracy* 16.3 (2005): 69–82. Web.

12. CNN.com. Europe Hails AKP Victory." November 4, 2002. http://edition.cnn.com/2002/WORLD/europe/11/04/turkey.elections/index.html (Accessed April 9, 2014).

13. http://www.tsk.mil.tr/eng/uluslararasi/isaf.htm (accessed March 1, 2007).

14. Interview with intelligence officials from the Turkish Ministry of Foreign Affairs.

15. Recep Tayyip Erdogan at the Council on Foreign Relations.

16. Speech by Prime Minister Recep Tayyip Erdogan at the Council on Foreign Relations in New York. September 27, 2007.

17. Sevgi Akarcesme. "A Decade of AK Party Governments: 2002–2012. *Today's Zaman.* November 2, 2012.

18. Stephen Kinzer. "The Big Change." *The New York Review of Books.* January 12, 2006

19. "The Big Change."

20. "The Big Change."

21. *Armenia Weekly*, January 4–10, 2003.

22. Cited by Adem Uzun in "Living Freedom." Berghof Foundation. Transition Series no. 11.

23. Scott Peterson. "The case of Orhan Pamuk is being watched as a test of political freedoms." *Reuters*. December 16, 2005.

24. Charges were brought under Article 301 of the Criminal Code.

25. "Help Expand The Public Library of US Diplomacy." *Cable: 02ADANA402_a*. N.p., n.d. Web. 27 May 2014. <https://www.wikileaks.org/plusd/cables/02ADANA402_a.html>.

26. *The Economist*. "Peace be unto you." August 20, 2005.

27. *The Economist*. "Peace be unto you." August 20, 2005.

28. Aksit, Sait, Ozgenhan Senyuva, and Cigdem Ustun. (n.d.): n. pag. *Acacdemia. edu*. Center for European Studies, Nov. 2009. Web. 27 May 2014. <http://sinan.ces.metu.edu.tr/dosya/turkey_watch_en.pdf>.

29. *Anatolian News Agency*. February 18, 2005.

30. Hugh Pope of the International Crisis Group; Dogu Ergil. "Don't Worry Turkey." Research paper presented at the National Endowment for Democracy in Washington, DC. February 12, 2006.

31. August 2, 1999.

32. Ibid.

33. Interview by the author with a DTP Member of Palriament. September 13, 2007.

34. Letter from Murat Karayilan to *Taraf*, 5 October 2011.

35. Interview with Ahmet Turk by the author. Diyarbakir, August 8, 2014.

36. Cited by Dogu Ergil in an interview with the author. August 9, 2014.

37. Interview with Cimsit Firat by the author. Diyarbakir, August 8, 2014.

38. "Living Freedom" The Evolution of the Kurdish Conflict in Turkey & the Efforts to Resolve It / By Adem Uzun." *Mesopotamische Gesellschaft* «. N.p., n.d. Web. 27 May 2014. <http://www.mesop.de/2014/03/19/living-freedom-the-evolution-of-the-kurdish-conflict-in-turkey-the-efforts-to-resolve-it-by-adem-uzun/>.

39. "Turkey Probes Mly's 2007 'e-coup'" *The News International, Pakistan*. N.p., n.d. Web. 27 May 2014. <http://www.thenews.com.pk/Todays-News-1-90893-Turkey-probes-mly%E2%80%99s-2007-%E2%80%98e-coup%E2%80%99>.

40. Yilmaz, Muzaffer Ercan. "The Rise of Political Islam in Turkey: The Case of the Welfare Party." *Turkish Studies* 13.3 (2012): 363–78. Web.

41. 20, Number 18 — May. "Turkey's Presidential Prospects." *Number 18 — May 2014 RESEARCH NOTES* (n.d.): n. pag. *Http://www.washingtoninstitute. org/uploads/Documents/pubs/ResearchNote18_Cagaptay.pdf*. May 2014. Web. 27 May 2014.

42. Interview by the author with a DTP Member of Parliament. September 13, 2007.

43. "Turkey's Maturing Foreign Policy." *Global*. N.p., n.d. Web. 29 May 2014. <http://www.foreignaffairs.com/articles/67974/mustafa-akyol/turkeys-maturing-foreign-policy>.

44. Ibid.

45. "Rhymes with Right." *Rhymes with Right*. N.p., n.d. Web. 27 May 2014. <http://rhymeswithright.new.mu.nu/world_affairs?page=4>.

46. Ellen Knickmeyer. "Gul Elected to Turkey's Presidency. The Washington Post. August 29, 2007. http://www.washingtonpost.com/wp-dyn/content/article/2007/08/28/AR2007082800223.html (accessed on April 13, 2014).

47. Turkey in veil controversy. *Asia News*. October 30, 2006.
48. "Gul Elected to Turkey's Presidency." *Washington Post*. The Washington Post, 29 Aug. 2007. Web. 27 May 2014. <http://www.washingtonpost.com/wp-dyn/content/article/2007/08/28/AR2007082800223.html>.
49. "Ruling party to face closure trial." Turkish Daily News. April 1, 2008. http://www.hurriyetdailynews.com/default.aspx?pageid=438&n=ruling-party-to-face-closure-trial-2008-04-01 (accessed April 13, 2014).
50. Associated Press. June 7, 2008.
51. "The battle for Turkey's soul (Democracy v secularism in Turkey)". *The Economist*. 2007-05-03.
52. "Bianet :: AKP:." *Bianet*. N.p., n.d. Web. 30 May 2014. <http://bianet.org/english/english/105640-akp-closure-trial-will-give-us-70-percent-of-the-vote>.
53. http://asbarez.com/74456/top-turkish-court-begins-hearing-dtp-closure-case-kurdish-clashes-continue/
54. Article 14 of the 1982 constitution.
55. Atacan, Fulya. "Explaining Religious Politics at the Crossroad: AKP-SP."*Turkish Studies* 6.2 (2005): 187–99. Web. <http://www.tandfonline.com/doi/abs/10.1080/14683840500119510#.VBHbQLywJvY>.
56. Erdogan at the TGNA, March 2008.
57. *Yeni Şafak*, 11 March 2009.
58. Turkey's govt to send bills on Kurdish opening to Parliament. *Azerbaijan Today*. 2010-01-09.
59. Kıvanç Ulusoy. "When did the 'democratic opening' start and where are we now?" *Today's Zaman*. June 14, 2011.
60. "The Democratic Initiative Process", AKP, Ankara, February 2010.
61. "Document 32008D0157." *EUR-Lex*. N.p., n.d. Web. 27 May 2014. <http://eur-lex.europa.eu/legal-content/EN/TXT/?uri=CELEX:32008D0157>.
62. "Ecoi.net - European Country of Origin Information Network." *IRB: Turkey: The Kurdistan Workers' Party (PKK), including Areas of Operation and Targets, Methods of Recruitment and Activities; State Response [TUR104075.E]* |. N.p., n.d. Web. 27 May 2014. <http://www.ecoi.net/local_link/220838/328082_en.html>.
63. Today's Zaman. PM Erdoğan: PKK leaked secret Oslo talks to media September 28, 2012.
64. "The Secret Oslo Talks That Might Have Brought Peace to Turkey." *Oslo Talks*. N.p., n.d. Web. 21 Apr. 2014. <http://www.chris-kutschera.com/A/Oslo.htm>.
65. Letter from Murat Karayilan to *Taraf*, 5 October 2011.
66. "Erdogan's Many Positions on the Kurdish Issue - Al-Monitor: The Pulse of the Middle East." *Al-Monitor*. N.p., n.d. Web. 30 May 2014. <http://www.al-monitor.com/pulse/originals/2013/04/erdogan-kurdish-issue-flip-flop-turkey-peace.html#ixzz2zXS9vtig>.
67. Ibid.
68. "Erdogan's Many Positions on the Kurdish Issue - Al-Monitor: The Pulse of the Middle East." *Al-Monitor*. N.p., n.d. Web. 30 May 2014. <http://www.al-monitor.com/pulse/originals/2013/04/erdogan-kurdish-issue-flip-flop-turkey-peace.html#ixzz2zXS9vtig>.

69.   Letter from Murat Karayilan to *Taraf*, 5 October 2011.

70.   "Turkish General Jailed over 'plot'" *BBC News*. N.p., n.d. Web. 11 Sept. 2014. <http://www.bbc.com/news/world-europe-23571739>.

71.   "Freedom at Issue: Insights on the Global Struggle for Democracy." *Freedom House*. N.p., n.d. Web. 29 May 2014. <http://www.freedomhouse.org/blog/ergenekon-case-and-turkey%25E2%2580%2599s-democratic-aspirations#.U1WLWFdPr3A>.

72.   "SHOAH | Archive | Turkey." *SHOAH | Archive | Turkey*. N.p., n.d. Web. 27 May 2014. <http://www.shoah.org.uk/category/europe/turkey/page/4/>.

73.   Interview with Abdulla Demirbas by the author. Diyarbakir, August 8, 2014.

8

From Syria's Ashes

The Damascus Declaration was signed by Kurds, Assyrians, Christians, Arabs, and tribal sheikhs on October 16, 2005.[1] Cooperation between opposition groups, standing against the government of President Bashar al-Assad, was inspired by the 2004 Qamishli Uprising.[2] The Damascus Declaration was an unprecedented joint appeal calling for an end to violence by the Assad regime. It demanded "a gradual and peaceful transition to democracy and the equality of all citizens in a secular and sovereign Syria."[3] Kurds wanted citizenship rights, repeal of the emergency law, and other reforms liberalizing the use of Kurdish language and freedom of assembly. Some Kurdish parties refused to sign the Damascus Declaration because it did not go far enough. They demanded recognition in the constitution as the largest ethnic minority in Syria.

Joining their brethren in Syria, Kurds in Diyarbakir and Erbil took to the streets. The uprising occurred weeks after the Transitional Administrative Law (TAL) was adopted by Iraqis on March 8, 2004. As an interim constitution for Iraq, the TAL formally recognized the autonomous Kurdistan Regional Government.[4] The TAL was a milestone for the Kurdish cause, inspiring Kurds everywhere. When the TAL was announced, Kurds celebrated in Syria and across the region. Syrian Kurds wanted what their brethren had achieved in Iraqi Kurdistan. The resulting unrest represented a major challenge to Damascus. Assad deployed extra troops to Kurdish regions and placed them on high alert.

The regime tried to decapitate the opposition by targeting its leaders. Sheikh Mashouq al-Khaznawi, a respected Sufi cleric and outspoken critic of the regime's discrimination, disappeared on May 10, 2005.[5] His disappearance was anticipated by his son, Sheikh Murad Khaznawi: "[Syrian intelligence] wrote a report saying he . . . should be stopped. They said he would start a revolution."[6] When Khaznawi's body was returned to the family, it had been brutally tortured. Khaznawi's son demanded an investigation and was arrested. In response, ten thousand

Kurds launched street demonstrations in Qamishli. Police responded by beating peaceful protesters. Kurdish shops were targeted and torched. Violent crackdowns became a pattern. When Kurds rallied in Damascus to protest the regime's confiscation of identification documents in 2006, they were beaten and dispersed.

A Washington Conference of Syrian Kurds was held on March 13, 2006.[7] Participants endorsed thirteen points, framing the struggle for human rights of Kurds in Syria. They also agreed to institutionalize their efforts by establishing an umbrella organization comprised of Kurdish NGOs, political parties, and independent activists. Some Kurdish groups were focused on cultural issues, such as the liberalization of the Kurdish language in education and official proceedings, as well as relaxed rules regulating cultural events like Newroz. Others were more focused on political rights. They demanded constitutional recognition of Kurds as a minority in Syria, as well as political and cultural autonomy. Despite differences, Syrian Kurds all shared a core objective: political and cultural rights as well as citizenship.

Damascus tried to exploit Kurdish factionalism and disrupt a follow-up meeting planned for May in Brussels. Syria's Vice President Najah al-Attar reached out to Syrian Kurds that the regime considered more moderate than those at the Washington conference. This contact was unprecedented. It was also an underhanded effort to dissuade Kurds from attending the Brussels Conference. While trying to discredit Kurdish cooperation, the regime was also ratcheting up pressure on Kurds by jailing their prominent leaders.[8] Led by Dr. Sherkoh Abbas, the Kurdistan National Assembly of Syria (KNA-S) was established at the Brussels conference to raise international awareness about the plight of Kurds in Syria.

Abbas and members of the Assembly's Executive Committee discussed Syria's state-sponsored terrorism with US officials, Members of Congress, and think tanks during a visit to Washington, DC in June 2006. Abbas presented a pro-democracy agenda for Syria. He embraced a federal state, with devolved asymmetric powers modeled on Iraq's 2005 constitution. In addition to individual rights, he proposed special measures to protect and promote the rights of minority groups.[9]

The Assembly found a receptive audience in Washington. The Project for a New American Century was established by neo-conservatives in the 1990s. It envisioned eliminating the Baath Parties in both Iraq and Syria, toppling Saddam Hussein, and overthrowing the regime of Bashar al-Assad. Though Iraq and Syria were different states, they shared a Baathist ideology. Neoconservatives viewed Baathism as a fascistic form of Arab exceptionalism. They believed that regime change in Iraq and Syria would catalyze democratic, pro-Western revolutions across the Middle East.

*****

Assad used both legal and extrajudicial measures to pressure the Kurds, whose ambitions represented a threat to his monopoly on power. Decree 49 was adopted on October 27, 2008. It required state approval of the sale and lease of land in the border regions of Syria. Crafted by Mohammed Talib Hilal, Kurds living on the Iraq-Turkey border were hardest hit. Decree 49 was a form of ethnic cleansing, effectively evicting the residents of border areas from their homes. It compounded problems for Kurds, who were already forbidden to transact property or leave it to their heirs. It also had a material impact by denying the livelihoods of Kurdish farmers and herders. Decree 49 was issued during a time of drought, forcing many Kurds to abandon their farms and villages,[10] leaving ancestral lands in search of jobs in Damascus.[11]

Talib Hilal is called the "Arabization mastermind."[12] In 1963, Talib Hilal published "A Study of the Jazira Province from National, Social and Political Aspects."[13] The so-called development prospectus was nothing more than a security plan for marginalizing and exterminating the Kurds of Syria. It proposed displacing Kurds and creating collective farms for Arabs. It proposed denying education and jobs to Kurds. Non-Arabs would be denied citizenship and non-Arabic speakers would be denied the right to vote or hold office. "Wanted" Kurds would be handed over to Turkey. Talib Hilal was a strong influence on Syrian President Hafiz al-Assad. He inspired Assad to establish the Arab Belt in 1976, which denuded traditional lands of Kurdish residents. Assad also imposed strong restrictions on the use of Kurdish language and expression.

Talib Hilal was the author of a racist anti-Kurdish propaganda campaign. As the head of internal security in Hasakah, he described Kurdish as an "unintelligible language which was used to conceal treason and separatist plotting."[14] He wrote, "The bells of Jazira sound the alarm and call on the Arab conscience to save this region, to purify it of all this scum, the dregs of history. As befits its geographical situation, it can offer up its revenues and riches, along with those of the other provinces of this Arab territory."[15] According to Talib Hilal, "The

Kurdish question, now that the Kurds are organising themselves, is simply a malignant tumor which has developed in a part of the body of the Arab nation. The only remedy which we can properly apply thereto is excision."[16]

Soon after adopting Decree 49, Assad reached out to Kurdish political factions. He hoped to cultivate pro-regime Kurdish groups in exchange for citizenship concessions. A meeting between Assad and Kurdish tribal leaders was planned, then cancelled.[17] Instead of being directly involved, Assad enlisted Issam Baghdy, a former parliamentarian, as a backchannel. In 2009, Baghdy contacted Abd al-Hakim Bashar, secretary general of the Kurdish Democratic Front (KDF), who represented a coalition of nine left-wing Syrian Kurdish parties. Baghdy assessed the possibility of negotiations between the KDF and Damascus. He sought the KDF's views on Syria's territorial integrity, continuity of the Assad regime, and the Damascus Declaration. He also wanted information on relations between Kurdish parties in Syria and counterparts in Iraq and Turkey.[18]

Syria was a haven for Saddam Hussein's loyalists and Iraqi Baathists who fled Iraq in 2003. They regrouped on Syrian soil and then launched an insurgency with money, weapons, and fighters flowing from Syria to Iraq. In turn, Iraq's instability spread to Syria, worsening tensions between ethnic and sectarian groups. Iran played a double game, colluding with both Assad and Arab Sunnis to support Iraqis resisting the US occupation of Iraq. Iran's Quds Force was focused on Tehran's core regional interest: preserving a corridor through the Shia crescent from Basra to Tehran, Damascus, and Beirut. The corridor was an essential portal for delivering arms to Hezbollah and other anti-Western and anti-Zionist terror groups.

Inspired by the Tunisian and Egyptian revolutions, Syrians declared a Day of Rage on February 4, 2011. Events in Daraa were the spark that lit a flame, causing a nationwide conflagration. At least fifteen teenagers were arrested for painting anti-government graffiti on the walls of their school on March 1, 2011.[19] The government's violent response left dozens dead after widespread rioting. It was unheard of for Syrians to oppose the regime. Events in Daraa shattered the people's "wall of fear," inspiring Syrians to oppose the regime's intimidation and oppression.[20]

Assad made a forty-five-minute television address to the nation on March 30, 2011. With deadly violence spiraling across the country, he admitted mistakes and hinted at reforms. Over the next weeks, Assad took steps to divide and mollify his opponents, focusing first on the Kurds. Building on the Baghdy back-channel, Assad addressed the citizenship issue. He promised "Syrian Arab" citizenship to some 225,000 Kurds on April 7, 2011.[21] Kurds were skeptical. Assad had made a similar promise in May 2011, but did nothing. Most Kurds affected by the decree were descendants of Kurds in Hasakah, declared "foreigners" and stripped of their citizenship in 1962. The April 2011 decree did not address the fate of another 75,000 "unregistered" Kurds who were stripped of their legal status by the 1962 census. In the end, only about 6,000 stateless Kurds actually received identification cards.[22]

Appeasing the Kurds was part of a broader effort to contain the rebellion that was sweeping across the country. On April 21, Assad lifted the forty-eight-year-old state of emergency and abolished the Higher State Security Court. He declared, "the right to peaceful protest as one of the basic human rights guaranteed by the Syrian Constitution."[23] He liberalized the establishment of new political parties. To shore up support among his core constituency of Alawite civil servants, Assad announced a salary increase for government employees. But concessions were too few and too late. Syrian opposition groups established the Syrian National Council (SNC) on October 2, 2011. The SNC declared its commitment to regime change and a new democratic order.

*****

Turkish Prime Minister Recep Tayyip Erdogan and Assad established good personal relations after the AKP came to power in 2002. Turkey's economic diplomacy included more than $1 billion of investment in Syria. Turkey's foreign ministry proposed a Free Trade Agreement, which would enable $5 billion in bilateral trade between Turkey and Syria.[24] Gaziantep became a major destination for Syrians purchasing consumer goods. Erdogan and Assad resolved the border dispute over Hatay province in Turkey and Alexandretta in Syria, which dated back to 1938 and intensified when Syria gained independence in 1946.[25] As a measure of their growing amity, Assad traveled to Turkey in 2004. It was the first time that a Syrian head of government had visited Ankara in sixty-eight years.[26] Assad visited Ankara again in November 2007 and pledged to intensify pressures on the PKK. About two hundred Syrian Kurds protested in Qamishli, but government security forces broke up the rally using truncheons and tear gas. One person was killed and four people seriously injured.[27]

In March 2008, security forces fired on Kurds celebrating Newroz, killing three people. In October 7, 2011, Mashaal Tammo, the leader of Kurdish Future Movement Party (KFMP), was assassinated in his Qamishli apartment by masked agents. Syrian security forces fired indiscriminately on fifty thousand Kurds who joined his funeral procession the next day. Five people were killed and scores injured. His son, Fares Tammo, urged Kurds to rise up: "My father's assassination is the screw in the regime's coffin. They made a big mistake by killing my father."[28]

With Syria's rebellion in full swing, Erdogan and Assad met again to discuss the escalation of violence on Turkey's border. Erdogan urged Assad to engage the Muslim Brotherhood in a governing coalition. Under the auspices of "democratization," Syria's Sunni Muslims could be coopted and hostilities ended. But it was a step that Assad was unwilling to take. Sunnis represent a majority of Syria's population, roughly 80 percent. Giving them representation would have overwhelmed Assad's Alawite government. Despite Assad's uncompromising stance, Erdogan stood by his man. He insisted, Assad is "a good friend of mine."[29] The two leaders had developed a personal rapport. Ahmet Davutoglu, then Turkey's foreign minister, visited Damascus more than forty times after the AKP came to power in 2002. Turkey-Syrian relations were central to Turkey's "zero problems with neighbors" policy. Ankara aspired to be a regional player and a Middle East peace broker. Ending Syria's civil war would open important trade routes for Turkey. Davutoglu coordinated five rounds of indirect talks between Syria and Israel. Though he did not succeed in arranging face-to-face negotiations, progress was reported on territorial and resource issues such as status of the Golan Heights and access to water supplies. Turkey's mediation broke down when violence flared between Israel and Gaza in December 2008.[30]

Erdogan reproached Assad for human rights abuses, but he did not publicly question the legitimacy of Assad's rule. Erdogan was much tougher on Hosni Mubarak, whom he condemned in the strongest terms for his crackdown against the Muslim Brotherhood in Egypt. While Erdogan called for Mubarak's resignation, he took a softer line toward Assad, publicly calling for reforms. Erdogan explained, "We had long discussions about lifting the state of emergency and the release of political prisoners. We discussed these issues and . . . changing the election system, allowing political parties. However, he was late in taking these steps."[31]

Despite private assurances, Assad continued his attacks against Syria's Sunni majority. Erdogan invested heavily in his personal relationship with Assad. He felt betrayed, humiliated, and enraged by Assad's uncompromising stance. Erdogan jumped on board when international public opinion turned against Syria. The Arab League, the Gulf Cooperation Council, and the Organization for Islamic Conference condemned Syria. Erdogan became one of Assad's most strident critics. While Ankara imposed bilateral financial sanctions against Syria on November 30, Erdogan was critical of the UN Security Council for failing to take collective action. He accused it of failing to protect civilians. He also blasted the world body for its unwillingness to adopt a Chapter 7 resolution under the UN Charter, authorizing the use of force to deliver humanitarian assistance and stop the slaughter. Assad continued his siege tactics to compel Syrians into submission. It was called "Kneel or starve."[32]

The Friends of Syria was a coalition of like-minded countries working for Assad's ouster. It recognized the SNC as the legitimate representative of the Syrian people at a conference in Istanbul on April 1, 2012. Abdulbaset Sieda, an ethnic Kurd, was elected the SNC's leader. Turkey became a hub for opposition to the regime. The SNC established its headquarters in Istanbul and its relief coordination center in Gaziantep. Leadership of the Free Syrian Army (FSA) was based on Turkish territory. Turkey's support for the Syrian opposition constituted a de facto declaration of war.

A peace conference was held in January 2012. It was called "Geneva I." UN Special Envoy Kofi Annan called for humanitarian access, the release of arbitrarily arrested detainees, and the start of a political dialogue. However, Damascus rejected the Annan peace plan, and Annan resigned in 2013. He was replaced by Lakhdar Brahimi, Algeria's former foreign minister and an experienced negotiator known for the Taif Accords that ended Lebanon's civil war. Brahimi understood that resolution of Syria's civil war would require an end to political Alawitism, and the end of Assad's dominance. Rebirth of the republic would empower the Sunni majority and uphold the rights of minorities, similar to arrangements in the Taif Accords.[33] Like Annan, however, Brahimi's efforts were stymied by Russia and China's obstructionism on the UN Security Council. And like Annan, Brahimi refused to renew his mandate. He stepped down in 2014.

It was hard to maintain the moral high ground and support Syria's rebels. A video surfaced of a jihadi, Abuu Saakar, executing a Syrian solider. He ripped the heart from his body and ate it, declaring: "I swear to God we will eat your hearts and livers."[34] The image went viral, further dampening calls to arm the rebels. Western countries were outraged when Turkish-backed jihadis executed sixty ethnic Armenians in the village of Kessab in March 21, 2014. Syria's Foreign Minister Walid al-Muallem blasted Davutoglu for supporting terror groups.[35] Davutoglu denied Turkey's links to the Muslim jihadi movement. Syria's combatants—Assad's regime, Assad's Iranian backers, Hezbollah, Al-Qaeda, and other members of the violent Sunni militant movement—shared hatred of the United States. Just as Ronald Regan refused to take sides in the Iran-Iraq war, Obama seemed content to let America's enemies fight it out. The dominance of jihadis was a result of the West's failure to support the FSA at the outset of Syria's civil war, when the Assad regime was most vulnerable.

Meanwhile, the humanitarian situation continued to deteriorate. As of September 1, 2014, the Syrian Observatory for Human Rights documented 190,000 deaths from the conflict. The UN High Commissioner for Refugees (UNHCR) estimated that nine million Syrians had been displaced. Lebanon received the most refugees then Turkey. As of September 1, the UNHCR indicated that 815,000 Syrian refugees were sheltered in camps in Turkey.[36] Another million people were urbanized refugees in Turkey's teaming cities. The border crossings between Turkey and Rojava, Syria's Kurdish region, were closed, preventing humanitarian supplies from getting in and Syrian Kurds from getting out.

Turkey was increasingly drawn into the conflict. In June 2012, Syria shot down a Turkish RF-4E Phantom reconnaissance plane that strayed into disputed airspace near the coastal city of Latakia. In response, Turkey deployed tanks and surface-to-air missiles to the border.[37] Ankara requested an urgent meeting of the North Atlantic Council. While NATO expressed solidarity with Turkey, it refused to adopt a Chapter 5 resolution committing the Alliance to join Turkey in the event of war with Syria. Emboldened by NATO's tepid response, Syria shelled the Turkish border town of Akcakale, killing five people in October 2012.[38] Turkey responded with a barrage of cross-border artillery attacks on Syrian targets. The Turkish Grand National Assembly (TGNA) passed a resolution giving the government permission to deploy Turkish troops, who were massing on the border. In May 2013, Reyhanli, a town in Hatay Province that shares a similar ethnic and sectarian mix to Syria's, was rocked by car bombings that killed

53 people and wounded another 140. Turkey downed a Syrian helicopter in Turkish airspace in September 2013, and it shot down a Syrian MIG-23 warplane over Hatay in March 2014.[39]

In addition to these incidents, Turkey became a direct party to the conflict through its support for Sunni armed groups in Syria. With the FSA increasingly marginalized, Turkey allegedly provided arms, ammunition, money, and logistical assistance to Sunni extremists.[40] It purportedly became the supply channel for al-Qaeda-affiliated groups including the Jabhat al-Nusra Front and the Islamic State in Iraq and Syria (ISIS), as well as Salafi groups such as Ahrar al-Sham. Cengiz Candar, the well-respected Turkish journalist, maintained that MIT helped "midwife" the Islamic state in Iraq and Syria, as well as other Jihadi groups.[41] The Islamic Front was established as an umbrella organization in November 2013. At the time, an estimated 700 to 1,500 jihadis were active in Syria. By Geneva II, which was convened in January 2014, as many as 5,000 al-Nusra fighters were in the field. They included more than 1,000 jihadis from European countries who learned skills to bring home for domestic terror attacks. According to Ambassador Robert S. Ford, former US ambassador to Syria, the brutal tactics of ISIS also attracted European jihadis to its ranks.

Prospects for political dialogue were growing increasingly remote. Assad offered lip service to reforms as a way to placate the opposition and counter-criticisms from the international community. Voters approved modifications to the constitution in a referendum on February 26, 2012.[42] The referendum was only held in government-controlled areas of Syria. This cosmetic concession did not dissuade the opposition from demanding Assad's resignation. They adamantly rejected any political solution that kept Assad in power. In early 2013, Assad ramped up criticism of the opposition, calling them "terrorists."

The SNC was envisioned as an inclusive government in exile, which would lead Syria after the fall of Assad. But internal power struggles undermined the SNC. The FSA was also undermined as more extremist groups emerged. The SNC also failed to address the unique requirements of Syria's minorities, especially the Kurds. The Kurdish delegation walked out of the National Syrian Salvation Conference of opposition groups in Istanbul in July 2011 because the SNC ignored Kurdish demands in its manifesto. These included constitutional recognition of Kurds as Syria's second-largest ethnic group and decentralization allowing greater self-rule by Kurds.[43]

Many Syrians viewed the SNC as increasingly irrelevant. Its members went to international conferences and stayed in five-star hotels while ordinary Syrians suffered desperate conditions on the ground. The SNC took steps to become more inclusive, establishing the National Coalition for Syrian Revolutionary and Opposition Forces at a meeting in Doha in November 2012. Mustafa Sabbagh became secretary general. Salih Moslem Mohamed, head of the Kurdish Democratic Union Party (PYD) was named general deputy coordinator of the National Coalition.

*****

Salih Moslem graduated in engineering from Istanbul Technical University in 1977. He speaks perfect Turkish.[44] Working in Saudi Arabia, he was contacted by PKK sympathizers and became a left-leaning political activist. Salih Moslem got more engaged in Kurdish politics when the PKK moved its base to Bekaa in 1980. At the time, Syrian Kurds represented about 20 percent of the PKK's rank and file. Hafiz al-Assad encouraged Syrian Kurds to join the PKK as part of a broader geopolitical struggle between Syria and Turkey, and to distract Kurds in Syria from Assad's oppressive domestic policies.

Under threat of war from Turkey, Assad signed the 1998 Adana Declaration recognizing the PKK as a terrorist organization, which led to the Ocalan's exile. That same year, Marwan Zourky established the National Democratic Coalition (NDC) as a Kurdish political organization in Syria with close ideological ties to the PKK. Zourky and members of the NDC were squeezed by the Assad regime. In 2004, the NDC evolved into PYD. The PYD was established at the 2004 PKK congress. Salih Moslem served as a member of the PYD Executive Committee until his arrest and yearlong detention in the summer of 2004. He was arrested again and jailed for two months in 2006. His wife was arrested and tortured for nine months in 2009. Salih Moslem was elected leader of the PYD in the Spring of 2011. The PYD's People's Protection Units (YPG) was an armed and effective fighting militia defending the Kurdish people.

There was no love lost between Syrian Kurds and Assad. Arab Sunnis and jihadis were also a threat to the Kurds. As Syrian armed forces withdrew and refocused their military assets in other parts of the country, the PYD filled the space. Damascus made no effort to contest the takeover of territories, leading to allegations of the PYD's collaboration with the regime. There are sixteen Kurdish parties in Syria, including a branch of Barzani's KDP. The PYD may be operationally independent from the PKK, but they share a common cause and ideology. The PKK is a pan-Kurdish organization, which inspires and assists the PYD.

The FSA fought the YPG in July 2011. Al-Nusra also confronted the YPG in a battle for control of the border town of Ras al-Ayn and other towns in Eastern Hasakah beginning in 2012. Ras al-Ayn had a plurality of Kurds, but it was also populated by Arabs, Assyrians, Syriacs, Armenians, and Chechens. It is a physically divided city linked to Ceylanpinar in Turkey via a border crossing. Al-Nusra and the YPG also fought over Tal Abyad, across the border from Akçakale in Turkey, which was liberated from rebel control. The YPG captured Kobani (Ayn al-Arab), Amude, and Efrin on July 19 and 20. Within a week, the YPG liberated the Kurdish-populated cities of Derika Hemko (al-Malikiyah), Sere Kainye (Ras al-Ayn), Dirbesi (al-Darbasiyah), and Girke Lege (al-Mabada). Fierce fighting erupted between al-Nusra and YPG at the Serekaniye border crossing on July 17, 2013.[45] By 2014, Hasakah and Qamishli were the only Kurdish-populated cities to remain under control of the government.

Battles also raged on the Iraq-Syria border. Jihadis pursued a strategy to control lands on both sides, spread their influence into a broader territory, and set up a transnational Islamic state. In February 2013, al-Nusra seized the Tabqa dam on the Euphrates River, the largest hydroelectric plant in Syria. ISIS took control of Raqah. It sought to establish a caliphate across the entire territory of Iraq and Syria.[46] Its leader, Abu Bakr al-Baghdadi, instructed ISIS fighters to establish Deir Ezzor as the main gateway between Iraq and Syria. ISIS quit cooperating with al-Nusra for being too moderate. Few ISIS fighters were actually from Syria. Most were foreigners from Saudi Arabia, Tunisia, Turkey, and Europe. The YPG fought effectively against al-Nusra, ISIL, and ISIS. It seized the Yaroubiyeh border crossing between Syria and Iraq in October 2013. However, it did not act alone. Eyewitnesses reported that both Syrian warplanes and Iraqi Army artillery bombed positions to support YPG ground operations.[47]

A clash of ideologies defined relations between the PYD and Islamic extremists. Jihadis view the Kurds as apostates and stooges of the West. In August 2013, ISIS issued a fatwa calling for the murder of Kurdish men, women, and children. Up to ten thousand Syrian Kurds suddenly fled across the just-opened pontoon bridge at Peshkabour to Iraqi Kurdistan on August 6, 2013.[48] ISIS reissued its fatwa a year later: "To all ISIS fighters, clean those areas (Syrian Kurdistan) of crusaders

161

and Kurdish traitors and all the militants of the 'Kafiristan' Workers' Party (PKK) and raise the Islamic flag."[49] "Kafir" is an Arabic term that means "disbeliever."

A struggle for resources also pitted jihadis against the PYD. The Kurds controlled border crossings and trade routes between Turkey and Syria. These crossings were essential supply routes for weapons and warriors. Salih Moslem stated, "We have clearly observed the relationship between armed religious groups and the Turkish government."[50] He added, "They are brutal force which wants to drag humanity back to the stone ages."[51]

Kurdish populated territories are mineral rich compared with most of Syria's dry and barren countryside. The PYD controlled the oil region of Rimalan. Jihadis were financed by wealthy sponsors and emirates, but they sought control of Rojava's energy fields to help pay for the long and grinding war. ISIS gained short-term benefits by selling oil to the Assad government. In return, it was exempted from air strikes by the regime and given access to electricity. As the international community debated assistance to the opposition, detractors pointed to the emergence of jihadis on the battlefield as rationale for not getting more involved in the conflict.[52]

Turkey also eyed the oil fields of Hasakah, as a supplement to its meager domestic supplies. International oil companies Royal Dutch Shell and Suncor helped develop Syria's fields. Royal Dutch Shell had participated in Syria's oil sector since the 1985. However, Syria's oil fields were already depleted and in decline before the uprising. Their output decreased from about four hundred thousand barrels per day in 2011 to less than eighty thousand barrels a day by the end of 2013. Declining production was partly a result of Syria's civil war, which took its toll on energy infrastructure and pipelines. With reduced productivity, Syria turned to Iran and Iraq for supplies.[53]

*****

The PYD gained popular support by protecting the local population and providing services. YPG fighters numbered twenty thousand. Women were half the force. In November 2013, the PYD declared the transitional administration of Rojava along the Turkish border in Western Kurdistan. As part of its "democratic self-management project," local legislative assemblies were created in the districts of Efrin, Kobani, and Cezire.[54] Syrian flags were removed and replaced by the Kurdish tricolor flag.

Regional finance committees managed the affairs of local administration. Local legislative assemblies were launched at an inclusive meeting of eighty-two men and women from thirty-five organizations and parties representing Kurds, Arabs, Syrians, and Turkmen from all three districts. The assemblies comprised equal numbers of men and women.

An electoral management body was created to consider the possibility, conditions, and timing for a regional election. As a political and social movement, the PYD included a political umbrella organization called the Rojava Democratic Society Movement (TEV-DEM), a youth movement and a women's movement.[55] The PYD opened schools and cultural centers, offering instruction in the Kurdish language. Cultural rights and decentralized governance in Rojava were recognized as a model for Syria as a whole.[56] Salih Moslem maintained, "We strongly believe that the model of democracy which we are developing today can serve as a model not only to the rest of Syria but in all of the Middle-East, therefore we must protect it and remain committed to it."[57]

He insisted, "Kurdish forces would be the region's military force that protect and provide the security," but they will "not be allowed to interfere in the administration's politics."[58] The PYD issued a Social Contract for Rojava in March 2014. It reads like an interim constitution, containing one hundred articles defining the competence of local governing bodies and enshrining human rights.[59] The social contract upholds minority rights consistent with international standards. In Rojava, Syriacs were already teaching in the Syriac language. The PYD protected local churches from terrorist attacks. According to a PYD official, "Rojava exists. It is as clear as the sun."[60]

With Syrians suffering severe deprivation, the PYD established public service and relief committees. Aid supplies came from Kurds in Iraqi Kurdistan and Turkey. PYD assistance was critical. Self-limiting UN agencies would deliver supplies only with permission of the Syrian government. Rojava's humanitarian hubs were islands of stability. "Kurdish regions have suffered the most and have been deprived of international aid and relief," maintained Salih Moslem. "Supplies are blocked by both the regime and the opposition." Turkey also blocked aid convoys from entering Rojava in order to marginalize the PYD, sealing its border with Rojava. According to Salih Moslem, "ISIS and al-Nusra accused the regional peoples administration as a step towards separation from Syria, while the jihadist established their Islamic emirates in neighboring region Al-Raqqa and wanted to establish Islamic state in Iraq and Syria."[61]

The PYD's muscular approach did not sit well with competing Kurdish groups in Syria, the KRG, or Turkey. The Kurdish National Council (KNC) was formed in 2011 through the initiative of Masoud Barzani and the KDP. Backed by Turkey, it comprised sixteen different Kurdish parties. The KNC was impressive on paper but wielded no real power. It had no military force or administrative capacity to counter the PYD. The KNC had contempt for the PYD, and the inverse was also true. According to a KNC member, "[The PYD] is nothing but an administration of regime allies."[62] The KNC tried to join the SNC, but its entreaties were rebuffed. Barzani brought Kurdish factions together in Erbil to discuss cooperation and the creation of a coordinating body. The Hewler Agreement was signed on July 11, 2012. It established the Kurdish Supreme Council (KSC), with ultimate authority to administer all Kurdish areas with protection from the YPG. Some political parties did not show up in Erbil. They joined the SNC, casting doubt on the Hewler Agreement.

Barzani rejected the PYD declaration of autonomy in November 2013. Turkey did not want the PYD, which it believed was under the PKK's control, to challenge the KRG. Barzani and Salih Moslem argued publicly. According to Masoud Barzani, "Only one Kurdish organization is in league with the regime and using armed force to control the region."[63] The KRG barred Salih Moslem from transiting through the airport in Erbil, forcing him to use the Baghdad airport instead. By August 2013, more than two hundred thousand Syrians—mostly Kurds—had crossed the border at Faysh Khabour to Iraqi Kurdistan.[64] In April 2014, the KRG dug a trench blocking the transit of people and goods. The trench extended for seventeen kilometers. It was three meters wide and two meters deep. The KRG explained that the trench was for security purposes.[65] Asked about Masoud Barzani, Salih Moslem responded: "I will be slave to no man."[66]

Despite personal antipathies, Barzani supported the PYD when jihadis attacked Syrian Kurds in the summer of 2013. On August 11, 2013, Barzani proclaimed, "The Kurdistan Region is ready to do everything in its power to protect the lives of the Kurds in western Kurdistan [from al-Qaeda terrorists]."[67] Soon after, Erbil was rocked by suicide car bombings that killed six people and wounded eighty-four, including forty-two security personnel. Gun battles erupted in the streets of Erbil's typically tranquil streets. The attackers were jihadis, linked to al-Qaeda fighting in Syria and based and in Nineveh Province.[68]

The SNC and KNC entered into a sixteen-point agreement on August 28, 2013. The deal included constitutional recognition of the Kurds. It pledged to rename the Syrian Arab Republic as the Syrian Republic. The KNC head, Abd al-Hakim Bashar, would become vice president of the SNC. Additionally, 11 KNC members would join the National Coalition's 114-member general commission, and 3 KNC members would join the more exclusive 19-member political commission.[69] Salih Moslem refused to recognize any agreement that did not treat the KNC as equal. He believed that subordinating Kurdish interests to the SNC was a betrayal of the Kurdish cause and the struggle of Syrian Kurds for constitutional rights.

The KRG wanted to have it both ways. It sought to control the Syrian Kurdish movement, thereby limiting the PKK's influence. Turkey supported the KRG in this goal. The KRG also sought to benefit from the PYD. The PYD could create a security buffer between Iraqi Kurdistan and extremists in Syria. Energy supplies from Iraqi Kurdistan need multiple pipeline routes to international markets. Oil could flow from Iraqi Kurdistan, through pipelines in Rojava, toward export terminals on the Lebanese coast. Iraqi Kurdistan accepted and bore the cost of up to 250,000 refugees from Syria. Just as the presence of the PKK in Qandil provided political leverage in the KRG's relations with Ankara, the PYD served a similar purpose to the KRG.

Turkey tried to foment competition and divide the Kurds, using its leverage with the Barzani's KDP. It sought to prevent Rojava's autonomy, which Ankara viewed as a stalking horse for the PKK. Ankara had good relations with the SNC and recognized the KNC as the sole representative of Syrian Kurds. Though Salih Moslem visited Turkey several times in 2013 and 2014, Erdogan remained deeply distrustful. When the PYD emerged immediately after the PKK withdrew from Syria in 1999, Ankara claimed it was a shell game with the PYD as a surrogate for the PKK. According to a Syrian Kurd independent of the PYD, "At least 400 new PKK came from Turkey and Iran [since 2013]."

Turkey blocked humanitarian convoys from traversing PYD-controlled territory. Denying humanitarian aid access made the provision of food and medical supplies a weapon of war. It also prevented Kurds from seeking medical assistance in Turkey. It built a seven-kilometer barrier between Nusaybin in Turkey and Qamishli to prevent the flow of Kurds from Syria. When UN Security Council Resolution 2139 (February 22, 2014) demanded humanitarian access to civilian populations in Syria, Ankara relented and temporarily opened its border at Qamishli.

A UN convoy crossed from Mardin to Qamishli in March 2014.[70] It was a symbolic and short-lived gesture of cooperation.

*****

Assad dashed any hope for reconciliation when his forces used chemical weapons on August 21, 2013. That day, At least 1,400 civilians died including 426 children.[71] According to rebels, the WMD attack was the fourteenth attack using chemical weapons. US Secretary of State John Kerry responded with outrage: "The indiscriminate slaughter of civilians, the killing of women and children and innocent bystanders by chemical weapons is a moral obscenity."[72] U.N. Secretary-General Ban Ki-moon called the use of chemical weapons a crime against humanity and demanded action.

President Obama warned during the Q&A part of a press conference that Assad's use of chemical weapons crossed a "red line." Despite overwhelming evidence of attacks using sarin gas and other chemicals, the British parliament rejected a resolution authorizing the use of force; Obama refused to intervene with support only from France. The American public was weary after ten long years of war in Iraq and Afghanistan. When Obama declared that the United States would not "put boots on the ground," Senator John McCain called on the administration to provide anti-tank and shoulder launched anti-aircraft missiles to the rebels. However, the Obama administration worried that sophisticated weapons would end up in the wrong hands to be used by extremists against the United States. Obama suffered withering criticism for halting efforts to train and equip the rebels, who were deeply disadvantaged in their battle with Syria's armed forces.

Kerry made a passing comment calling on the UN to sequester Assad's chemical weapons on May 4, 2013. Russia's Foreign Minister Sergei Lavrov seized the opportunity to propose a UN-led weapons inspections regime for Syria. The UNSC adopted a plan to eliminate Syria's chemical weapons stockpiles.[73] UN engagement represented a tactical victory for Syria. Assad created a problem that only he could solve. Ironically, Assad became indispensable to peace and disarmament in Syria. The plan to identify, transport, and destroy Syria's WMD actually strengthened the regime. Syria was able to avoid a chapter-seven resolution, which could lead to the use of "all necessary measures" to ensure the delivery of humanitarian supplies. Discussion about regime change all but ended.

Assad intensified military action, turning the tide of battle. Hezbollah entered the fray. The regime's use of barrel bombs was a particular heinous tool terrorizing civilians. Even after 90 percent of Syria's WMD stockpiles were removed, Syria's armed forces used chlorine bombs. Navi Pillay, the UN High Commissioner for Human Rights, cited "massive evidence" that the "the highest levels of the Syrian government" were responsible for war crimes.[74]

Cosponsored by the United States and Russia, plans were made for a peace conference known as Geneva II. The initiative was undermined by miscommunication and mismanagement, as well as by Assad's ongoing aggression. Kerry maintained there was "no way" that Assad would be part of a transitional government.[75] In response, Damascus threatened to cancel its participation in the conference. Ban Ki-moon surprisingly invited Iran to participate in Geneva II, with Turkey playing a role behind the scenes to encourage Tehran's participation. The SNC threatened to boycott the meeting, and the invitation to Iran was withdrawn. Geneva II was finally convened on January 22, 2014. The meeting was moved to Montreux because there were no hotel rooms in Geneva. A watch fair was previously scheduled.

The KNC and PYD met in Erbil to discuss Kurdish representation at Geneva II. The cosponsors told the PYD that its representatives could join the conference if they came as part of the SNC delegation. They refused. The PYD demanded a distinct Kurdish delegation. The KNC broke ranks and sent a group headed by Hamid Darwish. According to Darwish, "This legitimizes Kurdish demands and puts them forward on the international platform." Kurds protested across Europe, Turkey, and Syria. A PKK spokesman indicated, "The exclusion of the most basic democratization force—that is, the Kurds—from a conference on the future of Syria invalidates Syria's democratization from the very beginning. Those ostracizing the Kurds will be held responsible for this."[76]

The United States actively opposed the PYD's participation. Robert S. Ford criticized the PYD's declaration of autonomy. He also criticized the PYD for its intimidation of other Kurdish groups and for cooperating with the Assad regime. Salih Moslem applied for a visa at the US Embassy in Stockholm to attend a conference at Columbia University, but his application was not acted upon. The State Department could not reach consensus on whether to accept Salih Moslem's application. Nor was there consensus between the State Department and other agencies of the US government. Even if the US government decided to issue a visa to Salih Moslem, the Obama administration would not act without Ankara's agreement.

Washington opposed Rojava, which could accelerate the fragmentation of Syria. The Obama administration did not want its approach toward the PYD misconstrued as support for the PKK. Ford addressed a conference of Kurds on "Post-Assad Syria" in March 2013: "I am not pro-Kurdish. I am pro-Syrian."[77] His statement disappointed the Kurds. Obama's failure to follow through on threats to intervene militarily further upset the broader Syrian opposition, as well as their allies in Turkey and the Gulf States.

Notes

1. "The Damascus Declaration." *Carnegie Middle East Center*. N.p., n.d. Web. 09 June 2014. <http://carnegie-mec.org/publications/?fa=48514>.
2. Kurdwatch Is A Project Of The, European Center For Kurdish Studies, Emser Straße 26, and 12051 Berlin. *KURDWATCH•Report 4* (n.d.): n. pag. Web.
3. "The Damascus Declaration." *Carnegie Endowment for International Peace*. N.p., n.d. Web. 27 May 2014. <http://carnegieendowment.org/syriaincrisis/?fa=48514&reloadFlag=1>.
4. 12, 2006 December. *Kenneth Katzman and Alfred B. Prados* (n.d.): n. pag. Web. <http://fpc.state.gov/documents/organization/79340.pdf>.
5. Blanford, Nicholas. "A Murder Stirs Kurds in Syria." *The Christian Science Monitor*. The Christian Science Monitor, 16 June 2005. Web. 09 June 2014. <http://www.csmonitor.com/2005/0616/p01s03-wome.html>.
6. Ibid.
7. "In Memory of the Kurdish Patriot Ms Soraya Serajeddini (Nakshbandi)." *In Memory of the Kurdish Patriot Ms Soraya Serajeddini (Nakshbandi)*. N.p., n.d. Web. 09 June 2014. <http://www.kncna.org/docs/htm_asp_files/In_memory_of_Soraya_Nalshbandi.htm>.
8. "KurdishMedia.com: News about Kurds and Kurdistan." *KurdishMedia.com: News about Kurds and Kurdistan*. N.p., 21 May 2014. Web. 09 June 2014. <http://www.kurdmedia.com/article.aspx?id=16943>.
9. "World Media Watch for July 21, 2006." *World Media Watch for July 21, 2006*. N.p., n.d. Web. 09 June 2014. <http://www.truth-out.org/buzzflash/commentary/world-media-watch-for-july-21-2006/67-world-media-watch-for-july-21-2006>.
10. "Decree 49 – Ethnic Cleansing of Kurds in Syria." *Support Kurds in Syria RSS*. N.p., n.d. Web. 19 May 2014. <http://supportkurds.org/reports/decree-49-ethnic-cleansing-of-kurds-in-syria/#sthash.QtQNYX6O.dpuf>.
11. "World Directory of Minorities and Indigenous Peoples." *Minority Rights Group International : Syria : Kurds*. N.p., n.d. Web. 09 June 2014. <http://www.minorityrights.org/5270/syria/kurds.html#sthash.vWU4GrD7.dpuf>.
12. "Death of Arabisation Mastermind, Mohammed Talib Hilal." *KURDISTAN COMMENTARY*. N.p., n.d. Web. 09 June 2014. <http://kurdistancommentary.

wordpress.com/2011/02/13/death-of-arabisation-mastermind-moham-med-talib-hilal/>.

13. "Death of Arabisation Mastermind, Mohammed Talib Hilal." *KURDISTAN COMMENTARY*. N.p., n.d. Web. 09 June 2014. <http://kurdistancom-mentary.wordpress.com/2011/02/13/death-of-arabisation-mastermind-mohammed-talib-hilal/>.

14. "Death of Arabisation Mastermind, Mohammed Talib Hilal." *KURDISTAN COMMENTARY*. N.p., n.d. Web. 09 June 2014. <http://kurdistancom-mentary.wordpress.com/2011/02/13/death-of-arabisation-mastermind-mohammed-talib-hilal/>.

15. "Death of Arabisation Mastermind, Mohammed Talib Hilal." *KURDISTAN COMMENTARY*. N.p., n.d. Web. 09 June 2014. <http://kurdistancom-mentary.wordpress.com/2011/02/13/death-of-arabisation-mastermind-mohammed-talib-hilal/>.

16. Ibid.

17. KurdishMedia.

18. "THE RESURRECTION OF SYRIAN KURDISH POLITICS." *GLORIA Center*. N.p., n.d. Web. 1 June 2014. <http://www.gloria-center.org/2013/12/the-ressurection-of-syrian-kurdish-politics/>.

19. Sterling, Joe. "Daraa: The Spark That Lit the Syrian Flame." *CNN*. Cable News Network, 01 Mar. 2012. Web. 30 May 2014. <http://www.cnn.com/2012/03/01/world/meast/syria-crisis-beginnings/>.

20. International Crisis Group. "The Rising Cost of Turkey's Syrian Quagmire" *The Rising Costs of Turkey's Syrian Quagmire* 230 (2014): 39. 30 Apr. 2014. Web. <http://www.crisisgroup.org/~/media/Files/europe/turkey-cyprus/turkey/230-the-rising-costs-of-turkey-s-syrian-quagmire.pdf>.

21. "Alliance for Kurdish Rights." *Alliance for Kurdish Rights*. N.p., n.d. Web. 10 June 2014. <http://kurdishrights.org/2011/04/07/syria-to-grant-citizenship-to-some-of-its-stateless-kurds/>.

22. "The Evolution of Kurdish Politics in Syria | Middle East Research and Information Project." *The Evolution of Kurdish Politics in Syria | Middle East Research and Information Project*. N.p., n.d. Web. 09 June 2014. <http://www.merip.org/mero/mero083111?ip_login_no_cache=80d496e766fff3bf997ff4cb2f9358e3>.

23. "Syria Civil War Fast Facts." *CNN*. Cable News Network, 24 Feb. 2014. Web. 08 June 2014. <http://www.cnn.com/2013/08/27/world/meast/syria-civil-war-fast-facts/>.

24. "From Rep. of Turkey Ministry of Foreign Affairs." *Republic of Turkey Ministry of Foreign Affairs*. N.p., n.d. Web. 10 June 2014. <http://www.mfa.gov.tr/turkey_s-commercial-and-economic-relations-with-syria.en.mfa>.

25. "Is the Hatay/Alexandretta Problem Solved?" *:: Daniel Pipes*. N.p., n.d. Web. 10 June 2014. <http://www.danielpipes.org/blog/2005/01/is-the-hatayalexandretta-problem-solved>.

26. "Will Assad-Erdogan Love Affair Last?" *Ynet*. N.p., 30 May 2014. Web. 09 June 2014. <http://www.ynetnews.com/articles/0%2C7340%2CL-4051380%2C00.html>.

28. Blomfield, Adrian. "Thousands of Kurds Could Awaken against Syrian Regime." *The Telegraph*. Telegraph Media Group, 09 Oct. 2011. Web.

10 June 2014. <http://www.telegraph.co.uk/news/worldnews/middleeast/syria/8816825/Thousands-of-Kurds-could-awaken-against-Syrian-regime.html>.

29. "Erdogan: Assad Is a Good Friend, but He Delayed Reform Efforts." *Today's Zaman, Your Gateway to Turkish Daily News*. N.p., 30 May 2014. Web. 09 June 2014. <http://www.todayszaman.com/news-243660-erdogan-assad-is-a-good-friend-but-he-delayed-reform-efforts.html>.

30. "Will Turkey Bring Syria and Israel Back to the Table? Doubtful." *Foreign Policy*. N.p., n.d. Web. 10 June 2014. <http://blog.foreignpolicy.com/posts/2010/10/04/will_turkey_bring_syria_and_israel_back_to_the_table_doubtful>.

31. TodaysZaman

32. "Syria in Revolt." *Home*. N.p., 22 Aug. 2014. Web. 04 Sept. 2014. <http://bostonreview.net/world/sadik-al-azm-syria-in-revolt#.U_OfcBpzZLY.twitter>.

33. "Syria in Revolt." *Home*. N.p., n.d. Web. 05 Sept. 2014. <http://bostonreview.net/world/sadik-al-azm-syria-in-revolt#.U_OfcBpzZLY.twitter>.

34. Ibid.

35. International Crisis Group. "The Rising Cost of Turkey's Syrian Quagmire" *The Rising Costs of Turkey's Syrian Quagmire* 230 (2014): 39. 30 Apr. 2014. Web. <http://www.crisisgroup.org/~/media/Files/europe/turkey-cyprus/turkey/230-the-rising-costs-of-turkey-s-syrian-quagmire.pdf>.

36. "Needs Soar as Number of Syrian Refugees Tops 3 Million." *UNHCR News*. N.p., n.d. Web. 08 Sept. 2014. <http://www.unhcr.org/53ff76c99.html>.

37. "Russia Helped Syria Shoot down Turkish Plane, UK Newspaper Claims." *The Times of Israel*. N.p., 30 May 2012. Web. 09 June 2014. <http://www.timesofisrael.com/sources-russia-helped-shoot-down-turkish-plane/#ixzz33DTUAI46>.

38. Watson, Ivan, Gul Tuysuz, Talia Kayali, Richard Roth, Joe Vaccarello, Chris Lawrence, Nick Paton Walsh, Amir Ahmed, and Saskya Vandoorne. "Turkey Strikes Targets in Syria in Retaliation for Shelling Deaths." *CNN*. Cable News Network, 01 Jan. 1970. Web. 11 June 2014. <http://www.cnn.com/2012/10/03/world/europe/turkey-syria-tension/>.

39. International Crisis Group, 1

40. International Crisis Group, 31

41. "Will Turkey Midwife Independent Kurdistan? | RealClearWorld." *Will TurkeyMidwife Independent Kurdistan? | RealClearWorld*. N.p., n.d. Web. 09 Sept. 2014. <http://www.realclearworld.com/2014/07/17/will_turkey_midwife_independent_kurdistan_160143.html>.

42. "Syria Civil War Fast Facts." *CNN*. Cable News Network, 24 Feb. 2014. Web. 08 June 2014. <http://www.cnn.com/2013/08/27/world/meast/syria-civil-war-fast-facts/>.

43. "World Directory of Minorities and Indigenous Peoples." *Minority Rights Group International : Syria : Kurds*. N.p., 21 May 2014. Web. 09 June 2014. <http://www.minorityrights.org/5270/syria/kurds.html#sthash.vWU-4GrD7.dpuf>.

44. "Ocalan, the Names of the Same Frame!" *Ocalan, the Names of the Same Frame!* N.p., n.d. Web. 10 Sept. 2014. <http://www.habermonitor.com/en/haber/detay/ocalan-the-names-of-the-same-frame/155470/>.

45. "Jihadists Seek Islamic State on Syria-Iraq Border." *The Daily Star Newspaper*. N.p., n.d. Web. 1 June 2014. <http://www.dailystar.com.lb/News/Middle-East/2014/May-21/257245-jihadists-seek-islamic-state-on-syria-iraq-border.ashx#ixzz33QaYcYB4>.

46. Ibid.

47. "Flight of Icarus? The PYD's Precarious Rise in Syria." *International Crisis Group*. N.p., 8 May 2014. Web. 09 June 2014. <http://www.crisisgroup.org/en/regions/middle-east-north-africa/egypt-syria-lebanon/syria/151-flight-of-icarus-the-pyd-s-precarious-rise-in-syria.aspx>.

48. "Sudden, Massive Influx of Syrians into Iraq's Kurdistan Region." *UNHCR News*. N.p., n.d. Web. 1 June 2014. <http://www.unhcr.org/520e158f9.html>.

49. N.p., n.d. Web. 1 June 2014. <http://www.basnews.com/en/News/Details/ISIS-issues-Fatwa-against-Kurds-in-Syria/14192>.

50. Remarks by Salih Moslem Mohamed at the European Parliament on — 2013.

51. Remarks by Salih Moslem Mohamed at the European Parliament on — 2013.

52. "Jihadists Seek Islamic State on Syria-Iraq Border." *The Daily Star Newspaper*. N.p., n.d. Web. 1 June 2014. <http://www.dailystar.com.lb/News/Middle-East/2014/May-21/257245-jihadists-seek-islamic-state-on-syria-iraq-border.ashx#ixzz33QapIz8f>.

53. Hubbard, Ben, Clifford Krauss, and Eric Schmitt. "Rebels in Syria Claim Control of Resources." *The New York Times*. The New York Times, 28 Jan. 2014. Web. 1 June 2014. <http://www.nytimes.com/2014/01/29/world/middleeast/rebels-in-syria-claim-control-of-resources.html?_r=0>.

54. Crisis Group Middle East Report.

55. Crisis Group Middle East Report, 12.

56. Remarks by Salih Moslem Mohamed at the European Parliament on — 2013.

57. "PYD's Saleh Muslim Addresses The European Parliament." N.p., n.d. Web. 24 July 2014.

58. Crisis Group Middle East Reoprt, 15.

59. Crisis Group Middle East Report, 15.

60. Crisis Group Middle East, 23.

61. Email to the author. December __, 2013.

62. "Crisis Group Middle East, 16.

63. N.p., n.d. Web. 1 June 2014. <http://en.firatnews.com/news/news/barzani-accuses-pyd-of-collaborating-with-assad-regime.htm>.

64. Crisis Group Middle East Report, 10.

65. Crisis Group Middle East Report, 11.

66. Interview with the author, Brussels, December 5, 2013.

67. "Iraqi Kurdish Leader Vows to Aid Syrian Kurds." *Iraqi Kurdish Leader Vows to Aid Syrian Kurds*. N.p., n.d. Web. 1 June 2014. <http://www.kurdnas.com/en/index.php?option=com_content&view=article&id=580:iraqi-kurdish-leader-vows-to-aid-syrian-kurds&catid=3:newsflash&Itemid=54>.

68. "Peshmerga Role Expands with Iraqi and Syrian Violence | SOFREP." *SOFREP*. N.p., n.d. Web. 1 June 2014. <http://sofrep.com/29041/peshmerga-role-expands-iraqi-syrian-violence/#ixzz33PPeAV4m>.

69. "THE RESURRECTION OF SYRIAN KURDISH POLITICS." *GLORIA Center*. N.p., n.d. Web. 1 June 2014. <http://www.gloria-center.org/2013/12/the-ressurection-of-syrian-kurdish-politics/>.

70. "International Crisis Group, 27.
71. "More than 1,400 Killed in Syrian Chemical Weapons Attack, U.S. Says." *Washington Post.* The Washington Post, n.d. Web. 11 June 2014. <http://www.washingtonpost.com/world/national-security/nearly-1500-killed-in-syrian-chemical-weapons-attack-us-says/2013/08/30/b2864662-1196-11e3-85b6-d27422650fd5_story.html>.
72. "Transcript: Secretary of State John Kerry's Remarks on Alleged Syria Chemical Attack." *Washington Post.* The Washington Post, n.d. Web. 10 June 2014. <http://www.washingtonpost.com/world/national-security/transcript-secretary-of-state-john-kerrys-remarks-on-alleged-syria-chemical-attack/2013/08/26/40b0b4ea-0e8b-11e3-bdf6-e4fc677d94a1_story.html>.
73. "Syria Civil War Fast Facts." *CNN.* Cable News Network, 24 Feb. 2014. Web. 28 May 2014. <http://www.cnn.com/2013/08/27/world/meast/syria-civil-war-fast-facts/>.
74. Ibid.
75. "Tension High on First Day of Syrian Peace Talks." *PBS.* PBS, n.d. Web. 11 June 2014. <http://www.pbs.org/newshour/extra/daily_videos/tension-high-on-first-day-of-syrian-peace-talks/>.
76. "Syrian Kurds Feel Left out of Geneva II - Al-Monitor: The Pulse of the Middle East." *Al-Monitor.* N.p., n.d. Web. 5 June 2014. <http://www.al-monitor.com/pulse/originals/2014/01/geneva-ii-kurdish-international-community.html#ixzz33n6AFEDd>.
77. "Personal Website of Mutlu Civiroglu (Mutlu ÃǂiviroÄŸlu'nun KiÅŸisel SayfasÄ±)." *Personal Website of Mutlu Civiroglu Mutlu Ivirolunun Kiisel Sayfas.* N.p., n.d. Web. 11 June 2014. <http://civiroglu.net/tag/syrian-kurdish/>.

9

The Second Iranian Revolution

The Bush administration denied collaboration with The Party for a Free Life in Kurdistan (PJAK). However, the Iranian government and Turkish media insisted that the United States was covertly supporting PJAK as part of a broader strategy to undermine the regime in Iran.[1] Unconfirmed reports indicated that the United States and Israel provided weapons and financing to PJAK, and that US Special Forces were also on the ground coordinating with PJAK. The Pentagon allegedly provided "a list of targets inside Iran of interest to the U.S."[2] Covert activities require a presidential finding or Congressional oversight. Congressmen Dennis Kucinich wrote President George W. Bush requesting information on US ties to PJAK on April 18, 2006.[3] Both the United States and PJAK denied collaboration. According to a CIA spokesman, "The CIA does not, as a rule, comment on allegations regarding covert operations."[4]

Officials at the Office of the Vice President and the Department of Defense were zealous in their efforts to undermine Iran's theocratic rulers. They envisioned the overthrow of Saddam Hussein as the first domino in regional regime change agenda. The Bush administration cooperated with groups that used violence to advance their political goal and had committed crimes against the United States. These include Jundallah, a radical Sunni Baluchi group with links to al-Qaeda, which was listed as a Foreign Terrorist Organization (FTO) in 2010.[5] The Bush administration also engaged the People's Mujahedin of Iran (MEK), which provided secrets about Iran's nuclear program and organized attacks on Iranian facilities.[6] It is Iran's "largest and most militant group led by Massoud and Maryam Rajavi."[7] The MEK started as a radical student group which was used strategically by Ayatollah Khomeini against Pahlavi Shah, seizing hostages during the 1979 takeover of the US Embassy in Tehran. It was listed as an FTO in 1997.

In contrast, PJAK was never involved in attacks against US interests. Its armed struggle was focused on replacing Iran's theocracy with a "democratic and federal government," where "self-rule is granted to all ethnic minorities of Iran, including Ahwazi, Arabs, Azeris, Baluchis, and Kurds."[8] Clustered in Iran's border regions, non-Persian ethnic groups constitute about 40–50 percent of Iran's total population.[9]

Haji Ahmadi, PJAK's leader, visited Washington in August 2007. He sought meetings with US officials to propose security cooperation, including weapons supplies.[10] Ankara was incensed that Ahmadi was given a visa and lodged a formal diplomatic complaint. The United States tried to placate Turkey, its staunch ally and NATO member. After Haji Ahmadi's visit, PJAK accused the United States of providing Turkey and Iran with intelligence to support cross-border attacks against the PKK and PJAK in Qandil.[11] Commander of Turkish Land Forces General Ilker Basbug acknowledged that Turkey and Iran were coordinating strikes against PJAK. Their collaborative military action included airstrikes, cross-border artillery attacks, and an eight-day ground offensive in February 2008.[12]

Soon after President Barack Obama's inauguration in January 2009, the US Department of State formally listed PJAK as an FTO. The FTO listing put a freeze on PJAK's assets in the United States and barred US citizens from commercial contact with the organization. It was a symbolic move with little impact on PJAK. Listing PJAK as an FTO was intended to assuage Ankara's concerns. Nonetheless, charges of cooperation continued to swirl. In August 2011, Pentagon representatives allegedly met PJAK commanders in Iraqi Kurdistan to discuss military assistance.[13]

*****

Bush included Iran in the "axis of evil" during his State of the Union Address on January 29, 2002. "Prevent[ing] regimes that sponsor terror from threatening America or our friends and allies with weapons of mass destruction" emerged as the defining goal of his administration. Bush maintained, "Iran aggressively pursues these weapons and exports terror, while an unelected few repress the Iranian people's hope for freedom." He continued:

> States like these, and their terrorist allies, constitute an axis of evil, arming to threaten the peace of the world. By seeking weapons of mass destruction, these regimes pose a grave and growing danger.

They could provide these arms to terrorists, giving them the means to match their hatred. They could attack our allies or attempt to blackmail the United States. In any of these cases, the price of indifference would be catastrophic.[14]

Moderate Iranian officials felt betrayed. After the US invasion of Iraq in 2003, Iranians felt encircled by US troops in Iraq, Afghanistan, Pakistan, Kyrgyzstan, and Georgia.

The Iranian government's insecurity manifested as a campaign against internal dissent, NGOs, and PJAK. Iran and Turkey formalized a strategic alliance to combat terrorism during a visit to Tehran by Prime Minister Recep Tayyip Erdogan on July 27, 2004. As part of the deal, the Iranian Government declared Kongra-Gel[15] a terrorist organization.[16] Iranian armed forces launched an offensive against PJAK in the Sardasht region in July 2004. Clashes continued through 2005, with cross-border operations against PJAK and the PKK in Iraqi Kurdistan and Turkey.[17]

Iran's focus on a military solution to Kurdish issues intensified after the murder of Shivana Qaderi, a Kurdish human rights activist, by police in July 9, 2005, in Mahabad. Roj TV alleged that after Qaderi was shot, "Iranian soldiers tied [his] body to a military vehicle and dragged it through the city in a clear attempt to intimidate the population and deter further protests."[18] Demonstrations engulfed Kurdish towns such as Mahabad, Sanandaj, Sardasht, Piranshahr, Oshanavieh, Baneh, Bokan, and Saquiz during the summer of 2005. Protestors were brutally suppressed by Iranian police forces. They faced arbitrary arrest, torture, and murder.[19] Freedom of expression was under siege; Kurdish newspapers were closed, reporters and editors arrested.[20] Freedom of association suffered from a systematic crackdown on NGOs and civil society organizations. Cultural freedom was denied. Kurdish activists, writers, and teachers were arrested and sentenced to death.

The Majlis, Iran's parliament, set up an investigative committee to consider the security threat posed by Kurds. The Majlis attributed the high level of support for PJAK to disparities in economic development between Iranian Kurdistan and Kurdish-populated regions of Iraq and Turkey.[21] Instead of acting on the commission's findings, however, the Iranian government neglected Kurdish demands for increased investment, local resource ownership, and cultural rights. A 2008 Amnesty International report noted a pattern of discrimination. It accused the Iranian government of targeting the Kurds and found that "social, political, and cultural rights have been repressed, as have their economic aspirations."[22]

The abuse of political prisoners was a recruitment bonanza for PJAK. Kurds were incensed by the number of executions, which increased steadily after Mahmoud Ahmadinejad's election in 2005. Iran executed at least 94 people in 2005, 117 in 2006, 317 in 2007, and up to 370 in 2008."[23] For example, Mohammad Seddigh Kaboudvand was imprisoned in Tehran's notorious Evin Prison for establishing and serving as secretary of the Human Rights Organization of Kurdistan along with publishing *Payam-e Mardom,* a journal popular amongst Kurds.[24] He encouraged Kurds to boycott the presidential election of 2005 and was denied contact with his terminally ill son. Kaboudvand was convicted of "acting against the national security" and executed. Ehsan Fattahian, a Komala member, was convicted of transporting arms for an "illegal organization," sentenced to death for "enmity towards God," and hung in 2009.[25] Fasih Yasamani was tortured by authorities who tried to extract his confession in January 2010.[26] Farzad Kamangar, Ali Heydarian, Farhad Vakili, Mehdi Eslamian, and Shirin Alam Hooli were tortured, forced to confess their membership in PJAK, and executed in May 2010.[27]

Military operations intensified during the period before Iran's national elections in 2009, targeting both the PKK and PJAK's military wing, the East Kurdistan Defense Forces (HRK). Tehran demanded that the Kurdistan Regional Government of Iraq (KRG) impose restrictions on the HRK. Indiscriminate artillery shelling killed many civilians in Iraq and Iran. The crackdown increased support for the HRK, which grew to three thousand fighters with recruits from Iran, Turkey, Iraq, and Syria. About half of HRK's members were women, including members of the East Kurdistan Women's Union.[28] They had a reputation as the HRK's cruelest and fiercest fighters.

The Iranian Revolutionary Guard Corps (IRGC) launched a major ground offensive against HRK in response to its sabotage of oil pipelines. On August 16, 2011, five thousand IRGC poured across the border of Northwest Iran into Iraqi Kurdistan in hot pursuit of HRK fighters.[29] On September 5, 2011, "PJAK offered a unilateral cease-fire in response to Iran's increased efforts . . . displacing over a thousand Kurdish families."[30] Iran rejected the ceasefire, intensifying the attacks. PJAK's headquarters in the Jasosan heights fell after intense fighting, which killed 180 HRK members and wounded 300. According to Komala's leader, Abdullah Muhtadi: "If future governments in Iran are going to be hostile like the one today, then we will have no choice but to fight and shed blood until the end of the world."[31]

*****

Mahmound Ahmadinejad was President of Iran from 2005 to 2013. His repressive rule contrasted with the more moderate approach of his predecessor, Mohammad Khatami, who served from 1997 to 2005. Khatami spoke Kurdish. He appointed Abdollah Ramezanzadeh as the first Shia Kurdish governor of the Iranian Province of Kurdistan. Khatami's cabinet was relatively diverse, including both Shias and Sunnis. He also had Kurdish advisors. Khatami worked cooperatively with Kurds, permitting a Kurdish Caucus of twenty-one members in the parliament.

Many Kurds were disaffected by Khatami's poetic yet unfulfilled promises. They resented Ahmadinejad's discriminatory governance. Mir Hussein Mousavi and Mehdi Karroubi, leaders of the so-called reform movement, promised greater cultural rights for Iran's ethnic minorities as part of their campaign platforms in 2009. However, Kurds stayed away from the polls. While some Kurds joined the Green Movement, a pro-democracy youth movement, most stood on the sidelines. The Green Movement failed to articulate a strategy for addressing the aspirations of national minorities. Kurds did not join pro-democracy advocates who took to the streets protesting electoral fraud.

Kurds were similarly restrained in their support for Hassan Rouhani during presidential elections of June 2013. Like his predecessors, Rouhani pledged greater cultural rights for Kurds. However, Kurdish political leaders, such as Abdullah Muhtadi, were skeptical. He believed that Iranians voted for Rouhani because there was no better option.[32] According to Muhtadi, "Rouhani has never been a reformist, and he has never claimed to be one—never. What he claims to be is moderate. I'm sure Khamenei will oppose any serious and real change because he's not for a genuine rapprochement with the West—he thinks democratic values are corrupt Western values." He continued,

> We're for a democratic, secular, and federal Iran. We strongly believe in the separation between state and religion, and we are also for a system where every ethnic group—Kurds, Azerbaijanis, Baluchis— can have self-rule, governing their local and regional affairs through elected bodies. We believe in the importance of social, political, and

civil movements in a broad coalition to bring about powerful change in Iran for labor, women's and students' movements, and ethnic minorities. What we ask and fight for is a democratic Iran, where the rights and lives of Kurds and other minorities are respected by the constitution.[33]

Rouhani tried to send conciliatory signals. He downplayed Iranian nationalism, which both the Shah and the Ayatollah used to oppress minorities. Rouhani's platform pledged to empower local government and alluded to greater minority rights. Nonetheless, Khalid Azizi, secretary-general of the Kurdistan Democratic Party of Iran (KDPI), believed that, "The elections taking place will do little to improve Kurds' lot. I have not seen an agenda from the presidential candidates regarding the case of Kurdish people in Iran." He reflected on the limits of democracy given the vise grip on power of Iran's theocratic rulers. "It's not easy for a president to maneuver while the velayat-e faqih [guardianship of the jurist] will not allow him to practice his belief."[34] Azizi's doubts were well founded. No Kurd was appointed to Rouhani's cabinet. Instead of appointing a Sunni Kurd as governor or Iranian Kurdistan, he chose a Shiite. Rouhani maintained that no Sunni Kurd was as qualified.[35]

Executions of Kurdish political leaders continued after Rouhani assumed the presidency. Habibollah Golparipour and Shirko Moarefi were hanged in late 2013.[36] The government also continued its crackdown on NGOs. Since it is illegal to join a Kurdish political group, Kurds flocked to civil society organizations as a front for political mobilization. These too were suppressed.

*****

Divisions between Kurdish factions undermined their effectiveness. Komala had many historical divisions. Komala JK evolved into KDPI, and in 1988 a KDPI splinter group created KDPI: The Revolutionary Leadership. The two factions reunited in 1996. Again in 2006, a KDPI faction created the Kurdish Democratic Party (KDP). These groups share a similar goal—to establish a federal, democratic republic in Iran. However, personality conflicts and power struggles kept Iranian Kurds from cooperating.

In July 2013, Komala convened its fourteenth congress under the slogan of "unity and persistence."[37] KRG President Masoud Barzani invited thirty-nine Iranian Kurds to a reconciliation conference in Erbil on July 25, 2013. Building on the reconciliation process that Barzani set in motion, Komala, KDPI, and three other leading groups came together after a decade of bitter divisions to develop a common agenda for the Kurdish cause.[38] They also sought to establish coalitions with other ethnic groups and minorities in Iran. According to Muhtadi, Kurds are strengthened by working with Baluchis, Arabs, and Azeris. "It is true they are all Iranians, but a future Iran will not be democratic nor can it stay united if it doesn't grant its minorities their rights."[39]

PJAK jumped on the bandwagon of Kurdish unity. Its representative, Rezan Jawid, addressed an audience celebrating the organization's ten-year anniversary in Qandil: "The time has come for the Iranian Kurdish parties to meet and discuss solutions." Other Kurdish parties resented PJAK's presumption of leadership. They rejected PJAK's right to speak on their behalf. According to the KDPI, "Such a message shouldn't come from a group like PJAK. The Iranian Kurdish parties have been discussing this matter."[40]

There was context to tensions between PJAK and other Kurdish parties. In December 2012, PJAK accused rival Kurdish groups of fingering their membership to the security services and identifying the location of its military bases. PJAK was resented because of its popularity. Unlike other political parties, PJAK engaged and defeated the IRGC on the battlefield in 2011. According to Reza Mohammad Ismail, Mayor of Penjwin, a Kurdish area in Iraq near the Iranian border, PJAK is the only organization with the capabilities to engage in armed struggle and defend Kurdish rights.[41] Most Kurdish or political prisoners captured or murdered by the Iranian regime were from PJAK. PJAK was an active participant in the KCK, contacting Kurds at the grassroots. PJAK's support was especially strong in Shiite areas such as Kermanshah, Illam, and Lorenstan. PJAK also appealed to Kurdish youth who viewed Komala and DPKI as older and more traditional parties, which were ineffective advancing Kurdish interests.[42]

*****

Qassim Suleimani is commander of the Quds Force and major general of the IRGC, its highest rank. His portfolio includes Iraq, Syria, Afghanistan, Gaza, and Lebanon including liaison with

Hezbollah.[43] Suleimani is a hero and fixer of hotspots. He defended Iran against Iraq in the 1980s and confronted Afghan drug cartels on Iran's border in the 1990s. His tactical and operational assistance helped rescue the regime of Syrian President Bashar al-Assad from collapse in 2013. Under Suleimani's direction, the Quds Force orchestrated the deployment of Hezbollah fighters to Syria. Qassim Suleimani worked with Hezbollah to retake Qusayr from Syrian rebels, which divided their lines and turned the tide of battle in Assad's favor.[44]

Suleimani was also the point man expanding Tehran's influence over Iraq's internal affairs and mobilizing Shiite militia attacks against US forces. He arranged the delivery of rocket-assisted mortars and high penetration projectile improvised explosive devices that were used to kill Americans. He boasted, "I don't always kill people but when I do it's American soldiers in Iraq."[45]

Suleimani's actions helped drive US troops from Iraq. Tehran also scuttled negotiations over a Status of Forces Agreement that would have kept a residual US force in country to train the Iraqi Army and assist with counterterrorism operations.[46] Suleimani both foments and resolves crisis, keeping Iraq in a constant state of uncertainty, requiring Iran's assistance and his personal goodwill. Iran effectively turned Iraq into a vassal state.

Iran's core interests in Iraq are protecting Shiite sacred shrines in Samarra, Karbala, and Najaf. Iraq's Shiite militias are proxies for geopolitical confrontation between Saudi Arabia and Iran for regional influence. Iran also wants to preserve the corridor along the Shiite crescent to Beirut. The corridor is a critical supply route for weapons used to supply Hezbollah and Palestinian militants fighting for Israel's destruction.

Suleimani is no stranger to US officials. Ambassador Ryan C. Crocker met an Iranian delegation appointed by Suleimani in Geneva right after 9/11 to explore US-Iran cooperation against the Taliban in Afghanistan. In 2009, Ambassador Christopher R. Hill and General Raymond T. Odierno, the top civilian and military representatives in Iraq, met Suleimani.[47] Hill and Odierno denied the meeting. General David Petraeus, through intermediaries, had his own back-channel interactions with Suleimani. The US government considers Suleimani a terrorist for plotting to kill Saudi Arabia's ambassador to the United States.[48] Petraeus called him "a truly evil figure."[49]

In June 2014, Sunni jihadis from the Islamic State of Iraq and Syria (ISIS) poured across the Syrian border and routed the Iraqi army in Mosul, Iraq's second-largest city. ISIS raced across the desert, encountering little resistance in the Sunni heartland. They attacked Baquba, just twenty-five kilometers from Baghdad.[50] ISIS also advanced to the outskirts of Samarra, the site of the Great Golden Dome Mosque, one of Shia Islam's holiest shrines.[51]

The Iranian government reacted quickly to ISIS operations. Suleimani rushed to Baghdad to advise the Iraqi government on deterring ISIS. The day after he arrived, Ayatollah Ali al-Sistani issued a fatwa calling on Shiites to defend the country. Volunteers numbering in the tens of thousands rushed to the front line, including battle-hardened militias who had fought in Iraq's sectarian civil war.[52]

The Obama administration emphasized a political solution to the crisis, calling on Iraq's sectarian and ethnic groups to reconcile and share power. However, the US had scant influence over Prime Minister Nouri al-Maliki. Iraq has no tradition of reconciliation; Iraqis were at loggerheads for ten months after national elections in 2010. The impasse over government formation finally ended when Masoud Barzani mediated the Erbil Agreement.[53] The deal looked good on paper, but power sharing was never implemented in practice. Maliki went out of his way to antagonize other groups. He arrested Arab Sunni politicians and contested territories in Iraqi Kurdistan, including Khanaqin near oil-rich Kirkuk.[54]

The United States and Iran share an interest in deterring ISIS. Deputy Secretary of State William J. Burns attended P5+1 talks in Vienna on Iran's nuclear program. On the morning of the meeting, he met foreign Minister Javad Zarif on the margins to explore US-Iran cooperation stabilizing Iraq. According to Secretary of State John Kerry, "We're open to discussions if there is something constructive that can be contributed by Iran, if Iran is prepared to do something that is going to respect the integrity and sovereignty of Iraq and ability of the government to reform." Rear Admiral John Kirby, Pentagon press secretary and spokesman for Secretary of Defense Chuck Hagel, countered: "There is absolutely no intention and no plan to coordinate military activity between the United States and . . . Iran." Israel was concerned that the P5+1 would adopt a softer stance toward Iran's nuclear program in exchange for cooperation on Iraq.[55]

The State Department insisted that possible talks with Iran over Iraq would exclude military cooperation. However, members of the US Congress dismissed any idea of working with Iran. Senator John McCain called it the "height of folly." He added,

> This is the same Iranian regime that has trained and armed the most dangerous Shia militant groups, that has consistently urged Prime Minister Maliki to pursue a narrow sectarian agenda at the expense of national reconciliation, that supplies the rockets that have been fired at the US embassy in Baghdad, that has sponsored acts of terrorism throughout the Middle East and the world."[56]

Other US officials raised concern that US cooperation with Iran would radicalize the Arab Sunnis who participated in the Awakening Councils that fought al-Qaeda during the surge of 2007. Speaker John Boehner warned, "I can just imagine what our friends in the region, our allies, will be thinking by reaching out to Iran at a time when they continue to pay for terrorists and foster terrorism, not only in Syria and in Lebanon but in Israel as well."[57]

Maliki formally requested US air support against ISIS forces. He also invited the Quds Force to join the battle.[58] To counter Iran's influence, the US offered to expand surveillance and intelligence activities. It sent three hundred military advisers to Iraq. The aircraft carrier George H. W. Bush, sailed to the Persian Gulf.[59] During a press conference on June 19, 2014, Obama announced the possibility of targeted drone air strikes. Obama was a reluctant warrior. He ran on an antiwar platform, promising to withdraw troops from Iraq.

Notes

1. "Has the U.S. Played a Role in Fomenting Unrest During Iran's Election? - Foreign Policy Journal." *Foreign Policy Journal*. N.p., n.d. Web. 07 July 2014.
2. Hersh, Seymour M. (November 20, 2006). "The Next Act". The New Yorker. Retrieved 2006-11-19.
3. Letter from Congressman Dennis Kucinich to President Gorge W. Bush, April 18, 2006.
4. "U.S. Is Said to Expand Covert Operations in Iran." *Washington Post*. The Washington Post, 30 June 2008. Web. 20 June 2014. <http://www.washingtonpost.com/wp-dyn/content/article/2008/06/29/AR2008062901881.html>.
5. Ibid.
6. "ABC News Exclusive: The Secret War Against Iran." *ABC News*. ABC News Network, 03 Apr. 2007. Web. 07 July 2014.
7. Ibid.

8.   "Terrorism Monitor | The Jamestown Foundation." *Terrorism Monitor | The Jamestown Foundation*. N.p., n.d. Web. 20 June 2014. <http://www.jamestown.org/tm/?articleid=2370030>.
9.   "Nomads in Iran." *Nomads in Iran*. N.p., n.d. Web. 07 July 2014.
10. "Kurdish leader seeks U.S. help to topple regime." The Washington Times.
11. Statement issued October 18, 2008.
12. "Turkey and Iran Unite to Attack Kurdish Rebels." *The New York Times*. The New York Times, 05 June 2008. Web. 16 June 2014. <http://www.nytimes.com/2008/06/06/world/europe/06kurdish.html?ref=world&_r=0>.
13. PressTV, 10 August 2011.
14. "President Delivers State of the Union Address." *President Delivers State of the Union Address*. N.p., n.d. Web. 21 June 2014. <http://georgewbush-whitehouse.archives.gov/news/releases/2002/01/20020129-11.html>.
15. The Turkish Government considers the PKK to have been succeeded by KGK in 2003 though these Kurdish factions, themselves, do not partition these groups similarly and still acknowledge a PKK. This text will continue to adopt the acroynms "PKK" and "KGK" in discussions after 2003.
16. "Kongra-Gel (KGK) - Terrorist Groups." *Kongra-Gel (KGK) - Terrorist Groups*. N.p., n.d. Web. 07 July 2014.
17. "Iran's Kurdish Threat: PJAK." *The Jamestown Foundation*. N.p., n.d. Web. 07 July 2014.
18. "Shivan Qaderi | Online References | Cyclopaedia.net." *Shivan Qaderi | Online References | Cyclopaedia.net*. N.p., n.d. Web. 07 July 2014.
19. Ibid.
20. Ibid.
21. "IRAN." *Operational Guidance Note* 26 (2007): 1–26. Asylum and Appeals Policy Directorate, 27 Feb. 2007. Web. 7 July 2014.
22. "Gallery - Kurds in Iran." *Gallery - Kurds in Iran*. N.p., n.d. Web. 20 June 2014. <http://www.lightrocket.com/galleries/2983/kurds-in-iran>.
23. "Unrepresented Nations and Peoples Organization." *UNPO: Iranian Kurdistan*. N.p., n.d. Web. 05 June 2014. <http://www.unpo.org/members/7882>.
24. "Mohammad Sadiq Kaboudvand To Resume Hunger Strike." *International Campaign for Human Rights in Iran*. N.p., n.d. Web. 07 July 2014.
25. "Iran: COI Compliation." *Austrian Red Cross Accord* 10.4 (2013): 101. The European Refugee Fund, UNHCR and the Ministry of the Interior, Austria., Sept. 2013. Web.
26. "Iran Executes Kurdish PJAK Member Fasih Yasamani without Any Trial or Legal Formalities." *Iran Executes Kurdish PJAK Member Fasih Yasamani without Any Trial or Legal Formalities*. N.p., n.d. Web. 07 July 2014.
27. "News." *Iran Executes Five Political Prisoners*. N.p., n.d. Web. 07 July 2014.
28. "PJAK." - *Encyclopine*. N.p., n.d. Web. 07 July 2014.
29. "Iranian Repression of Kurds Behind Rise of Militant PJAK." *Rudaw*. N.p., n.d. Web. 03 June 2014. <http://rudaw.net/english/middleeast/iran/23012014>.
30. "Kurdish PJAK Rebels Deny Iranian Military Success." *Kurdish PJAK Rebels Deny Iranian Military Success*. N.p., n.d. Web. 07 July 2014.
31. "Five Kurdish Groups in Iran Working for United Front, Komala Leader Says." Rudaw. October 26, 2013.

32. "Five Kurdish Groups in Iran Working for United Front, Komala Leader Says." *Rudaw.* N.p., n.d. Web. 8 June 2014. <http://rudaw.net/english/middleeast/iran/26102013>.

33. N.p., n.d. Web. 8 June 2014. <http://www.ekurd.net/mismas/articles/misc2013/6/irankurd943.htm%20%28Accessed%20June%208%2C%202014%29.>.

34. Ibid.

35. "Kurdpress News Aganecy - I'm a Kurd, No Difference among Iranian Races: Interior Minister." *Kurdpress News Aganecy - I'm a Kurd, No Difference among Iranian Races: Interior Minister.* N.p., n.d. Web. 05 June 2014. <http://www.kurdpress.com/En/NSite/FullStory/News/?Id=6093#Title=I%19m%20a%20Kurd,%20no%20difference%20among%20Iranian%20races:%20interior%20minister>.

36. "Iran: Kurds Tortured, HangedZainab Jalaian and Mansur Arvand." *Iran: Kurds Tortured, Hanged: Zainab Jalaian and Mansur Arvand.* N.p., n.d. Web. 05 June 2014. <http://www.gatestoneinstitute.org/4213/iran-kurds-tortured-hanged>.

37. "Komala Party and Its 14th Congress." *Komala Party and Its 14th Congress.* N.p., n.d. Web. 08 July 2014.

38. Ibid.

39. Statement by Komala leader Abdullah Mohtadi. June 29, 2013.

40. "Iranian Kurdish Parties Say Talks with Iran Must Be Open and Direct." *Iranian Kurdish Parties Say Talks with Iran Must Be Open and Direct.* N.p., n.d. Web. 8 June 2014. <http://www.ekurd.net/mismas/articles/misc2013/2/irankurd918.htm>.

41. Ibid.

42. "Iranian Kurdish Group Shifts Policy, Seeking Democratic Autonomy." *Rudaw.* N.p., n.d. Web. 05 June 2014. <http://rudaw.net/english/middleeast/iran/06052014>.

43. "Dexter Filkins: Qassem Suleimani, the Middle East's Most Powerful Operative." *The New Yorker.* N.p., n.d. Web. 08 July 2014.

44. Filkins, Dexter (30 September 2013). "The Shadow Commander". *The New Yorker.*

45. Lee Smith. June 23, 2014. Vol. 19, No. 40.

46. "McClatchy DC." *Unofficial Translation of U.S.-Iraq Troop Agreement from the Arabic Text.* N.p., n.d. Web. 08 July 2014.

47. Iraq and its neighbours: A regional cockpit *The Economist.*

48. Designation of Iranian Entities and Individuals for Proliferation Activities and Support for Terrorism". United States Department of State. 25 October 2007 (Accessed June 19, 2014).

49. Michael R. Gordon. "Iran's Master of Iraq Chaos Still Vexes U.S." The New York Times. October 2, 2012.
http://www.nytimes.com/2012/10/03/world/middleeast/qassim-suleimani-irans-master-of-iraq-chaos-still-vexes-the-us.html?pagewanted=all&_r=0 (Accessed June 19, 2014).

50. "Iraq Rebels Battle for Baquba City." - *Middle East.* N.p., n.d. Web. 08 July 2014.

51. "ISIS Blow Up 'Heretical' Shia Mosques In Mosul." *The Huffington Post UK*. N.p., n.d. Web. 08 July 2014.

52. "Iraq Shia Cleric Issues Call to Arms." *BBC News*. N.p., n.d. Web. 08 July 2014.

53. Erbil, 7. November 2010. *Erbil Agreement* (n.d.): n. pag. Web.

54. "IRAQ." *CORI Country of Origin Research and Information* (2012): 1–15. *Refworld*. 5 Oct. 2012. Web. 8 July 2014.

55. Ybarra, Maggie. "Pentagon, State Dept. at Odds over Coordinating with Iran on Iraq Crisis." *Washington Times*. The Washington Times, 16 June 2014. Web. 19 June 2014. <http://www.washingtontimes.com/news/2014/jun/16/pentagon-state-dept-odds-over-coordinating-iran-ir/#ixzz355rzMAnE>.

56. *The Independent*. Independent Digital News and Media, n.d. Web. 20 June 2014. <http://www.independent.co.uk/news/world/middle-east/iraq-crisis-prompts-reconciliation-between-iran-and-the-western-powers-it-used-to-vilify-9541891.html>.

57. Parkinson, John. "Boehner Says Obama Should 'Absolutely Not' Coordinate With Iran On Iraq Crisis." *ABC News*. ABC News Network, 18 June 2014. Web. 21 June 2014. <http://abcnews.go.com/Politics/boehner-obama-absolutely-coordinate-iran-iraq-crisis/story?id=24193518>.

58. Mark Mazzati and Michael R. Gordon. "Beleaguered Iraqis Court Mastermind of the Shiites Who Fought the U.S." The New York Times. June 14, 2014. Pg. A9

59. *The Independent*. Independent Digital News and Media, n.d. Web. 08 July 2014.

Part Four

Peril and Opportunity

10

The End of Iraq

Everything changed after the Islamic State in Iraq and Syria (ISIS) overran Mosul and declared a caliphate with jurisdiction over Muslims worldwide. As the conflict in Syria and Iraq converged, ISIS created facts on the ground, all but annulling borders established by the Sykes-Picot Agreement and postwar mandates. The ISIS terror state stretched from Baghdad's outskirts through Anbar, to Aleppo in Syria.[1]

*****

ISIS took Mosul, Iraq's second-largest city, on June 10, 2014. The Iraqi army completely collapsed.[2] Nearly 30,000 soldiers deserted in Mosul.[3] Governance and security structures disintegrated, as terrified police officers removed their uniforms and tried to blend into the local population. The armed forces showed scant resistance or resolve to retake territory by force. A quarter of army brigades in Iraq were determined "combat ineffective."[4]

After Mosul, Tikrit, and Tal Afar fell in rapid succession.[5] ISIS seized the Baiji power plant that supplies electricity to the provinces of Baghdad, Salahuddin, and Kirkuk, Iraq's largest oil refinery, and advanced on a major dam near Haditha where many oil pipelines intersect. It secured border crossings between Iraq and Syria[6] and between Iraq and Jordan.[7] ISIS forces made their way down the Tigris River Valley to the outskirts of Samarra, seventy kilometers from Baghdad, and to Baquba, twenty-five kilometers from the capital.[8]

ISIS fundamentally changed the political geography in Iraq. As a result of battlefield victories by ISIS, Iraqi Kurdistan shared a one-thousand-kilometer border with the so-called Islamic State. Its forces cut off Iraqi Kurdistan from Shiite-majority parts of Iraq.[9] ISIS demonstrated remarkable command and control, strategic and tactical capabilities, and an ability to fight on many fronts—Iraq, Syria, and

Lebanon—and against multiple adversaries: Shiites, Alawites, Kurds, Christians, and other Sunni jihadi groups.

ISIS was growing daily, rolling up territory and attracting recruits using social media to highlight its brutal tactics. The ranks of 10,000 ISIS fighters were augmented by 2,500 jihadis freed from local jails.[10] It was also joined by opponents of the Shiite-led government—Sunni Baathists with ties to the Saddam regime and fighters affiliated with local tribal sheikhs. By September, the CIA estimated that ISIS ranks had swelled to 31,500.[11]

As ISIS advanced, its arsenal was augmented by sophisticated weaponry abandoned by the Iraqi armed forces. ISIS seized equipment including tanks, Humvees, artillery, and howitzers. Weaponry was state of the art, made in the USA. The United States spent $25 billion between 2005 and 2012 to equip and train the Iraqi armed forces.[12]

ISIS was suddenly flush with weapons, fighters, and cash. Seed funding for ISIS came from Saudi Arabia and other wealthy emirates. ISIS expanded its revenue by operating like a criminal gang. It raised funds through extortion and kidnapping. Additional revenue was derived by selling oil from wells in Raqaa and Jazeera to the Syrian government. ISIS also robbed banks, seizing at least $425 million from the central bank in Mosul and untold millions from other banks in Nineveh.[13]

Brutal tactics terrorized Iraqis living under the control of ISIS. Sharia law was imposed on the local population. Abu Bakr al-Baghdadi declared a caliphate with himself at the head. Anyone who resisted the Islamic State was executed. Its Taliban-like list of rules included a ban on cigarettes and alcohol. Sexual violence was widespread. Local women were allocated to ISIS fighters as "jihadi brides." Christians in Mosul were told to convert, pay a tax, or face death. ISIS was so extreme it broke from al-Qaeda, which it accused of being too moderate.[14]

Sunnis in Iraq initially welcomed ISIS. Excluded by the government of Prime Minister Nouri Al-Maliki, they turned to ISIS for emancipation. But differences gradually emerged between ISIS and Iraq's Sunnis. Former Baathists and local Sunni militants resented outsiders seizing control. According to cleric Khaled al-Mulla, ISIS "killed and displaced hundreds of thousands of other Sunnis in Iraq."[15] Over three hundred Sunni imams and clerics were killed over their different interpretation of Islam. Non-Salafists, including Wahhabis, were considered apostates and killed.

*****

Peshmerga moved quickly to strengthen control of Iraqi Kurdistan's borders when ISIS invaded. Within days of Mosul's fall, peshmerga took Kirkuk and consolidated control in Khanaqin and parts of Diyala.[16] They seized an airbase in Kirkuk that was abandoned by the Iraqi armed forces, as well as the Al-Kasik military base between Mosul and Tal Afar. They took cities in Diyala, consolidating control over disputed internal boundaries. They also occupied the Rabia border crossing on the Tigris River.[17] Taking Tuz Khurmatu allowed peshmerga to create a security belt from Dohuk south to the Sinjar Mountains and east to Tal Afar. Iraqi Kurdistan expanded to include territory from the border with Syria in the West to its border with Iran in the East.

US forces, Iraqi troops, and peshmerga jointly patrolled territories in Nineveh and Diyala provinces until 2011. Only peshmerga remained after Iraqi armed forces fled in June 2014. Kirkuk was the most important acquisition. Taking Kirkuk preempted implementation of Article 140 in the constitution, which promised a referendum on Kirkuk's status. Maliki protested. He maintained that taking Kirkuk violated an agreement between Baghdad and the KRG. Peshmerga in Saadiya, south of Kirkuk, were attacked by an Iraqi helicopter gunship on June 14. Six peshmerga were killed and twenty-five wounded. Though Baghdad claimed it was an accident, the friendly-fire incident deepened mistrust between Baghdad and the KRG.[18]

Masoud Barzani did not want to take sides in the civil war between Sunnis and Shiites. An ISIS courier conveyed a message to the KRG: "If you don't attack us, we would not attack you."[19] ISIS offered the Kurds a truce on June 14, 2014.[20] When Islamic State fighters stalled outside Samarra, they pivoted to attack Kurds in the Syrian cities of Kobane and Hasakah, and then attacked Sinjar in Iraqi Kurdistan on August 3, 2014.

Yazidis, an ethnic and religious minority who follow an ancient religion with links to Zoroastrianism, fled Sinjar, Zumar, and Jawhar Ali Begg. Yazidi prisoners were ordered to convert to Islam, pay a huge tax, or face death. Islamic fighters killed Yazidi men, keeping their women for jihadi marriage. About two hundred thousand Yazidis were displaced, many heading to Erbil. Up to fifty thousand climbed to Mount Sinjar, seeking sanctuary from Islamic State fighters.[21]

The International Rescue Committee, a leading international humanitarian agency, issued a situation report on August 11:

> Since June 6, fighting between armed opposition groups, including Islamic State (IS), and Iraqi forces have led to a rapid deterioration of

the security situation throughout much of Iraq. Within the two months following, an estimated 850,000 women, men and children have fled their homes. Waves of violence continue to crash through Iraqi cities and towns as the IS attempts to solidify its stronghold on key areas. On 3 August, IS launched a new offensive, capturing three additional Iraqi towns—Sinjar, Zummar, and Wana—all in Ninewa governorate. . . . Following heavy fighting in Sinjar on 3 August, up to 200,000 people (mainly of the Yazidi minority) ran for their lives. An estimated 35,000 to 50,000 people—those without immediate access to transportation—fled north into the mountains that cradle the city. They became trapped when IS took control of the two access roads. Many thousands of women, men and children currently remain besieged in the mountains. . . . Beyond threats of violence, there are very real threats of dehydration and heat stroke that have led to the deaths of multiple children. The distance between Sinjar and Yarubia, the border crossing into Syria, is approximately 60 km. Some people have been driven but others have crossed this distance on foot. Some have stayed in Syria; the remainder has fled back across the border into the Kurdistan region of Iraq, mainly Duhok.

The People's Protection Units (YPG) of the Democratic Union Party (PYD) and PKK fighters opened a humanitarian corridor from Mount Sinjar, through Rojava to KRG-controlled towns of Dohuk and Zakho. The YPG and PKK escorted more than ten thousand Yazidis off the mountain. Their extensive experience with guerrilla warfare and solid discipline helped blunt ISIS. The YPG is battle hardened from fighting Syria's armed forces and Sunni extremists in Kobani and Hasakah for more than a year. It engaged Islamic State fighters in Shengal, a triangle of territory on the border of Iraq, Turkey, and Syria, with about 1,500 fighters. The Islamic State tried to impose a cordon around Shengal, but the YPG broke their lines in Rabiya.

The KRG tried to absorb as many displaced persons as possible, but it was overwhelmed by the sheer number of displaced. A cordon was established twenty kilometers around Erbil to manage the population flow. Single men and those who could not prove they had family in Iraqi Kurdistan were turned away. The KRG was already struggling to assist many Syrian refugees at the Domiz camp in Dohuk.[22]

No one expected Islamic State fighters to sweep across Iraqi Kurdistan and vanquish the vaunted Kurdish peshmerga. ISIS was a foreign army with no stake in Iraq other than destroying the country, redrawing colonial borders, and reversing a century of Arab humiliation by foreign powers. Islamic State fighters occupied Makhmour, just thirty kilometers from Erbil, and were on the verge of overrunning the capital of Iraqi Kurdistan.

*****

US officials had been losing confidence in Maliki since 2011. John McCain and other senators threatened to withhold support for Iraq unless Maliki stopped suppressing Sunni and Kurdish minorities. They wrote in October 2011, days before Maliki's visit to Washington, that Maliki was "pursuing a sectarian and authoritarian agenda." If Maliki failed to share more political power with Sunni Iraqis, resolve territorial disputes with Kurdish leaders and ensure free and fair elections the following year, "no amount of security assistance will be able to bring stability and security to Iraq."[23] Maliki was simply incapable of coalition politics that required sharing power with key groups and constituencies.

Iraq experienced a steady erosion of its institutions during Maliki's eight-year rule. Increased suicide bombings and deteriorating security conditions undermined confidence among Iraqis in their government. Shiite factions accused Maliki of corruption, partisanship, and ineffectiveness for failing to deliver public services or provide security. Sunnis accused Maliki of exclusion and marginalization. Kurds resented Maliki for centralizing power and monopolizing unfair distribution of economic resources. Condoleezza Rice told Maliki, "You're a terrible prime minister. Without progress and without an agreement, you'll be on your own, hanging from a lamppost."[24]

George W. Bush initiated plans to withdraw US forces by 2011. However, America's retreat from Iraq occurred during the Obama administration. Obama tried to negotiate a Status of Forces Agreement (SOFA) that would leave a residual force of about ten thousand troops to continue training of the Iraqi armed forces and to act as a rapid counterterrorism response. But Maliki could not deliver a parliamentary majority to endorse the SOFA, and provide immunity for US troops and contractors. Maliki proposed a diplomatic note promising immunity, but administration lawyers rejected his offer. Failure to establish the SOFA provided justification to Obama and his advisers who wanted to pull the plug on America's involvement in Iraq.

Defense Secretary Leon E. Panetta attended the flag-lowering ceremony in Baghdad on December 15, 2011.[25] The solemn occasion marked the formal withdrawal of US forces from Iraq after nearly nine years of war. All told, more than 4,500 American soldiers died and 30,000 Americans were wounded. The financial cost of the war was $2 trillion. More than 134,000 Iraqis were killed and millions displaced.[26]

Panetta said, "After a lot of blood spilled by Iraqis and Americans, the mission of an Iraq that could govern and secure itself has become real. This is a time for Iraq to look forward. This is an opportunity for Iraq to forge ahead on a path to security and prosperity. We owe it to all of the lives that were sacrificed in this war not to fail."[27] Panetta echoed Obama's remarks to troops in North Carolina: "Everything that American troops have done in Iraq, all the fighting and dying, bleeding and building, training and partnering, has led us to this moment of success." He told troops to leave with "heads held high." He also commended the Iraqi government for its just administration, fair representation, and inclusivity. He characterized Iraq as "sovereign, stable and self-reliant, with a representative government that was elected by its people."[28]

*****

Iraqis went to the polls on April 30, 2014. The election was a referendum on Maliki's eight years in power. His State of Law Coalition surpassed expectations, winning ninety-two seats. The second largest block won just thirty-three seats, putting Maliki in a strong position to form a government.[29] Sunnis were largely not engaged in the political process. ISIS was already in control of Fallujah and Ramadi. It threatened voters, resulting in a reduced number of polling stations. Candidates also withdrew under threat of death.

After Mosul fell, Maliki emphasized a security solution to the ISIS crisis. Once ISIS was defeated, Iraqis could enter into a political dialogue on government formation. The Iraqi parliament convened to establish a new government on July 2. The Iraqi constitution stipulates that lawmakers have two weeks to name a president and two vice presidents after the speaker is selected. Once the president is named, lawmakers have another month to select a prime minister.[30]

Negotiations were acrimonious. The Rule of Law Party was reluctant to remove Maliki, lest it be seen as a victory for the terrorists. Sunnis were ready to present their candidate for speaker of the parliament, but only after Shiites offered a candidate for prime minister. Sunni lawmakers declared their support for any Shiite except Maliki. Negotiations broke down after a half-hour; parliament adjourned in disarray. Sistani called on Iraqis to create a government with "broad national support."[31]

The Obama administration grew increasingly skeptical that Maliki could deliver a coalition to govern Iraq, and engage the Sunnis in a united front against ISIS. John Kerry declared on June 23, "The United States would like to see the Iraqi people find leadership that is prepared to represent all the people of Iraq."[32] But Maliki rejected a government of "national salvation." He proclaimed: "I will continue to fight."[33] The Dawa Islamic Party had won the most seats; Maliki refused to step aside.[34]

With Iraqis at loggerheads, President Fuad Masum—a Kurd—designated Haider al-Abadi, a member of the Dawa Islamist Party, to form a new government. Maliki rebuked the move, claiming it violated Iraq's constitution. Amidst rising tensions over the possibility of a coup, Maliki shut Baghdad's airport and deployed elite forces on Baghdad's streets.[35] Maliki also threatened legal action to prevent Abadi from taking office. With Iraq on the brink, the Dawa Islamic Party, the security services, and Maliki's backers in Iran dropped their support. Sistani also played an influential role behind the scenes convincing Maliki to step down.

Government formation was the first hurdle. Abadi was also tested to implement the power sharing that gives Arab Sunnis and Kurds a meaningful role. The KRG insisted that the new government be responsive to its core concerns. Kurds demanded the right to sell oil, buy weapons, and conduct referenda in Kirkuk and other formerly disputed territories. They insisted on a mechanism to prevent "abuses of power by Baghdad."[36]

Sunnis are suspicious of Baghdad. Sheikh Mohammed al-Bajari, a member of the local council in Fallujah, called Abadi's designation "a simple change of faces." Sunnis set the bar high. They demanded the withdrawal of all army divisions from Anbar, disbanding of militias, the release of thousands of Sunni detainees, and compensation to the "families of martyrs for their psychological, material and moral sufferings."[37] They also demanded repeal of the de-Baathification law and Article 4 of the Anti-Terrorism Law, as well as a new constitution granting Sunni provinces more autonomy.

The Awakening was critical to a successful surge in 2007. After helping to defeat al-Qaeda in Mesopotamia, the precursor to ISIS, Sunni Arabs felt betrayed by the Iraqi government. Awakening members were not paid. Nor were they integrated into the Iraqi Army, which was dominated by Shiites. Marginalized and shut down by the Iraqi government, Awakening members developed a deep resentment toward Baghdad and a distrust of Shia-dominated security and intelligence services. To help reconcile sectarian groups and engage Sunnis in the security service, Abadi created a new National Guard. Its members were drawn from local tribes, controlled by provincial governors, and tasked with fighting ISIS. The Iraqi government agreed to pay their salaries and pensions.

*****

Kurds distinguish between the period before Mosul and after. Kurds woke up one morning to find ISIS as their neighbor. According to Fuad Hussein, Masoud Barzani's chief of staff and national security adviser, "values" separate the Kurds from ISIS. "ISIS is against civilized values, democracy, human rights and religious freedom. They are anti-West, anti-American, and anti-world while the Kurds are on a democratic path and committed to international cooperation."[38]

ISIS created a new reality. Masoud Barzani stated, "Iraq is falling apart. It's obvious that the federal or central government has lost control over everything. Everything is collapsing—the army, the troops, the police." Barzani maintained, "The time is now for self-determination." He proposed a referendum "for the Kurdistan people to determine their future."[39]

Duress brought the Kurds together. The KRG Foreign Minister Falah Mustafa Bakir asserted, "Everyone is for independence. We are tired of thinking and talking about Baghdad."[40] The KRG established a broad-based cabinet, including different parties and factions. For years, Kurds were discussing how to achieve independence in a deliberative and democratic manner. They considered details from establishing a central bank to aviation guidelines. Fuad Hussein said, "Believe me. We were studying everything. Now we need a plan to implement it."[41]

Kurds want to make sure they are not perceived as dividing Iraq. Barzani insisted, "We did not cause the collapse of Iraq. It is others who did. And we cannot remain hostages to the unknown."[42] The KRG was willing to participate in negotiations about forming a government, but Masoud Barzani made clear that he would not lead the process or sacrifice core national interests for the unity of Iraq.

Notes

1. Sly, Liz. "Islamic Law Comes to Rebel-held Syria." *Washington Post.* The Washington Post, 09 July 2014. Web. 09 July 2014.
2. "Why the Iraqi Army Can't Defeat ISIS." *Vox.* N.p., n.d. Web. 07 July 2014.
3. Ibid.
4. "FP's Situation Report: Kerry Arrives in Iraq; Nat-sec Luminaries Pop Popcorn for New Afghanistan Combat Film; Bergdahl Becomes an."*Foreign Policy.* N.p., n.d. Web. 10 July 2014.
5. Chulov, Martin. "Iraqi City of Tal Afar Falls to Isis Insurgents." *The Guardian.* Guardian News and Media, 17 June 2014. Web. 09 July 2014.
6. "Floodgates Open as ISIS Bridges Victories between Syria and Iraq." - *12 News KBMT and K-JAC. News, Weather and Sports for SE Texas.* N.p., n.d. Web. 09 July 2014.
7. "Floodgates Open as ISIS Bridges Victories between Syria and Iraq." - *12 News KBMT and K-JAC. News, Weather and Sports for SE Texas.* N.p., n.d. Web. 09 July 2014.
8. Chulov, Martin, and Rory Carroll. "Isis Captures More Iraqi Towns and Border Crossings." *The Guardian.* Guardian News and Media, 23 June 2014. Web. 07 July 2014.
9. Cooper, Helene, and Michael R. Gordon. "Iraqi Kurds Expand Autonomy as ISIS Reorders the Landscape." *The New York Times.* The New York Times, 29 Aug. 2014. Web. 05 Sept. 2014. <http://www.nytimes.com/2014/08/30/world/middleeast/iraqi-kurds-expand-autonomy-as-isis-reorders-the-landscape.html>.
10. "ISIS: Tough Warriors or Guardsmen?" *The Daily Star Newspaper.* N.p., n.d. Web. 10 July 2014.
11. "CIA Reveals ISIS Ranks Have TRIPLED to More than 30,000 Fighters - including 2,000 Westerners." *Mail Online.* Associated Newspapers, 12 Sept. 2014. Web. 12 Sept. 2014. <http://www.dailymail.co.uk/news/article-2753004/CIA-believes-ranks-ISIS-fighters-swollen-TRIPLE-number-previously-thought-31-500-fighters-2-000-Westerners.html>.
12. Schmitt, Eric, and Michael R. Gordon. "The Iraqi Army Was Crumbling Long Before Its Collapse, U.S. Officials Say." *The New York Times.* The New York Times, 12 June 2014. Web. 10 July 2014.
13. "ISIS Just Stole $425 Million, Iraqi Governor Says, and Became the 'world's Richest Terrorist Group." *Washington Post.* The Washington Post, n.d. Web. 10 July 2014.
14. "Why ISIS Is More Dangerous than Al Qaeda and What America Must Do About It." *Breitbart News Network.* N.p., n.d. Web. 10 July 2014.
15. "Sunni Mufti: ISIS and Affiliates Have Killed over 300 Sunni Imams, Preachers." *Breitbart News Network.* N.p., n.d. Web. 10 July 2014.
16. "Kurdish Forces Take Kirkuk as ISIS Militants Push towards Baghdad | News | DW.DE | 12.06.2014." *DW.DE.* N.p., n.d. Web. 20 June 2014.
17. Slater, Andrew. *The Daily Beast.* Newsweek/Daily Beast, n.d. Web. 30 June 2014.
18. "Analysis: The Kurds Take Kirkuk, Now What?" - *Middle East.* N.p., n.d. Web. 20 June 2014.

19. "ISIS Proposes Truce to Kurdish Peshmerga South of Kirkuk." *Rudaw*. N.p., n.d. Web. 16 June 2014.

20. "ISIS Proposes Truce to Kurdish Peshmerga South of Kirkuk." *Rudaw*. N.p., n.d. Web. 14 July 2014.

21. Lister, Tim. "Dehydration or Massacre: Thousands Caught in ISIS Chokehold." *CNN*. Cable News Network, 01 Jan. 1970. Web. 12 Sept. 2014. <http://www.cnn.com/2014/08/10/world/meast/iraq-isis-sinjar/>.

22. "Iraq | Refugees International." *Iraq | Refugees International*. N.p., n.d. Web. 10 July 2014.

23. Margaret Talev and David Lerman. "Obama and Maliki Meet as Iraq Seeks Additional U.S. Aid." Bloomberg News. Nov 2, 2013.

24. Baker, Peter. "For 2 U.S. Presidents, Iraqi Leader Proved a Source of Frustration." *The New York Times*. The New York Times, 11 Aug. 2014. Web. 05 Sept. 2014. <http://www.nytimes.com/2014/08/12/world/middleeast/for-2-us-presidents-iraqi-leader-proved-a-source-of-frustration.html?action=click&contentCollection=Middle%20East*ion=Footer&module=Top News&pgtype=article>.

25. "Leon Panetta Photos on Townhall." *Townhall*. N.p., n.d. Web. 10 July 2014.

26. Trotta, Daniel. "Iraq War Costs U.S. More than $2 Trillion: Study." *Reuters*. Thomson Reuters, 14 Mar. 2013. Web. 10 July 2014.

27. Greene, Richard Allen, This Article Is Based on Reporting by Mohammed Tawfeeq, Arwa Damon in Baghdad, Moni Basu in Atlanta, Zain Verjee in London, and Tom Cohen in Washington. "Muted Ceremony Marks End of Iraq War." *CNN*. Cable News Network, 15 Dec. 2011. Web. 29 June 2014.

28. "US Flag Ceremony Ends War in Iraq." *BBC News*. N.p., n.d. Web. 10 July 2014.

29. "Analysis: Maliki Bolsters Iraq Re-election Chances." *BBC News*. N.p., n.d. Web. 10 July 2014.

30. "Full Text of Iraqi Constitution." *Washington Post*. The Washington Post, 12 Oct. 2005. Web. 13 July 2014.

31. "Embattled Iraqi Prime Minister Nouri Al-Maliki 'will Not Go Quietly,' Foes and Friends Say." *Washington Post*. The Washington Post, n.d. Web. 7 July 2014.

32. Alissa J. Rubin. "MIliytant Take Major Border Post; Kedrry Hints U.S. Is Open to a New Premier." The New York Times. June 23, 2014. Pg. A9.

33. "Iraq's PM Al-Maliki Refuses to Step Down: 'I Will Continue to Fight'" *The Christian Science Monitor*. The Christian Science Monitor, n.d. Web. 13 July 2014.

34. "Iraqi PM's Bloc Wins Most Parliamentary Seats." *The Big Story*. N.p., n.d. Web. 13 July 2014.

35. "Iraq's Maliki Rejects Nomination of New PM." *Middle East Eye*. N.p., n.d. Web. 08 Sept. 2014. <http://www.middleeasteye.net/news/iraqs-maliki-vows-stay-despite-international-backing-rival-1597125558#sthash.RTsKlROj.dpuf>.

36. Cooper, Helene, and Michael R. Gordon. "Iraqi Kurds Expand Autonomy as ISIS Reorders the Landscape." *The New York Times*. The New York Times, 29 Aug. 2014. Web. 05 Sept. 2014.

37. "Sunnis Do Not Believe Abadi Is a Solution to Iraq's Crises." N.p., n.d. Web. 22 Aug. 2014. <http%3A%2F%2Fwww.al-monitor.com%2Fpulse%2Foriginals%2F2014%2F08%2Fsunnis-solution-abadi-maliki-problems.html%3Futm_source%3DAl-Monitor%2BNewsletter%2B%255BEnglish%255D%26utm_campaign%3Dbc2ac65823-August_22_2014%26utm_medium%3Demail%26utm_term%3D0_28264b27a0-bc2ac65823-93077049%23ixzz3B8m87wvn>.

38. Interview with KRG National Security Adviser Fuad Hussein by the author, July 1, 2014 (Washington, DC).

39. "EXCLUSIVE: Iraqi Kurdistan Leader Massoud Barzani Says 'the Time Is Here' for Self-determination." *Amanpour RSS.* N.p., n.d. Web. 2 July 2014.

40. Interview with KRG Foreign Minister Falah Mustafa Bakir by the author, July 1, 2014 (Washington, DC).

41. Interview with Dr. Fuad Hussein, Chief of Staff to the Presidency of KRG, by the author, July 1, 2014 (Washington, DC).

42. "EXCLUSIVE: Iraqi Kurdistan Leader Massoud Barzani Says 'the Time Is Here' for Self-determination." *Amanpour RSS.* N.p., n.d. Web. 2 July 2014.

11

International Response

Abu Bakr al-Baghdadi declared himself "caliph," renamed ISIS the Islamic State, and called on Muslims worldwide to accept his authority.[1] Baghdadi even demanded that al-Qaeda recognize his leadership. He endorsed holy war against the forces of "disbelief and hypocrisy."[2] He implored "Rush O Muslims to your state."[3] Events in Iraq fueled international concern as allies and front-line states moved to protect their national interests in the wake of Iraq's catastrophic collapse.

The United States

The KRG warned Iraqi and US officials that ISIS was massing on the border to attack Mosul. According to Fuad Hussein, natural security adviser and chief of staff to KRG President Masoud Barzani, "US officials did not want to listen." Even after ISIS occupied Anbar and declared a caliphate, Washington did not grasp the urgency of the situation or the potential role of Kurds in countering ISIS.[4] "It is not clear to us how [the United States] defined [its] interests in Iraq," said Fuad Hussein.[5] Washington was reacting to events, rather than shaping them. The Obama administration's "one-window policy" focused solely on Baghdad.[6]

John Kerry visited Baghdad and Erbil on June 23 and 24, 2014. He emphasized the need for a united front of Shiites, Sunnis, Arabs, and Kurds to drain the swamp of support for ISIS. He asked Masoud Barzani to facilitate power-sharing negotiations. Kerry raised "the elephant in the room." He called on Barzani to act like a "statesman" and reject independence for Iraqi Kurdistan.[7] Barzani was courteous but noncommittal. US leverage had been dramatically reduced when American troops withdrew in 2011, leaving Iraqis to provide for their own security and manage their political affairs.

Iraqi Kurds were always called upon to sacrifice their self-interest for the unity of Iraq. Kurds helped establish Iraq's system of governance by taking a leading role during negotiations over the 2005 constitution, which established a federal, democratic republic. Barzani brokered the Erbil Agreement in 2010, which averted a political crisis by allocating leadership positions to Iraq's different groups. But that was a different time. Barzani told Kerry, "We are facing a new reality and a new Iraq."[8] He asked, "How many more years do you want us to wait after all the sacrifices?"[9]

Instead of supporting Iraqi Kurdistan, the United States sought to limit its opportunities. Iraq's Federal Court upheld the KRG's right to sell oil. However, the Obama administration opposed the export of Kurdish oil.[10] It believed that the KRG's direct access to energy markets would accelerate the break up of Iraq. When oil from Kurdistan arrived in Ceyhan for export to Morocco, US officials approached the government of Morocco to try and block the sale.[11] Washington also pressured the Turkish government not to buy oil from Iraqi Kurdistan. Oil revenue was critical. Baghdad was supposed to distribute 17 percent of the country's total oil income to the KRG, but it always distributed less than what was owed.[12] Moreover, it suspended payments entirely in January 2014. The United States not only blocked oil sales, it intervened to prevent governments from selling weapons to the KRG, which the peshmerga needed for self-defense.

Obama insisted that Iraqis establish an inclusive government before the United States would consider "targeted military action."[13] Cooperation proved a tall order. Iraq is a deeply divided society with no tradition of inclusion. Tribal leaders believe that inclusion threatens their authority, and that compromise means weakness.[14] But Obama was adamant. "Only leaders that can govern with an inclusive agenda are going to be able to truly bring the Iraqi people together and help them through this crisis."[15] He wanted Iraqis to sort it out. "We do not have the ability to simply solve this problem by sending in tens of thousands of troops."[16] He added, "It is not our job to choose Iraq's leaders. . . . [They] must rise above their differences and come together."[17] Obama's talking points were the same as ten years ago.[18]

The United States faced a stark choice. Either the United States would re-engage in a war that Obama opposed from the start, or the US would allow Iraq to fall into an abyss of sectarian slaughter, leading to its eventual collapse and fragmentation. After Mosul, Washington announced plans to send three hundred military advisers.[19] They were deployed to help secure the US Embassy/Baghdad and the Baghdad Airport.[20] Some went to Kurdistan, which faced regular attacks by ISIS. Unlike the Iraqi troops, peshmerga were known to be capable and highly motivated to defend their homeland.

Pentagon planners presented a sliding scale of military options to Obama. However, he resisted even limited air strikes. Obama took the measure of US public opinion, heading into midterm elections. Most Americans opposed US military re-engagement in Iraq. Obama resisted military action, even when Islamic State fighters overran Sinjar and displaced two hundred thousand Yazidis.[21] He insisted that Iraqis form a government of national unity. The plight of fifty thousand Yazidis clinging to life on Mount Sinjar proved hard to ignore. When Islamic State fighters advanced to within thirty kilometers of Erbil, Obama finally authorized air strikes.[22]

Addressing the nation to explain reasons for America's military action in Iraq, Obama cited the protection of US officials at the consulate in Erbil. He underscored the need to prevent the genocide of Christians and Yazidis. Obama offered that military intervention would create space for a political solution, making Iraqis stakeholders in the country's future. He believed that Sunni political engagement would turn them against ISIS.

US air strikes came just in time to save Erbil from being overrun, but warplanes alone were insufficient. General Martin E. Dempsey, Chairman of the Joint Chiefs of Staff, noted that air strikes had blunted the Islamic State's momentum. He announced weapon supplies to the KRG.[23] The Pentagon provided rocket-propelled grenades and heavy machine guns. The EU held an extraordinary meeting on August 12, deciding that member states could directly supply weapons to the KRG. France, Britain, Italy, Denmark, Canada, Croatia, and Albania stepped up.[24] More than small arms, the peshmerga needed sophisticated weapons—artillery, mortars, Humvees and APCs—to deter ISIS. Germany sent thousands of machine guns and hand grenades, as well as antitank missiles. The peshmerga proved to be motivated and capable when properly equipped. Their ranks total about two hundred thousand, including special counterterrorism forces.[25]

US intervention started as a way to prevent further advances by ISIS. The mission morphed into preventing genocide and regaining territory. C-17 and C-130 transport planes dropped water and food rations for Yazidis on Mount Sinjar. Britain, France, and Australia joined the humanitarian operation, providing twenty-eight air drops of food and supplies, including 35,000 gallons of water and 115,000 MREs ("meals ready to eat.")[26] Getting people off the mountain to safety was a more challenging task. Obama talked about opening a humanitarian corridor, but it was the People's Protection Forces (YPG) of the PYD who successfully escorted as many as ten thousand Yazidis down from the mountain, through treacherous territory, and across the border to Rojava.[27]

The beheading of James Foley and Steven J. Sotloff was a wake-up call for US officials. Obama initially disparaged ISIS as "the JV team."[28] After the slaughter of Foley and Sotloff, Defense Secretary Chuck Hagel said, "[ISIS] is like nothing we've seen before."[29] US officials recast their view of ISIS, calling it as a direct threat to US national security. ISIS had become an international organization with worldwide membership. Its ranks include more than one hundred US citizens, more than five hundred British citizens, up to nine hundred French citizens, as well as fighters from Turkey, Jordan, Tunisia, Chechnya, and Saudi Arabia. ISIS went from being a gang contained in Syria to a terror group with global reach. Jihadis learned skills in Syria and Iraq that they might use at home.[30] US intelligence agencies believe that fifteen thousand foreign fighters had joined ISIS in Iraq and Syria.[31]

Obama acknowledged: "We do not have a strategy, yet."[32] From rescuing civilians, the mission expanded to regaining territory. The United States replicated the model of US air strikes complementing peshmerga on the battlefield.[33] Peshmerga, with assistance from Iraqi Special Forces and US air strikes, launched a major counteroffensive and captured the Mosul Dam on August 18, 2014.[34] It included ninety-one bombing attacks. In September, an operation to retake the Haditha Dam included seventeen bombing operations. Plans were made to recapture Mosul and roll back other gains in Northern and Western Iraq.[35]

Obama unveiled a long-term plan to degrade, dismantle, and destroy the Islamic State at the NATO Summit in Wales on September 4, 2014. The campaign emphasized a multilateral approach based on a "coalition of the willing." To complement air strikes, coalition members pledged to train and equip the peshmerga, Iraqi armed forces, and Sunni tribes. The coalition did not, however, reach an agreement to expand strikes against Islamic State targets on the Syrian side of the border.[36]

The Obama doctrine on the use of military force foreswore the use of military power except for self-defense or when US interests or American citizens were threatened. Obama was a firm believer in mul-tilateral diplomacy. He reframed military action as a type of soft power. Obama addressed cadets at the US Military Academy at West Point on May 28, 2014: "The US would not become isolationist. America must always lead on the world stage. If we don't, no one else will." According to Obama, "Our military became the strongest advocate for diplomacy and development."[37]

The US approach was self-contradictory. Washington was a de facto ally of violent Sunni groups like ISIS in Syria, where both were seeking to overthrow Assad. In Iraq, the United States supported the central government and launched air strikes against ISIS. Washington did not object when Syrian warplanes launched a cross-border raid on ISIS positions in Iraq. However, it protested when Syrian warplanes dropped barrel bombs on Sunni strongholds in Syria.

As the death toll mounted, critics blasted the Obama administration for ignoring its "responsibility to protect." They lamented America's inconsistency and diminished status as a superpower. NATO spearheaded the intervention in Libya, where in the words of a National Security Council official, the United States was "leading from behind."[38] Obama described his approach to foreign policy: "Don't do stupid stuff."

A chorus of former cabinet members criticized Obama. Former Secretary of State Hillary Clinton maintained, "Great nations need organizing principles, and 'Don't do stupid stuff' is not an organizing principle."[39] Former Defense Secretary and CIA Director Leon E. Panetta noted Obama's failure to define "America's role in the world in the twenty-first century."[40] Robert M. Gates, the former defense secretary, criticized the administration's overly cautious approach in Afghanistan and other crises.

Obama's ambivalence was most glaring in his approach toward Syria. In 2012, he pledged to back the Free Syrian Army but delivered little more than rhetorical support. Obama drew a red line and threatened air strikes when Syria used chemical weapons on civilians:

> Well over 1,000 people were murdered. Several hundred of them were children—young girls and boys gassed to death by their own government. This attack is an assault on human dignity. It also presents a serious danger to our national security. It risks making a mockery of the global prohibition on the use of chemical weapons. It endangers our friends and our partners along Syria's borders, including Israel, Jordan, Turkey, Lebanon and Iraq. It could lead to escalating use of chemical weapons, or their proliferation to terrorist groups who would do our people harm. In a world with many dangers, this menace must be confronted.

The red line shifted in the sands. The US embraced Russia's proposal for a UN-led initiative to sequester and dispose of Syria's chemical weapon stockpile. The arrangement made Assad indispensable to disarming Syria of its WMD. Assad created a crisis that only he could solve. Meanwhile Syria's conventional war raged on. The Syrian Army retook Qusair, Homs, and major suburbs of Damascus. Humanitarian access was denied.[41] Syria's slaughterhouse proved to be a fertile field for the Islamic State.

Events in Syria and Iraq invited closer scrutiny of Obama's plan to withdraw from Afghanistan. Obama publicly declared the drawdown of American forces to ten thousand by the end of 2014, with a fixed timetable for complete withdrawal by 2016.[42] The American public was weary of war in Afghanistan after nearly fifteen years. The drawdown schedule was announced for domestic consumption. The timetable was taken on board by the Taliban, which readied for renewed operations after America's withdrawal.

Rather than project American power and influence, Obama's foreign policy choices were largely shaped by domestic considerations. The disapproval rating for foreign policy reached 60 percent in September 2014.[43] While Americans are wary of conflict in distant land, they rejected Obama's foreign policy, which was too deliberative, cautious, and defined by limitations.

After long and careful consideration, Obama addressed the nation from the Oval Office on September 10, 2014.[44] He spoke on the eve of the thirteen-year anniversary of the September 11 terror attacks. Putting the United States on an open-ended war footing, Obama announced a long-term campaign to "degrade and destroy" ISIS. He authorized air strikes against the Islamic State fighters in Syria. He also requested that Congress authorize $500 million for a train and equip program benefitting moderate Syrian opposition and $5 billion for counterterrorism activities. The United States resisted military action in Syria for more than three years. However, the beheadings of Foley and Sotloff demanded a response. Obama's declaration of war signaled a new phase in America's fight against extremists in Iraq and Syria.

Turkey

ISIS abducted thirty-one Turkish truck drivers in Mosul on June 9, 2014.[45] The next day, it seized the Turkish Consulate and took forty-nine hostages, including Consul General Ozturk Yilmaz.[46] It humiliated Turkey by turning its diplomatic facility into ISIS headquarters, removing the Turkish flag and replacing it with the black terror flag. The day after the Turkish hostages were taken, the story totally disappeared from television news in Turkey. The Turkish government imposed a gag order, claiming that coverage would disrupt sensitive negotiations.[47] The cover-up was an effort to mitigate the sense of outrage, humiliation, and concern felt by Turks. It was also intended to limit political fallout for Erdogan, who was gearing up to run for president.

Ahmet Davutoglu said, "No one should try to test the limits of Turkey's strength."[48] But ISIS ignored Turkey's warnings. It attacked Tal Afar, a town populated by four hundred thousand Turkmen. Turkish opposition parties, the Republican People's Party and the Nationalist Movement Party, blasted Erdogan and Davutoglu's "zero problems with neighbors" policy. They blamed Erdogan for the kidnapping of Ozturk Yilmaz and called for military intervention to liberate Mosul.[49] The opposition strongly criticized the government's overall approach to Syria.

Turkey's National Intelligence Agency (MIT) was the "midwife" that helped birth the Sunni armed movement fighting to depose Syrian President Bashar Al-Assad.[50] Beginning in 2012, the government allegedly operated a cross-border supply channel funneling arms, ammunition, money, and providing logistical assistance to Jabhat al-Nusra Front, Ahrar al-Sham, and ISIS.[51] Turkey's goals were twofold. It aimed to support jihadis fighting the Syrian regime. It also sought to abort the birth of an autonomous Kurdish region in Syria.

ISIS turned on Turkey in September 2013. It threatened suicide attacks in Istanbul and Ankara. It also carried out twin car bombings in Reyhanli, a town in the southern province of Hatay, that killed 53 people and injured 140 on May 11, 2013.[52] After Reyhanli, Turks grew wary of entanglements in Syria's civil war. By the end of 2013, the cost of providing for eight hundred thousand refugees was $1.5 billion.[53] Erdogan was criticized for the refugee crisis and its cost.[54]

The Turkish government was also blamed for the plight of Iraqi Turkmen, ethnic brethren in the Kurdistan region of Iraq. In June 2014, the Turkish Red Crescent built a camp for twenty thousand internally displaced Turkmen.[55] The camp was set up in Iraqi Kurdistan to keep Turkmen from crossing the border into Turkey. It was the second time Turkmen had been displaced. Tens of thousands fled their homes in Tal Afar between Sinjar and Mosul when the Islamic State attacked on June 10. Instead of zero problems with neighbors, Turkey had two failed states on its borders.

Voters turned a blind eye in the local and presidential elections of 2014. Running on Erdogan's record of prosperity and improved services, the AKP scored a resounding victory in local elections on March 30, 2014. Turkey's pious entrepreneurial class, which forms the core of

Erdogan's constituency, turned out in large numbers. The BDP, however, swept local elections in municipalities on the Iraq and Iranian borders. It demanded "the construction of Kurdish autonomy" in municipalities under its control.[56] Abdullah Ocalan indicated that the AKP needed to remain in power for political dialogue to continue.[57]

Turks went to polls to directly elect their president for the first time on August 10, 2014. Erdogan won in the first round, with 51.95 percent of the vote.[58] By avoiding a runoff, Erdogan claimed to represent the "national will." Obama sent a presidential delegation to attend Erdogan's inauguration on August 28, 2014. In a sign of deteriorating US-Turkey relations, a midlevel official, Mr. Jess L. Bailey, chargé d'affaires of the US Embassy in Ankara, headed the delegation.[59]

Sellahatin Demirtas, the BDP presidential candidate, received 9.71 percent. He ran on a platform of greater political and cultural rights for Kurds and peace with the PKK. Demirtas also appealed to mainstream Turkish voters as a moderate, progressive, and charismatic leader. Despite efforts to characterize Demirtas as the PKK candidate, he substantially increased support for the BDP in several provinces outside the Kurdish region. Demirtas celebrated the "victory of democracy and equality" despite "an unfair and unequal election campaign." He maintained, "The messages we wanted to convey have reached all of Turkey. Our presidential election campaign has reached its goal."[60] The BDP was in the system, campaigning under a Turkish flag.

Erdogan's sweeping victory puts him in position to dominate Turkish politics for years to come. Erdogan seeks to rival Ataturk's legacy and preside during the centennial of the Republic's founding in 2023. If the AKP wins national parliamentary elections in 2015, Erdogan will renew efforts to amend Turkey's 1982 constitution and establish a more powerful presidential system with himself at the helm. Under these conditions, the current de-facto presidential system will be legally established. Erdogan's victory was no surprise. Nor was the margin of victory. Erdogan is a masterful politician. One way or another, he was sure to win.

The AKP consolidated its support, despite recent difficulties and setbacks. Demonstrations over a commercial development project in Istanbul's Taksim Square spiraled into violent protests in sixty cities across the country during the summer of 2013. Police brutality enraged protesters, adding fuel to the fire. Erdogan impugned protesters, calling them thugs, hooligans, looters, and agents of foreign powers.[61]

The government restricted freedom of expression in the media and civil society. Dissenting opinions were silenced via criminal prosecutions. The government refused to repeal regressive legislation that limits freedom of expression and marginalizes political opposition. It limited press freedom, building a cohort of propagandists disguised as columnists. Article 8 of the Anti-Terror Act is used to suppress dissent, and Article 301 of the Penal Code makes it a crime to "denigrate Turkishness."[62] Judicial proceedings were used to eliminate political opponents. The AKP also attacked the judiciary, a bastion of secularism. It confronted the military under the guise of democratization and eliminating the deep state.

Erdogan was caught up in a corruption scandal, implicating his son and inner circle. Four cabinet ministers resigned. Erdogan fell out with his longtime friend and ally, Fetulleh Gulen, and launched a campaign to remove hundreds of police and prosecutors involved in investigations. Members of parliament requested information, but they were denied access to police reports and court records.[63]

When Erdogan visited Soma, scene of Turkey's worst mining accident, which killed 301 miners in May 2014, he shirked responsibility, stating: "These types of incidents are ordinary things." He was jostled and jeered by family members of the miners, after attributing the accident to the will of God. The AKP had ties to the mining company. The AKP block in parliament helped defeat demands by miners to investigate mine safety and working conditions in 2013.[64]

Erdogan curried favor with voters by injecting huge sums into the Turkish economy. Economic growth was fueled by public spending, which was tied to public borrowing. A $400 billion public works program included large infrastructure projects—a $10 billion airport for Istanbul, a $3 billion bridge across the Bosphorus, and a forty-kilometer canal linking the Black Sea with the Sea of Marmara. In 2012, $4.7 billion was spent on construction projects in Istanbul alone. Corporations that supported the AKP were first to receive government contracts.[65]

Instead of recognizing the legitimate grievances of Kurds, Turks blame PKK terrorism for threatening Turkey's peace and progress. Some Turkish officials claim that reforms would undermine Turkey's territorial integrity and cause disintegration. They blame outsiders for fanning the flames of Kurdish dissatisfaction and trying to divide the country. US-Turkish relations suffered after Iraq's 2003 invasion. While Turks admire America, they resent attitudes of superiority, arrogance, and bullying.[66]

Rather than a true strategic partnership, US-Turkish relations became transactional. Instead of friendship and a shared global vision, cooperation was based on interests. Washington's view of Erdogan deteriorated dramatically after the Gezi Park crackdown. Erdogan deepened the distrust of Turks toward the United States by insinuating that Washington supported the creation of an independent Kurdistan and the division of Turkey.

Turkey is indispensable to Obama's "coalition of the willing." Multilateral measures to degrade and destroy the ISIS would be much more effective with Turkey's participation. Turkey is a valued member of NATO. It also shares a border with both Syria and Iraq.

ISIS is a conundrum. Turkey delayed action, first citing presidential elections in August and then pointing to the plight of Turkish hostages. Past those milestones, Turkey has no more excuses to explain its ambivalence.

Secretary of Defense Chuck T. Hagel met Erdogan in Ankara on September 8, 2014. They explored ways that Turkey can contribute to Obama's multilateral coalition without directly engaging in combat operations. Incirlik Air Force Base in Southeast Turkey is minutes away from the frontline. It is an ideal staging ground for reconnaissance drones, as well as refueling and resupplying of US and British warplanes. Incirlik can also serve as a hub for delivering humanitarian supplies to the KRG, which has sheltered nearly one million people displaced by the ISIS. Turkey can curtail income of the Islamic State by refusing to buy oil from its wells in Raqqa and Jazirah in Syria, and wells in Iraq. In addition, Turkey also can take additional steps to seal its border with Syria to prevent new fighters from entering the battlefield. The "jihadi highway" is a portal for extremists from around the world to travel through Turkey to Syria and Iraq.

Erdogan made no commitments. He insisted that the United States recommit itself to Geneva II, which calls for regime change in Damascus. Hagel was pressed on how the United States could go to war with the ISIS, attacking positions in Syria, without inadvertently aiding Bashar al-Assad. Erdogan also expressed concern that weapons supplied from the US to the KRG could fall into PKK hands. Turkey opposes rapprochement between Washington and the PYD, which is played an important role fighting ISIS in both Syria and Iraq.

Erdogan and Davutoglu thought they could diversify alliances and build bridges to the Middle East. Turkey curried favor with Muslim Brotherhood affiliates in the region and worldwide. From the Western perspective, Turkey looks like a Middle Eastern country. Viewed from the Middle East, Turkey is decidedly Western. Most Arabs view Turks as Westernized degenerates.

Turkey also underestimated the animosity between Arabs and Turks. The Ottoman caliphate was forcibly moved from Cairo to Istanbul in the sixteenth century. The heist was about political power, not religious devotion. Arabs resented Ottoman imperialism. Muhammad Wahhab denounced influences on Islam that corrupted the Qur'an, including Ottomanism. In the eighteenth century, he killed thousands of Shiites in Karbala and drove Ottoman armies from Medina. The 1916 Arab revolt was brutally suppressed by Ottoman forces.

The end of the Ottoman Empire was a tragic period for Turks. The empire shrunk to a third of its size and millions of Turks were killed or displaced. The Empire's collapse effected Turks from the Balkans, to the Black Sea, and the deserts of Arabia. Humiliation was enshrined by the Treaty of Sevres. The so-called Sevres Syndrome results from collective suffering and loss. Turks feel they are surrounded by foes real and imagined, both within and outside the country.[67] Erdogan's charisma helped Turks overcome insecurities that date back to the end of the Ottoman Empire.

Saudi Arabia

King Abdullah ibn Abdilaziz of Saudi Arabia sees himself as the leader of the Sunni world. Saudi Arabia, with its vast petroleum wealth, has the means to support its leadership. It is the biggest backer of Egypt's new government that outlawed the Muslim Brotherhood. Saudi Arabia also supported Sunni Muslim fighters engaged in Syria's civil war. Financial support did not mean loyalty. Islamist militants took the money while denouncing the Saudi royal family for its ties to the West.

The United States, Saudi Arabia, and Iran were regional allies and partners until the overthrow of the Shah in 1979. While Saudi Arabia maintained close cooperation with Washington in the energy and security fields, Iran became America's adversary. The United States relied on the Saudi monarchy to offset Iran's regional influence. By supporting Saudi Arabia, the United States benefitted from energy security. Saudi Arabia is the world's largest oil producer and leader of OPEC.

Since 1979, Saudi Arabia and Iran have competed for influence in the Persian Gulf, with Iraq as a staging ground for their regional rivalry. Saudi Arabia provided Iraq with $30 billion in its war with Iran. Iraq remained a battleground between Saudi and Iranian proxies after the overthrow of Saddam in 2003. Saudi Arabia sided with Sunni Muslims in Syria and Lebanon. The Saudi royal family sees the Kingdom as the seat and defender of Sunni Islam's greatest shrines in Mecca and Medina.

The Arab Spring of 2012 was deeply troubling to Saudi Arabia. Riyadh championed the old order as a source of stability. It was concerned about US support for revolts in Tunisia, Libya, and Egypt, publicly criticizing the Obama administration for pulling the rug out from under Hosni Mubarak. Saudi troops intervened to stabilize the regime in Bahrain when pro-democracy activists and members of the Shiite minority rebelled. Saudi Arabia was the first country to withdraw its ambassador from Syria when civil war broke out in 2012. Saudi Arabia also supported Sunnis seeking to stem Hezbollah's influence in Lebanon.[68] The Saudi government, the royal family, and wealthy Wahhabi businessmen allegedly finance ISIS and other radical Sunni groups in Syria and Iraq. These organizations are seen as a counterweight to Iran. Riyadh fears that geopolitical trends are aligning against it. This trend potentially threatens both Saudi Arabia's regional standing as well as the Kingdom's domestic security.

Sponsorship of ISIS and other militant Sunni groups was expedient because they were fighting Assad's regime, which was backed by Iran. However, Saudi Arabia grew concerned that Sunni extremists might challenge the royal family or Saudi Arabia's position as leader of the Sunni world. Saudi Arabia's Grand Mufti, Sheikh Abdul Aziz Al ash-Sheikh, issued a statement on August 9, 2014 branding the Islamic State and al-Qaeda "apostates" and calling on Muslims to oppose their extreme Salafist doctrine.[69] Saudi Arabia offered bases to train the moderate Syrian opposition.

In response to the challenges of Sunni militancy, Saudi Arabia gave $100 million to the United Nations Counter-Terrorism Center. The center is designed to build national capacity in the fight against terrorism by targeting the financing and information campaigns of terror groups. These are the same groups that Saudi Arabia helped create. Saudi Arabia also pledged $500 million to assist Iraqis displaced in 2014, "regardless of sect or ethnicity."[70] Many Syrians and displaced Iraqis have sought sanctuary in Iraqi Kurdistan. Saudi Arabia's humanitarian contribution is a statement of support to the KRG, which both stands against Sunni militants and serves as a counterweight to Iran's influence in Baghdad. Saudi Arabia also represents an alternative to Turkey, on whom the Kurds rely for international access.

Jordan

ISIS declared the death of Sykes-Picot, endorsing a caliphate in Iraq and Al-Sham, an Arabic term referring to lands encompassing Iraq, Syria, Jordan, Lebanon, and Palestine. ISIS issued "a call to arms in Jordan" and opened an unofficial branch in Amman.[71] When ISIS seized the Karama and Treibel border crossings, Jordan mobilized its army and intelligence services to preempt the possibility of an attack. Jordan also imposed travel restrictions on men of military age born between 1976 and 1996, requiring a valid military service certificate. King Abdullah II ibn-al Hussein assumed powers to appoint heads of the armed forces and the General Intelligence Department, shifting Jordan from a constitutional monarchy to a presidential monarchy.

Extremist ideology in Jordan is fueled by oppression and frustration that arises from unemployment and the high cost of living. Many Jordanians feel like outcasts, neglected by their government. They are sympathetic to ISIS and embrace Islamism as an antidote to their ills. Not only did Jordanians fight in Syria's civil war, they rallied to assist up to one million Syrian refugees who resettled in Jordan.

Jordan includes nearly two million Palestinian refugees, half of Jordan's existing population. Jordan is under pressure from extremists. The Amman suburb of Zarqan is riddled with al-Qaeda. Abu Musab Al-Zarqawi ("one from Zarqa") formed al-Tawhid wal-Jihad in the 1990s. An offshoot of al-Qaeda, it was known for videotaping suicide bombings and beheadings of hostages. Zarqawi opposed the presence of US forces in Iraq. He was committed to the destruction of Israel and the overthrow of regimes, such as the Hashemite Kingdom of Jordan, that made peace with Israel. Salafis in Jordan represent a fifth column that might rise up if the Islamic State invaded.

King Abdullah views ISIS as part of a wider threat. Jordan is a buffer for Saudi Arabia to the south and Israel to the west. He advocates a robust response to ISIS in Iraq and Syria, and to extremism in the region.

Iran

The historic rivalry between Iran and Iraq peaked during the Iran-Iraq War of 1980–88. Today, Iran's top priority is preventing Sunni terrorists from occupying Iraq. When Mosul was overrun by ISIS, General Qassim Suleimani rushed to Baghdad to advise the Iraqi government. The day after Suleimani's arrival in Baghdad, Ayatollah Ali al-Sistani issued a fatwa calling on Shiites to defend Iraq. "He who sacrifices for the cause of defending his country and his family and his honour will be a martyr." The government offered to equip any citizen willing to fight.[72] Thousands of volunteers turned up at the Imam Ali Shrine in Najaf. They included battle-hardened fighters who participated in Iraq's sectarian civil war.[73] Suleimani planned to embed militias with army units to strengthen their resolve and fighting mettle.[74] He stated that Iran would help Iraq using the same methods it deployed against Sunni opposition forces in Syria.

Muqtadar Al-Sadr rejected Sistani's appeal. He refused to subordinate his Mahdi Army to the Iraqi state. Sadr insisted that the Mahdi Army was a purely Shiite force, independent of formal military structures. Volunteers were zealous, but they had no combat experience. In contrast, the Mahdi Army included proven fighters who engaged US troops in Sadr City and confronted other Shiite militias between 2006 and 2008. Sadr's refusal to submit his forces to Maliki's command revealed fault lines between Shiites. Factionalism created conflicts within conflicts. Divisions further undermined the Iraqi state and exacerbated the challenge of holding Iraq together.

Backed by the Quds Force, Shiite militias vowed to defend shrines in Samarra, Karbala, and Najaf. Karbala is the site of a great battle where Hussein, Mohammed's grandson, was betrayed and slain by Sunnis. The cousin of the Prophet Mohammed is buried at the Imam Ali Shrine in Najaf. The Al-Askari Golden Dome Mosque in Samarra is the resting place of two prominent Shia imams. Protecting these shrines is a sacred duty for Shiites. Iraq's sectarian civil war started in 2006 when Sunni militants destroyed part of the golden dome.

Iran deeply distrusts the United States. Reflecting Iran's sense of victimization, Supreme Leader Ayatollah Ali Khamenei maintained, "Americans are trying to undermine the stability and the territorial integrity of Iraq, in which the last remnants of Saddam Hussein's regime are used as proxies and those formerly outside this network of power are treated as pawns." He believes that al-Qaeda, the Taliban, and ISIS were created by the US as a counterweight to Iran. An officer of the Islamic Revolutionary Guard Corps (IRGC) maintained, "The ISIS conflict is an American and Zionist conspiracy to reverse Islamic awakening in the Middle East. Command centers for the ISIS fighters are in the White House and Saudi Arabia."[75]

Iraq's crisis was an opportunity for reconciliation between Iran and the West. Tehran's distrust did not prevent it from coordinating battlefield operations with the United States via the Iraqi government and the KRG. Iran and the United States were involved in a joint operation to break the siege of Amerli, a Turkmen Shiite community of fifteen thousand people North of Baghdad. Amerli was surrounded by Islamic State fighters. Shiite militias joined peshmerga and Iraqi armed forces to punch through ISIS lines in late August 2014. Iranian military advisers were in the field working with Asa' Ib Abl al-Haq, a military group associated with Sadr's militias. Both Iran and the United States deny coordination, but there was a clear convergence of interests in Amerli as well as the broader battle against ISIS.

ISIS could potentially disrupt the corridor if it expands territory under its control. Iraq is a geopolitical battleground. While wealthy emirates sponsor armed Sunni terrorists, Iran supports Assad in Damascus and the Shiite prime minister in Baghdad as a counterweight to Saudi influence. Tehran also competes for influence with Turkey-Iran is wary of Turkey's neo-Ottoman ambitions, and rapprochement with Iraqi Kurdistan. Cooperation with Turkey turns Iraqi Kurdistan toward the West, and makes Iraqi Kurds less reliant on Iran. When Islamic State fighters advanced on Erbil, Iran was the first country to send weapons to the Kurds.

Prime Minister Heidar Al-Abadi comes from the same party as Maliki, the Dawa Islamic Party. Maliki's bid to resist Abadi's appointment collapsed when Iran withdrew its support. Tehran read the writing on the wall. It switched its support to Abadi when his ascendance became clear. Abadi would not have gained the post if Iran was not confident of his cooperation.Iran does not take a public position on the independence of Iraqi Kurdistan. It plays both sides, working with Baghdad and cooperating with the KRG.

Iran is concerned that developments in Iraqi Kurdistan could inspire unrest among Iranian Kurds. About ten million Kurds live across the Iran-Iraq border in Iranian Kurdistan and Kermanshah. The Party for a Free Life in Kurdistan (PJAK) has been fighting to replace Iran's theocracy with a democratic and federal government.

Lebanon

The 2010 Erbil Agreement was modeled on the 1988 Taif Accord that ended Lebanon's long civil war. The Taif Accord, otherwise known as the National Reconciliation Accord, allocated governance responsibilities to different sects and recognized the ascendance of Lebanon's

Muslim majority. It also sought to restore Lebanon's sovereignty and territorial integrity by addressing the presence of foreign forces on Lebanese territory. The Taif Accord established a schedule for Syria's withdrawal from the Bekaa Valley and called for the withdrawal of Israeli troops from South Lebanon.

Power sharing provided "the basis for ending the civil war and the return to political normalcy in Lebanon."[76] However, Lebanon's stability was challenged by sectarian groups acting as proxies for Iran, Saudi Arabia, and other international interests. These same countries worked through surrogates in Syria's civil war. The March 14 Alliance, which is backed by Saudi Arabia, became the leading proponent of Sunni participation, while the Iranian-backed March 8 Alliance supported Damascus. The conflict in Syria inflamed tensions in Lebanon, polarizing Lebanese politics, spilling over into Lebanon, and leading to a resurgence of sectarianism.

Hezbollah also entered the fray. In May 2013, elite fighters of Hezbollah engaged rebels in Homs province. They liberated the Qusayr corridor, a route running from Damascus to the coast along the border with Lebanon. The battle for Qusayr swung the tide in Assad's favor. Hezbollah and the United States found themselves on the same side against ISIS. Assad's overthrow would change the balance of power to disadvantage Hezbollah's sponsor, Iran. While most Shiites supported Hezbollah's engagement with Sunni rebels, some viewed Hezbollah's role in Syria's civil war as a distraction from Hezbollah's core mission: to defeat and destroy Israel.

Lebanon became a haven for Syrians fleeing deadly conflict. Approximately 1.2 million Syrian refugees are in Lebanon, which has provided sanctuary to more refugees than any country. Before the Syrian conflict, Lebanon's total population was about 4.5 million, including 450,000 Palestinian refugees. Lebanon is a fragile state. Lebanese fear that volatility in the region could be contagious, sparking violence and resulting in Lebanon's fragmentation.

On August 4, ISIS seized the Lebanese town of Arsal in the Bekaa Valley. Over three days of fighting, fourteen soldiers were killed, eighty-six wounded, and twenty-two captured by ISIS. At least one Lebanese solider was beheaded. Fighting was sparked by the arrest of Imad Ahmad Jomaa, the local emir and commander of Syrian Islamist rebel group.[77] General Jean Kahwaji, chief of staff of the Lebanese Armed Forces, maintained that the attack was intended to renew sectarian

216

strife in Lebanon. In response, Saudi Arabia gave $1 billion to bolster Lebanon's armed forces.

Israel

Israel and Iraqi Kurdistan have common interests. ISIS represents a risk to both. Israel supports the Iraqi Kurds, as a bulwark against Islamic extremism. Moreover, Kurds are the only group with the commitment and capabilities to confront Islamic State fighters.

ISIS seized territory in the Golan Heights and border crossings between Iraq and Jordan. Both are springboards for attacks on Israel. Israel has taken steps to counter ISIS by discreetly cultivating ties with moderate Syrian rebel groups. It is also finding common cause with moderate Arab States who fear the tide of radical Islam. Saudi Arabia was virtually silent during Israel's clash with Hamas in 2014. Other Arab states—Egypt, Jordan, and the United Arab Emirates—have silent sympathy with Israel. They view radical Islam as the vanguard of Islamist efforts to destabilize the region.

Israel and Arab states share a deep distrust of Iran. Prime Minister Benjamin Netanyahu is convinced that the goal of Iran's nuclear program is to develop a nuclear bomb. A nuclear-armed Iran is an existential threat to Israel's survival. Whereas Israel historically looked to the United States for support, Netanyahu is wary of Obama's willingness to negotiate with enemies and give away his bottom line. He fears that the United States will seek a regional accommodation with Iran.

In remarks on June 28, 2014, Netanyahu endorsed the "Kurdish aspiration for independence," citing the "collapse" of Iraq. According to Netanyahu, Kurds are a "fighting people that has proved its political commitment, political moderation, and deserves political independence." Israeli President Shimon Peres told Obama, "The Kurds have, de facto, created their own state, which is democratic." According to Foreign Minister Avigdor Lieberman, "The creation of an independent Kurdish state is a foregone conclusion."[78] President Shimon Perez established, "It is upon us to support international efforts to strengthen Jordan and support the Kurds' aspiration for independence."[79]

About two hundred thousand Jews of Kurdish descent live in Israel.[80] They are an important constituency advocating Kurdish interests. Israel and Iraqi Kurdistan are both small nations, surrounded by hostile neighbors. Israeli-Kurdish cooperation dates back to the 1960s, when Israel built peripheral alliances with non-Arab entities in the region—Iraqi Kurdistan, Turkey, and Iran. Israel helped train Mustafa Barzani's peshmerga in the 1960s. Israel provided humanitarian relief to Kurds after the Gulf War in 1991. Israeli dry-land farmers export technology and expertise to partners in Iraqi Kurdistan.

Israel and Iraqi Kurdistan are also working together in the energy sector. Israel was the first customer buying oil from Iraqi Kurdistan. At least four tankers delivered oil from Ceyhan to the southern port of Ashkelon between January and June 2014. The transactions were arranged by a Turkish company, Powertrans, which acts as the KRG's agent selling oil via tenders to traders. The KRG is discreet about its contact with Israel. It does not want "to offend anyone."[81]

Notes

1. *Al Arabiya News.* N.p., 09 Sept. 2014. Web. 09 Sept. 2014.
2. Ibid.
3. "ISIS Leader Al-Baghdadi Calls on Muslims to Rush to 'Your State,'" NBC News." *NBC News.* N.p., n.d. Web. 2 July 2014.
4. Interview with KRG Chief of Staff of the Presidency, Dr. Fuad Hussein, by the author, July 1, 2014 (Washington, DC).
5. Gordon, Michael R. "In U.S. Exit from Iraq, Failed Efforts and Challenges." *The New York Times.* The New York Times, 22 Sept. 2012. Web. 2 July 2014.
6. Interview with KRG Chief of Staff of the Presidency, Dr. Fuad Hussein, by the author, July 1, 2014 (Washington, DC).
7. Weinberg, Ali. "Biden, Kerry Work the Phones to Unite Iraqi Politicians." *ABC News.* ABC News Network, 02 July 2014. Web. 13 July 2014.
8. Gordon, Michael R. "Kerry Implores Kurdish Leader to Join a Government and Not Break Away." *The New York Times.* The New York Times, 24 June 2014. Web. 08 July 2014.
9. Interview with KRG Foreign Minister Falah Mustafa Bakir by the author, July 1, 2014 (Washington, DC).
10. "Iraqi Kurds Say Will Sue Baghdad If It Blocks Oil Sales." *Reuters.* Thomson Reuters, 03 July 2014. Web. 13 July 2014.
11. Payne, Julia. "Israel Accepts First Delivery of Disputed Kurdish Pipeline Oil." *Reuters.* Thomson Reuters, 20 June 2014. Web. 11 July 2014. <http://www.reuters.com/article/2014/06/20/us-israel-iraq-idUSKBN0EV0X620140620>.
12. "Kurdistan Premier: We Will Never Give Up Control of Our Own Oil." *Rudaw.* N.p., n.d. Web. 11 July 2014. <http://rudaw.net/english/kurdistan/29052014>.
13. "Obama Sending up to 300 Military Advisers to Iraq." *Obama Sending up to 300 Military Advisers to Iraq.* N.p., n.d. Web. 10 July 2014.
14. "What Iraq's New Prime Minister Can Learn from Nelson Mandela." *Cognoscenti.* N.p., n.d. Web. 05 Sept. 2014. <http://cognoscenti.wbur.org/2014/08/20/iraq-inclusion-al-abadi-timothy-phillips>.

15. "Embattled Iraqi Prime Minister Nouri Al-Maliki 'will Not Go Quietly', Foes and Friends Say." *Washington Post*. The Washington Post, n.d. Web. 7 July 2014.

16. Ibid.

17. Ibid.

18. Interview with a State Department official who was not authorized to speak on-the-record, July 1, 2014.

19. Lewis, Paul, and Spencer Ackerman. "Obama to Send up to 300 'military Advisers' to Help Iraqi Army Repel Isis." *The Guardian*. Guardian News and Media, 20 June 2014. Web. 13 July 2014.

20. Ackerman, Spencer. "Pentagon Says Growing US Forces in Iraq Need 'flexibility' for Mission." *Theguardian.com*. Guardian News and Media, 01 July 2014. Web. 13 July 2014.

21. *US News*. U.S.News & World Report, n.d. Web. 09 Sept. 2014. <http://www.usnews.com/opinion/mercedes-schlapp/2014/08/08/yazidis-and-christians-have-been-abandoned-by-obamas-iraq-retreat>.

22. Miller, Zeke. "Obama Authorizes Air Strikes, Humanitarian Aid in Iraq." *Time*. Time, 7 Aug. 2014. Web. 09 Sept. 2014. <http://time.com/3090310/iraq-yazidi-isis-barack-obama-us-military-airstrikes/>.

23. V, Tom, and En Brook. "130 More U.S. Military Advisers Arrive in Northern Iraq." *USA Today*. Gannett, 13 Aug. 2014. Web. 13 Aug. 2014. <http://www.usatoday.com/story/news/world/2014/08/12/advisers-sent-northern-iraq-help-plan-refugee-evacuation/13970545/>.

24. Cited in The New York Times, "U.S. Mobilizing Allies to Widen Assault on ISIS." August 27, 2014. Pg. A1.

25. Anderson, Liam D., and Gareth R. V. Stansfield. *Crisis in Kirkuk: The Ethnopolitics of Conflict and Compromise*. Philadelphia, PA: U of Pennsylvania, 2009. Print.

26. "Local & North Carolina State News from Raleigh, NC | NewsObserver.com." *Local & North Carolina State News from Raleigh, NC | NewsObserver.com*. N.p., n.d. Web. 12 Sept. 2014. <http://www.newsobserver.com/2014/09/10/4139818/pentagon-us-warplanes-have-taken.html>.

27. Tharoor, Ishaan. "A U.S.-designated Terrorist Group Is Saving Yazidis and Battling the Islamic State." *Washington Post*. The Washington Post, n.d. Web. 09 Sept. 2014. <http://www.washingtonpost.com/blogs/worldviews/wp/2014/08/11/a-u-s-designated-terrorist-group-is-saving-yazidis-and-battling-the-islamic-state/>.

28. Carter, Chelsea J., Elise Labott, Susan Garraty, Jim Acosta, Josh Levs, Brian Stelter, Samira Said, and Tim Lister. "ISIS Video Shows Beheading of American Journalist Steven Sotloff." *CNN*. Cable News Network, 01 Jan. 1970. Web. 08 Sept. 2014. <http://www.cnn.com/2014/09/02/world/meast/isis-american-journalist-sotloff/index.html>.

29. Smith-Spark, Laura, Andrew Carey, Hamdi Alkhshali, Jason Hanna, Richard Allen Greene, and Mariano Castillo. "UK Raises Terror Threat Level, Citing Risks out of Syria, Iraq." *CNN*. Cable News Network, 01 Jan. 1970. Web. 10 Sept. 2014. <http://www.cnn.com/2014/08/29/world/meast/isis-iraq-syria/index.html>.

30. Ibid.

31. "Somini Sengupta. "Nations Working to Stop Citizens from Aiding ISIS." The New York Times. September 13, 2014. Pg. A1. M.

32. Carter, Chelsea J., Chelsea J. Carter, Catherine E. Shoichet Reported, Wrote from Atlanta. Hamdi Alkhshali Reported from Atlanta. Barbara Starr, Jim Acosta in Washington, Anna Coren in Irbil, Iraq, and Jethro Mullen in Hong Kong. "Obama on ISIS in Syria: 'We Don't Have a Strategy Yet'" CNN. Cable News Network, 01 Jan. 1970. Web. 10 Sept. 2014. <http://www.cnn.com/2014/08/28/world/meast/isis-iraq-syria/index.html>.

33. "Isis Besieges Town of Amerli amid Fears of Repeat of Sinjar Massacre. Hardline Islamists Are Surrounding the Town of Amerli â" Sparking Concern for the Safety of the 18,000 Shia Turkmen Residents, and Fears of a Repeat of the Mount Sinjar." ISISwatch. N.p., n.d. Web. 09 Sept. 2014. <http://isiswatch.org/2014/08/isis-besieges-town-of-amerli-amid-fears-of-repeat-of-sinjar-massacre/>.

34. "Iraqi Forces Recapture Strategic Mosul Dam with Help From U.S. Airstrikes." ABC News. ABC News Network, n.d. Web. 09 Sept. 2014. <http://abcnews.go.com/International/video/iraqi-forces-recapture-strategic-mosul-dam-us-airstrikes-25028097>.

35. "U.S. Airstrikes on ISIS Part of Operation to Retake Key Iraqi Dam." FOX2now-com. N.p., n.d. Web. 09 Sept. 2014. <http://fox2now.com/2014/08/16/u-s-airstrikes-on-isis-part-of-operation-to-retake-key-iraqi-dam/>.

36. "Could Iran Be Part of America's New Coalition of the Willing?" Slate Magazine. N.p., n.d. Web. 09 Sept. 2014. <http://www.slate.com/blogs/the_world_/2014/09/05/could_iran_be_part_of_america_s_new_coalition_of_the_willing.html>.

37. Hudson, David. ""America Must Always Lead": President Obama Addresses West Point Graduates." The White House. The White House, 28 May 2014. Web. 10 July 2014.

38. "Leading From Behind." The New Yorker. N.p., n.d. Web. 10 July 2014.

39. "Hillary Clinton Splits with Obama on Foreign Policy." CNN Political Ticker RSS. N.p., n.d. Web. 11 Aug. 2014. <http://politicalticker.blogs.cnn.com/2014/08/10/hillary-clinton-splits-with-obama-on-foreign-policy/comment-page-1/>.

40. Landler, Mark. "A Rift in Worldviews Is Exposed as Clinton Faults Obama on Policy." The New York Times. The New York Times, 11 Aug. 2014. Web. 12 Aug. 2014. <http://www.nytimes.com/2014/08/12/world/middleeast/attacking-obama-policy-hillary-clinton-exposes-different-worldviews.html?action=click&contentCollection=Middle%20East*ion=Footer&module=MoreInSection&pgtype=article>.

41. "Syrian Arab Republic." UNHCR News. N.p., n.d. Web. 05 Sept. 2014. <http://www.unhcr.org/pages/49e486a76.html>.

42. "Troop Drawdown: Obama Says U.S. Finishing Afghan Job - Hamodia." Hamodia. N.p., n.d. Web. 10 July 2014.

43. "Obama Job Approval - Foreign Policy - Polls - HuffPost Pollster." The Huffington Post. N.p., n.d. Web. 05 Sept. 2014. <http://elections.huffingtonpost.com/pollster/obama-job-approval-foreign-policy>.

44. "Obama Job Approval - Foreign Policy - Polls - HuffPost Pollster." *The Huffington Post.* N.p., n.d. Web. 05 Sept. 2014. <http://elections.huffingtonpost.com/pollster/obama-job-approval-foreign-policy>.

45. "More Than 30 Turkish Truck Drivers Freed in Iraq." *Time.* Time, n.d. Web. 13 July 2014.

46. Yeginsu, Ceylan. "Militants Storm Turkish Consulate in Iraqi City, Taking 49 People as Hostages." *The New York Times.* The New York Times, 11 June 2014. Web. 13 July 2014.

47. "Turkish Media Banned from Reporting on Mosul Hostage Crisis - Al-Monitor: The Pulse of the Middle East." *Al-Monitor.* N.p., n.d. Web. 13 July 2014.

48. Ibid.

49. "World Socialist Web Site." *The Crisis in Iraq and the Response of the Turkish Ruling Class -.* N.p., n.d. Web. 10 Sept. 2014. <http://www.wsws.org/en/articles/2014/06/19/turk-j19.html>.

50. "Will Turkey Midwife Independent Kurdistan? | RealClearWorld." *Will Turkey Midwife Independent Kurdistan? | RealClearWorld.* N.p., n.d. Web. 09 Sept. 2014. <http://www.realclearworld.com/2014/07/17/will_turkey_midwife_independent_kurdistan_160143.html>.

51. "Syrian Kurds Continue to Blame Turkey for Backing ISIS Militants - Al-Monitor: The Pulse of the Middle East." *Al-Monitor.* N.p., n.d. Web. 13 July 2014.

52. "42 Killed, 140 Injured in Turkey Blasts." *PressTV.* N.p., n.d. Web. 13 July 2014.

53. "Turkey Looks for International Aid, and Countries to Host Refugees, in Syrian Crisis." *Washington Post.* The Washington Post, n.d. Web. 13 July 2014.

54. "POLITICS - PM ErdoÄŸan Slams Opposition Parties over Response to Mosul Kidnappings." *PM ErdoÄŸan Slams Opposition Parties over Response to Mosul Kidnappings.* N.p., n.d. Web. 13 July 2014.

55. "Turkey to Build Camp inside Iraq for Turkmen Refugees - Yenisafak.com.tr - 09.08.2014." *Turkey to Build Camp inside Iraq for Turkmen Refugees - Yenisafak.com.tr - 09.08.2014.* N.p., n.d. Web. 10 Sept. 2014. <http://english.yenisafak.com/news/turkey-to-build-camp-inside-iraq-for-turkmen-refugees-09.08.2014-3753>.

56. "Pro-Kurdish BDP to Push for Autonomy following Local Elections." *Pro-Kurdish BDP to Push for Autonomy following Local Elections.* N.p., n.d. Web. 13 July 2014.

57. Murat Yetkin. "Next Issues: Presidential Polls, Kurdish Autonomy and Syria. *Turkish Daily News.* April 1, 2014.

58. BECATOROS, SUZAN FRASER and ELENA. *Yahoo! News.* Yahoo!, 10 Aug. 2014. Web. 10 Sept. 2014. <http://news.yahoo.com/pm-erdogan-wins-turkeys-presidential-election-194352738.html>.

59. "President Obama Announces Presidential Delegation to Turkey to Attend the Inauguration of His Excellency Recep Tayyip Erdoğan." *The White House.* The White House, n.d. Web. 04 Sept. 2014. <http://www.whitehouse.gov/the-press-office/2014/08/26/president-obama-announces-presidential-delegation-turkey-attend-inaugura>.

60. Letsch, Constanze. "Erdogan Emerges Victorious in Turkish Presidential Elections amid Low Turnout." *The Guardian.* Guardian News and Media, 11 Aug. 2014. Web. 12 Aug. 2014. <http://www.theguardian.com/world/2014/aug/10/turkey-presidential-election-ergodan>.

61. "Why Are Turks So Angry? | World Policy Institute." *Why Are Turks So Angry? | World Policy Institute.* N.p., n.d. Web. 13 July 2014.

62. Document, Public, March 2006, and Eur 44/003/2006. Turkey: Article 301: How the Law on "denigrating Turkishness" Is an Insult to Free Expression (n.d.): n. pag. Web.

63. "Turkey Ministers Resign amid Scandal." *BBC News.* N.p., n.d. Web. 13 July 2014.

64. Scott, Alev. "Erdoğan's Self-defence over Soma's Mining Disaster Was Badly Misjudged." *Theguardian.com.* Guardian News and Media, 15 May 2014. Web. 3 July 2014.

65. "Why Are Turks So Angry? | World Policy Institute." *Why Are Turks So Angry? | World Policy Institute.* N.p., n.d. Web. 13 July 2014.

66. American Foreign Policy. The Sevres Syndrome: Turkish Foreign Policy and its Historical Legacies. Dietrich Jung. August 2003. Thewww.unc.edu/...**sevres**/jung_**sevres**.html.

67. HakanYilmaz, "Two Pillars of Nationalist Euroskepticism in. Turkey: The Tanzimat and *Sevres Syndromes.*" 2006. *hakanyilmaz.info/.../HakanYilmaz-2006-TanzimatSevresSyndromes-Eng...*

68. "Global Public Square." *Global Public Square RSS.* N.p., n.d. Web. 30 July 2014. <http://globalpublicsquare.blogs.cnn.com/>.

69. "No End in Sight for Islamic State's Attack on Iraq - Al-Monitor: The Pulse of the Middle East." *Al-Monitor.* N.p., n.d. Web. 22 Aug. 2014. <http://www.al-monitor.com/pulse/originals/2014/08/iraq-sunnis-targeted-by-islamic-state.html?utm_source=Al-Monitor+Newsletter+%5BEnglish%5D&utm_campaign=bc2ac65823-August_22_2014&utm_medium=email&utm_term=0_28264b27a0-bc2ac65823-93077049#ixzz3B8knNJJC>.

70. "Ban Ki-moon Credits Saudi Arabia for Supporting UN Aid Effort in Iraq." *Ptvnews.* N.p., n.d. Web. 30 July 2014. <http://ptvnews.ph/bottom-news-life2/12-12-world/35021-ban-thanks-saudi-arabia-for-backing-un-aid-effort-in-iraq#sthash.D1FMex9W.dpuf>.

71. "After Success in Iraq and Syria, ISIL Will Find It Tougher to Crack Jordan | The National." *After Success in Iraq and Syria, ISIL Will Find It Tougher to Crack Jordan | The National.* N.p., n.d. Web. 4 July 2014.

72. "Top Shiite Cleric Urges Iraqis to Fight Advancing Militants - Hindustan Times." *Http://www.hindustantimes.com/.* N.p., n.d. Web. 10 July 2014.

73. Ibid.

74. "Qassem Suleimani Has Brought Iran Much Grief." *The Daily Star Newspaper.* N.p., n.d. Web. 10 July 2014.

75. IranWire. *The Daily Beast.* Newsweek/Daily Beast, n.d. Web. 4 July 2014.

76. Krayem, Hassan. "The Lebanese civil war and the Taif agreement". American University of Beirut.

77. Saad, Hwaida, and Rick Gladstone. "Border Fighting Intensifies Between ISIS and Lebanon." *The New York Times*. The New York Times, 04 Aug. 2014. Web. 13 Aug. 2014. <http://www.nytimes.com/2014/08/05/world/middleeast/isis-lebanon-syria.html?_r=0>.

78. "Israeli PM Netanyahu Endorses Kurdish Independence Citing Chaos in Iraq."- *RT News*. N.p., n.d. Web. 4 July 2014.

79. "McClatchy DC." TEL AVIV: Netanyahu's Call for Kurdish Independence Sparks Questions about a Unified Iraq. N.p., n.d. Web. 4 July 2014.

80. "National News from McClatchy DC News | Washington DC." National News from McClatchy DC News | Washington DC. N.p., n.d. Web. 12 Sept. 2014. <http://www.mcclatchydc.com/2014/07/01/232057/netanyahus-call-for-kurdish-independence.html>.

81. Interview with KRG National Security Adviser Fuad Hussein by the author, July 1, 2014 (Washington, DC).

12

The Path to Independence

Masoud Barzani made a closed-door address to the Kurdistan Parliament on July 2, 2014.[1] He outlined plans for self-determination and a referendum. That day, Barzani's chief of staff and national security adviser, Fuad Hussein, met Vice President Joe Biden and Deputy National Security Adviser Anthony Blinken at the White House. Fuad Hussein came out of the meeting and briefed the press about the KRG's conditions for participating in the new Iraqi government: "We are once again going to give a chance to the political process in Baghdad." As a starting point, Baghdad must "recognize the border of Kurdistan [and] the independence of our economy." The KRG set a deadline for conducting a referendum should Baghdad fail to address their core demands. If Prime Minister Heidar al-Abadi could not govern inclusively, talks with Baghdad would be about "divorce" rather than power sharing.[2]

Traditionally Kurds and Shiites were in coalition, working together to depose Saddam Hussein. Losing the Kurdish block would destabilize Iraqi politics, further polarizing Arab Shiites and Sunnis. Iraq's Shiite parties are proxies of Iran, which opposes Kurdish independence. Though Kurds and Sunnis shared frustration during the mandate of Prime Minister Nouri al-Maliki, Sunnis oppose Kurdish independence. They support the concept of Iraqi unity, which was propagated under Saddam. ISIS is also against Kurdish independence. Islamic State fighters targeted the Kurds for being pro-Western, pro-American, and pro-democracy apostates.

Practical obstacles impede the national aspirations of Iraqi Kurds. Though Baghdad is obligated to distribute 17 percent of Iraq's total oil income to the KRG, it suspended payments in January 2014.[3] The KRG needs to sell its oil and gas to offset the loss of revenue. However, it faces legal and procedural obstacles to monetizing Iraqi Kurdistan's energy wealth. Large energy companies, like Exxon Mobil and Chevron, have positions in Iraqi Kurdistan, but they are hedging their bets pending a hydrocarbons and revenue sharing law between Baghdad and the KRG.[4] Meanwhile, the KRG is at a disadvantage. It has oil but lacks delivery and storage capacity. The KRG also lacks the legal and political basis for consistent, large-scale exports. Ongoing violence poses a further problem; the northern pipeline has been regularly sabotaged.[5]

Turkey allows the transport of oil from Iraqi Kurdistan to Ceyhan. However, it does not purchase the oil for domestic consumption. A tanker of Kurdish oil was stranded off the coast of Morocco for days, because Iraq threatened a legal challenge against the buyer. The United States also pressured the government of Morocco not to offload the oil.[6] Ownership of Kurdish oil in a tanker outside Galveston, Texas, was tied up for months in US courts. A deal to deposit oil revenues in the New York account of Iraq's Central Bank collapsed when Turkey insisted on placing funds in escrow at state-owned Halkbank.[7] The Obama administration discourages customers. It thinks that sale of oil from Iraqi Kurdistan would accelerate Iraq's fragmentation.

The KRG has a cash-flow problem, stemming from Baghdad's revenue cutoff and problems selling Kurdish oil. The KRG did not pay salaries to civil servants for months due to its budget crisis. Predictability is critical to trade and investment. Iraqi Kurdistan's vibrant economy slowed when ISIS attacked. Scarce supply of processed fuels, like petrol, led to rationing and long lines at the pump.[8]

Kurds will not be easily deterred from their national aspirations. Kurds are virtually unanimous in support for independence as the best way to ensure their security and political and cultural rights. Kurdish culture has always been under threat from Iraq's Arab majority, which treats them like second-class citizens. Iraqi Kurdistan is a progressive society. Women in Suleimani are often seen without a hijab, strolling with unmarried male companions. Kurdish businessman and politician Cimsit Firat describes cultural differences between Kurds and Arabs: "Kurds are joyful and love life. Kurds go to parties; they dance. The women dress colorfully." He contrasts them with Shiite women, who wear all black and are covered from head to toe, and Arab Sunni women, who are subordinated to their husbands and patriarchy. "Arabs have a culture of killing that dates back to the battle of Karbala" and the slaying of Ali and Hussein.[9]

Conservative social values and identity politics intensify when people feel isolated from the world. Iraqi Kurdistan may be landlocked, but Kurds have overcome isolation through the Internet. About 70 percent of Iraqi Kurds are under the age of twenty-five. They are increasingly connected to the global community via social media.[10] Access to information is an antidote. Kurds feel kinship with the West. Turkey represents a portal to Europe, European culture, and an eventual customs union between the KRG and the European Union. Globalization enhances Iraqi Kurdistan's secular pro-Western orientation.

Tragedy dominates the Kurdish historical narrative. Kurds have a history of betrayal, which dates back to the early twentieth century. More recently, the 1988 chemical weapons attack on Halabja left a deep scar on the Kurdish psyche. Halabja is commemorated every year on its anniversary.[11] Memories of Halabja reinforce a widespread and deeply rooted insecurity among Kurds that a similar event is imminent.

Despite their national tragedy, Kurds are an optimistic and proud people. They have withstood betrayal by great powers, atrocities by Saddam, and false promises by the United States. Independence is not just a political state. It is a state of being. Independence would right a historical injustice, manifesting the pride of Kurds and fulfilling their destiny as a people. Kurds believe that independence is the only credible guarantor of security. Only Kurds can protect Kurds.

*****

Iraq appeared on the verge of collapse when ISIS seized Mosul on June 10, 2014, and Islamic State fighters raced across the desert to the gates of Baghdad. Peshmerga consolidated control of Kirkuk and extended Iraqi Kurdistan's boundaries. However, dreams of independence were shattered when ISIS attacked Kurdistan, declaring an Islamic State, occupying Sinjar, threatening Dohuk, and seizing Makhmour, just thirty kilometers from Erbil.[12]

Kurds have not abandoned their goal of independence. However, events have delayed its realization. The Kurdish economy was badly affected. Peshmerga need time to develop into a more effective military. The KRG still relies on the United States for support and protection. Without US assistance, Erbil would have fallen, and thousands killed

Independence is based on several assumptions. First, the KRG can defend its territory and citizens. Second, the KRG can sell its oil and gas on international markets. Third, revenue from energy sales would be adequate to support KRG operations. Fourth, Turkey is an ally and friend. Events cast serious doubt on these assumptions.

Turkey is most problematic. Its lack of response to ISIS raised serious questions about its reliability. Concern was exacerbated by Turkey's reluctance to sign the Jeddah declaration on September 10, 2014, as well as its reluctance to join Obama's coalition of countries opposing ISIS. Rumors swirled about Turkey's assistance to ISIS, including financial and logistical support for jihadis transiting from Turkey to Syria. According to Thomas L. Friedman, "Erdogan stands for authoritarianism, press intimidation, crony capitalism, and quiet support for Islamists including ISIS." He asked, "What's in his soul?"[13]

Unilateral Declaration of Independence (UDI)

The KRG is seeking a genuine partnership with the Iraqi government. It maintains that partnership should be rooted in principles of equality and justice. The Iraqi government must uphold the constitution, especially federalism. The unique characteristics of Kurds should be protected and preserved. Measures marginalizing the Kurds or any group are unacceptable. Government institutions should be inclusive and professionalized. Simply put, Iraqi Kurds demand a say in their future. The KRG articulated benchmarks clarifying its core demands. Baghdad must distribute Kurdistan's share of the national budget, 17 percent. The KRG should be allowed to sell Kurdish oil. The Iraqi government must provide equipment and budgetary support to the peshmerga, which would become a national guard responsible for security in Kurdistan.

Heidar al-Abadi, who replaced Nouri al-Maliki, is more conciliatory by nature. Maliki's erratic behavior and polarizing personality pushed the Kurds toward a UDI. Maliki blamed the Kurds for allowing ISIS to advance. He called Erbil the "headquarters of ISIS, Baath, and al-Qaeda."[14] Maliki thought he could score political points by accusing the Kurds, but Barzani would have none of it. Barzani responded, "Kurdistan is proud that Erbil has always served as a refuge for oppressed people, including yourself when you fled the former dictatorship."[15]

Kurds have always maintained they will not be blamed for Iraq's break up. The KRG will not move precipitously unless the crisis grows more urgent, or it has international support. To succeed, a UDI requires recognition by the international community The Obama administration made clear its opposition to Kurdistan's independence, under current circumstances.

Coordinated Declaration of Independence (CDI)

All diplomatic efforts must be exhausted prior to a CDI, which would require a country or countries to take the lead in close coordination with the KRG. Iraqi Kurdistan's CDI will require Turkey's participation. Ankara was silent when peshmerga seized Kirkuk, but it opposed Masoud Barzani's plan for a referendum on self-determination.[16] President Erdogan did not rule out the possibility of independence for Iraqi Kurdistan. At the Council on Foreign Relations on September 22, 2014, he expressed a willingness to discuss independence, with Iraq's territorial integrity as the starting point.[17]

The KRG initiated contingency planning discussions with then-Foreign Minister Ahmet Davutoglu in 2012. They discussed how Turkey would react to different scenarios whereby Iraqi Kurdistan achieved independence.[18] Beginning in 2012, Turkey and Iraqi Kurdistan forged a strategic partnership based on common commercial interests. In 2013, $15 billion in Turkish goods were sold in Iraqi Kurdistan. Turkish construction companies signed lucrative contracts to build skyscrapers, airports, and highways. A new oil pipeline with the capacity to transport 200,000 barrels/day was opened to Ceyhan on May 2, 2014. Up to one million barrels/day can be delivered by 2015. More is potentially on the way; Iraqi Kurdistan has forty-five billion barrels of oil reserves.[19]

Prime Minister Nechirvan Barzani championed the strategic partnership between Ankara and Erbil. Nechirvan insisted that Kurds could count on Turkey's protection. However, the KRG grew wary of Turkey's golden handcuff. It does not want to gain independence from Iraq and become dependent on Turkey.

Kurds were deeply disappointed in Turkey's complicity and neglect as the ISIS crisis escalated in August 2014. A KRG envoy met Turkish officials in Istanbul. He asked Turkish forces based in Iraqi Kurdistan to intervene. Short of their direct involvement, he asked Turkey to supply weapons to the peshmerga. Ankara demurred, using the upcoming presidential elections as an excuse to remain uninvolved. Later, Ankara would use the fact that ISIS held Turkish hostages to resist Kurdish entreaties.[20]

Erdogan's democratic credentials were increasingly questioned. Despite his strong electoral mandate, Erdogan refused to allow greater political and cultural rights for Kurds in Turkey. He sought constitutional reforms establishing an executive presidency, but rejected Kurdish demands for decentralization and enhanced powers for local government. Though the PKK maintained its ceasefire and withdrew forces from Turkey, Erdogan continued to call the PKK a terrorist organization. The Turkish government rejected amnesty for PKK commanders.[21] It refused to release jailed political prisoners as a sign of goodwill toward the peace process. Regressive legislation, such as Article 8 of the Anti-Terror Act and Article 301 of the Penal Code, remained in force.[22]

Saudi Arabia also opposes an independent Kurdistan. It fears that independence would result in the fragmentation of Iraq into Shiite and Kurdish regions. The emergence of "Shiastan" in Iraq's Southeast could inspire a rebellion by Shiites in the Kingdom, resulting in instability and potential fragmentation. The United States is unlikely to oppose Ankara and Riyadh, by participating in a CDI for Iraqi Kurdistan.

Mutual Agreement

Negotiations between Baghdad and the KRG could result in a mutual agreement to disassociate. However, a civilized divorce is unlikely. Breaking up states through mutual agreement is a rarity. Czechs and Slovaks negotiated their disassociation in 1993; Norway held a referendum on independence from Sweden in 1905.[23] But disassociation is usually the result of conflict rather than cool-headed negotiation.

Maliki intimated that he would let go of Iraqi Kurdistan. "Good riddance," he implied. But Maliki insisted that Kirkuk and other disputed internal boundaries remain a part of Iraq. Kirkuk is a deal breaker. No Kurdish leader would give away Kirkuk and Khanaqin, which are presently under the KRG's control.

More than political will, separation will require agreement on a number of technical and financial issues. The two sides must demarcate the boundaries of Iraqi Kurdistan. A security pact would be required. Negotiations must address the division of assets and liabilities, revenues, and resources including water supply as both the Tigris and Euphrates Rivers flow through Iraqi Kurdistan to the Mesopotamian plains. A customs union would be needed to manage comingled economic interests. Both Iraq and Iraqi Kurdistan benefit from trade with one another.

Moreover, Iraqi Kurdistan needs revenue to be viable. The KRG requires $1.2 billion each month to pay salaries and expenses.[24] Oil is king in Kurdistan. To date, however, the Iraqi government has obstructed oil exploration, production, and transport. Once pumped out of the ground, Kurdish oil must gain access to the sea. The current pipeline runs through Turkey to Ceyhan. Though Turkey needs additional energy supplies, it refuses to buy Kurdish oil. It could shut down the pipeline at any time. Iraqi Kurds cannot count on Turkey. The KRG has learned not to put all its eggs in one basket.

The KRG and Iran have historically enjoyed good relations. However, Iran's abusive approach toward Iranian Kurds is a bone of contestation for all Kurds. Likewise, PJAK's use of Iraqi Kurdistan as a base for its political and military operations concerns the Iranian government. The plight of Iranian Kurds and PJAK's status must be addressed in the context of Tehran's regional and international relations.

Successfully completing an accord with the P5+1 on its nuclear program would allow Iran to normalize its international relations and benefit from the lifting of sanctions. An accord would strengthen the forces of reform in Iran, with broad bearing on Iran's domestic politics and international relations. If the nuclear negotiations culminate in an accord, Rouhani and Iran's reform forces will be emboldened. A stronger and more progressive middle and merchant class would emerge. The Iranian government would have incentive to pursue a path of democratization, adopting more liberal policies including autonomy and decentralization for non-Persian communities.

If talks on the nuclear program flounder, however, Ayatollah Khamenei and the conservative Guardian Council will marginalize Rouhani and crack down on internal dissent. The United States would shift from diplomacy to a strategy of regime change. This could involve ratcheting up political support for prodemocracy activists and dissident ethnic groups. A new US administration might even consider covert activities, assisting PJAK and other armed militants to put more pressure on the regime.

KRG-Rojava relations have improved. Masoud Barzani was a vocal supporter of foreign intervention when ISIS attacked Kobani canton.[25] Peshmerga joined the battle. Kurds fought side by side against ISIS in Shengal. Kurdish oil could flow from Iraqi Kurdistan through Rojava toward the Mediterranean . However, Rojava has no access to the sea. The distance between Rojava's boundary to a port is about thirty kilometers, running through Latakia and Alawite lands controlled by the Syrian government.

State Formation

In any scenario, the KRG must act like a state rather than a region or militia. The KRG needs strong institutions. It must get its affairs in order and gradually assume the trappings of statehood. No marching bands or fanfare in this scenario. As Iraq falls down, Iraqi Kurdistan would stand up, gaining greater credibility, respect, and international recognition.

The KRG needs a more modern macroeconomic policy. Oil is owned and traded by the KRG. This leaves little room for a diversified private sector and foreign direct investment outside the energy sector. To function like a normal economy, the KRG requires a system to assess and collect taxes, with taxes from oil revenues going to support the national budget. A sovereign wealth fund could be established, drawing on the Norwegian model.

Iraqi Kurdistan also needs a more diversified economy. Construction is the second greatest contributor to GDP, but construction has created a potential real estate bubble.[26] Electricity sales are also a source of revenue; Iraqi Kurdistan produces more electricity than it uses, with the excess sold in Iraq. Communications, cement, and agro industries are other noteworthy activities. Smuggling beer and cigarettes to Iran is also big business.[27]

Iraqi Kurdistan has virtually no banking system. Since most of the KRG's income comes from oil, which is traded in dollars, the KRG could dollarize the Kurdish economy. Converting all of its currency into dollars would outsource central banking functions to the US Federal Reserve. This would strengthen ties with the United States and help develop liquidity arrangements with central banks around the world, assuring the international exchange of funds.[28]

The World Bank and International Monetary Fund (IMF) can become more engaged with the KRG. The IMF has expertise to advise on fiscal policy. Though membership is not presently possible, the KRG can encourage the World Bank/IMF to set up working groups on Iraqi Kurdistan. Working groups would include a point person to interact with a KRG counterpart, and liaison offices in Erbil.

In parallel, the KRG could establish a core team of international economic advisers working with World Bank/IMF representatives on the KRG's central banking, treasury operations, trade relationships, and the energy sector. Creating the team would be a big step toward functioning like a country. Merely announcing the team would send a signal of seriousness to the international community.

Greater consensus among Iraqi Kurds is the foundation of getting Iraqi Kurdistan's house in order. Rivalry between the KDP and PUK has been a serious impediment to progress. The 1995 Kurdish civil war resulted in the establishment of parallel statelets, rather than genuine power sharing. Therein lies a conundrum. Power sharing is critical to

Iraqi Kurdistan's democratic development. However, Iraqi Kurdistan needs a strong state to address challenges on the path to independence.

A national vision would transcend party and tribal loyalties. It would also counteract nepotism, which lies at the root of corruption and has a corrosive effect on governance. To be sure, nepotism and corruption are widespread throughout the Middle East. They are also prevalent in Kurdish society, where kinship ideology and tribal loyalties run deep.[29]

Cash contributes to corruption and the abuse of power, which is an impediment to independence. The windfall from construction and consumer goods has created a cash-based economy. Corruption has been sustained by Baghdad's 17 percent payout. Government decisions are based on a web of personal relationships. A strong PUK and the rise of Gorran have improved transparency and held the KDP-led government accountable. However, Gorran is now a part of the system, which has affected its independence and undermined popular support. While the KDP has demonstrated the capacity for effective governance, it trends toward monolithic rather than inclusive rule.

A sense of entitlement exists among Kurds who struggled and fought for liberation. Many loyalists are given positions but do not work. At the Ministry of Anfal Affairs, personnel just show up and collect paychecks. The KDP and PUK are hiring too many people. The absence of meritocracy fuels inefficiency and undermines the development of a work ethic. The KRG needs a more competitive hiring process and fundamental reforms, including steps to shrink government and reduce the public debt.[30] About 70 percent of the work force in Iraqi Kurdistan is employed by the KRG. Underemployment is widespread among Kurdish youth. Persons under twenty years old are about half the total population. A culture of materialism and conspicuous consumption is widespread.[31]

A big and inclusive "Kurdish national conference" was planned for 2013. Abdullah Ocalan was driving the agenda, which appeared to lay the ground for a Greater Kurdistan. Not surprisingly, the KRG cancelled the conference in the face of opposition from Washington and Ankara.[32] According to Osman Baydemir, the former mayor of Diyarbakir, a consensus-building conference would be useless without participation of the PKK, PJAK, and the PYD.[33] He wants to revitalize the initiative including all parties and factions. To create a comfort zone, the conference should focus on cross-border cooperation in the Kurdish neighborhood rather than redrawing borders.

Masoud Barzani wants to lead a united front of Kurdish groups. However, the PYD resisted Barzani's role. The KRG and PYD have compelling reasons to cooperate. Both are under attack by ISIS. Both Iraqi Kurdistan and Rojava have established local administration over territories. Future oil transport from Iraqi Kurdistan may require cooperation of the authorities in Rojava. A positive precedent was set when the KRG and PYD beat back ISIS in Shengal. The PYD and KRG have already demonstrated the capacity to overcome their differences and develop cross-border cooperation to enhance mutual security, humanitarian assistance, and local administration.[34]

Unity is critical, especially during times of crisis. Differences between Masoud Barzani and the PYD's Salih Moslem Mohamed are superficial, not substantive. The PYD must not resist Barzani's leadership or undermine the Syrian branch of the KDP. Nor should Iraqi Kurds disparage or resist cooperation with Salih Moslem. As Kurds in Syria come together to defend their communities from attacks by both ISIS and Assad's forces, Barzani can assist the PYD's People's Protection Units. The ISIS succeeded in bringing Kurds together to fight terrorism.

The Kurdish neighborhood would be a space for expanding cross-border trade and cultural affinities as the base of a greater, virtual Kurdistan. Like letting steam out of the kettle, practical cooperation in the Kurdish neighborhood would diminish threats to territorial integrity rather than exacerbate differences between states where Kurds reside. Democratic development of Iraqi Kurdistan would serve as an inspiration to Kurds in the region, as well as a model for states.

*****

It would be best if Iraqis come together in common cause. Abadi may succeed in fostering national reconciliation. The Iraqi army may succeed in regrouping and reclaiming territories seize by ISIS. However, these goals may be wishful thinking In any event, stabilizing Iraq will take time. A clear victory against the Islamic State may be out of reach. Ending Syria's grinding civil war is a distant goal. Coalitions of the willing are basically symbolic. Eradicating Islamic extremism through education and economic development is a generational endeavor.

The KRG has set a deadline for Baghdad to address its core concerns. If Abadi fails to achieve consensus and satisfy the Kurds, Washington will have to face the fact that Iraq is simply not viable as a coherent and sovereign state. The United States is making a good-faith effort to save Iraq. But if Iraq fails, the US should organize countries to support Iraqi Kurdistan's independence. Meanwhile, the Obama administration should stop blocking the sale of oil from Iraqi Kurdistan so that Kurds have revenue to invest in state building. To enhance its train and equip program, Washington should seek a Status of Forced Agreement with the KRG. Even a small US force in Iraqi Kurdistan would help defend Kurds from the ISIS and show Tehran that the United States is still relevant.

The United States should focus its efforts in the region on the Kurds. The State Department should remove the PKK from the list of Foreign Terrorist Organizations (FTO). The PKK has complied with its ceasefire obligations and commitment to withdraw forces. It has become a force for good in the region, effectively opposing ISIS, saving Yazidis in Sinjar and Kurds in Kobani. If Ankara is talking to Ocalan, there is no reason for the US government to keep the PKK on the FTO list. Likewise, the EU and other states should delist the PKK. Delisting the PKK would recognize its positive contribution, galvanizing peace talks and putting a deal within reach. The PKK seeks a dignified peace. Eliminating indignities will shape its approach going forward.

Progress on the PKK would allow further progress with the PYD. Likewise, better relations would the PYD would affect relations between Western countries and the PKK. Salih Moslem should be given a visa to visit the United States for official meetings, including discussions at the Pentagon.[35] If the Peoples Protection Unites oppose ISIS, the US should not hesitate to assist. Even if Turkey objects, Washington should embrace the PYD for opposing Assad and battling Sunni extremists. The so-called moderate Syrian opposition is a myth. Friends of the West are few and far between in Syria.

America's best and only friends in Iraq are the Kurds. Washington must initiate reality-based contingency planning, and get ahead of events. Instead of trying to placate its enemies, the United States should support its friends. The Kurds used to have "no friend but the mountains." In Iraq and Syria today, the United States has no friend but the Kurds.

Notes

1. "Kurdistan Region-Iraq News in Brief. July 2, 2014." *Kurdistan Region-Iraq News in Brief. July 2, 2014.* N.p., n.d. Web. 12 Sept. 2014. <http://www.ekurd.net/mismas/articles/misc2014/7/kurdlocal1655.htm>.
2. Gordon, Michael R., and Alissa J. Rubin. "Kurdish Officials Seek More Autonomy in Any Deal With a New Government." *The New York Times.* The New York Times, 03 July 2014. Web. 7 July 2014.

3. "Iraq: Select Issues." *IMF Country Report* 13.218 (2013): n. pag. July 2013. Web. <http://www.imf.org/external/pubs/ft/scr/2013/cr13218.pdf>.

4. "Resetting the U.S.-Kurdish-Baghdad Relationship." - *The Washington Institute for Near East Policy*. N.p., n.d. Web. 26 Sept. 2014. <http://www. washingtoninstitute.org/policy-analysis/view/resetting-the-u.s.-kurdish-baghdad-relationship>.

5. *The Wall Street Journal*. Dow Jones & Company, n.d. Web. 14 July 2014.

6. "Iraqi Kurdistan's Oil Tanker Leaves Moroccan Port without Unloading - News." *Iraqi Kurdistan's Oil Tanker Leaves Moroccan Port without Unloading - News*. N.p., n.d. Web. 14 July 2014.

7. "Kurdistan Oil Export: A Game Changer." *American Center for Democracy*. N.p., n.d. Web. 14 July 2014.

8. Arango, Tim, and Clifford Krauss. "Poised to Gain in Iraq Crisis, Kurds Face New Barriers to Autonomy." *The New York Times*. The New York Times, 04 July 2014. Web. 7 July 2014.

9. Interview with Cismat Firat by the author. August 7, 2014.

10. Abc News Poll: Iraq – Where Things Stand, and Embargoed For Release After 6:30 P.m., Monday, March 15, 20. *EMBARGOED FOR RELEASE AFTER 6:30 P.M., Monday, March 15, 2004 While Ambivalent About the War, Most Iraqis Report a Better Life* (n.d.): n. pag. Web.

11. "Associates." *International Network of Museums for Peace*. N.p., n.d. Web. 14 July 2014.

12. "Saturday 9 August 2014." *Support Kurds in Syria RSS*. N.p., n.d. Web. 26 Sept. 2014. <http://supportkurds.org/news/saturday-9-august-2014/>.

13. Thomas L. Friedman. "ISIS Crisis." *The New York Times*. September 24, 2014.

14. Alissa J. Rubin and Alan Cowell. Kurdish Government Calls on Maliki to Quit as Premier." The New York Times. July 11, 2014. Pg. A6.

15. "Iraq's Maliki 'hysterical' Says Kurdish Leader | MidEast | Daily Sabah." *Dailysabah.com*. N.p., n.d. Web. 14 July 2014.

16. http://www.theguardian.com/world/2014/jul/03/kurds-independence-referendum-iraq-massoud-barzani

17. Remarks by President Recep Tayyip Erdogan at the Council on Foreign Relations. New York, September 22, 2014.

18. "MIDEAST - Ankara 'will Not Block Kurdish State in Iraq'" *Ankara 'will Not Block Kurdish State in Iraq'* N.p., n.d. Web. 14 July 2014.

19. "ISIL in Iraq Series: Iraq-Turkey Economic Ties Survive ISIL - Global Risk Insights." *Global Risk Insights*. N.p., n.d. Web. 14 July 2014.

20. "Turkey Just Got Forty-Six Hostages Back From ISIS. How Did That Happen?" *Slate Magazine*. N.p., n.d. Web. 26 Sept. 2014. <http://www. slate.com/blogs/the_world_/2014/09/22/isis_hostages_turkey_just_got_46_ hostages_back_from_the_terror_group_how.html>.

21. Gordts, Eline. "PKK Rebels Start Withdrawal From Turkey, Officials Says." *The Huffington Post*. TheHuffingtonPost.com, 08 May 2013. Web. 26 Sept. 2014. <http://www.huffingtonpost.com/2013/05/08/pkk-starts-withdrawal-turkey_n_3237178.html>.

23. Bennhold, Katrin. "From Kurdistan to Texas, Scots Spur Separatists." *The New York Times*. The New York Times, 10 Sept. 2014. Web. 26 Sept. 2014.

<http://www.nytimes.com/2014/09/11/world/europe/separatists-around-the-world-draw-inspiration-from-scotland.html?_r=0>.

24. "Iraq's Kurds Vow to Keep Kirkuk Oil Fields Until Referendum."*Bloomberg.com*. Bloomberg, n.d. Web. 26 Sept. 2014. <http://www.bloomberg.com/news/2014-06-30/iraq-s-kurds-vow-to-keep-kirkuk-amid-referendum-plans.html>.

25. Reuters. "Kurdish Forces Fight Off ISIS Attack On Kobani." *The Huffington Post*. TheHuffingtonPost.com, 25 Sept. 2014. Web. 25 Sept. 2014. <http://www.huffingtonpost.com/2014/09/25/kobani-isis_n_5879964.html>.

26. "Iraqi Kurdistan's Real Estate Market: A Bubble about to Burst?" *Iraqi Kurdistan's Real Estate Market: A Bubble about to Burst?* N.p., n.d. Web. 26 Sept. 2014. <http://www.ekurd.net/mismas/articles/misc2012/9/state6521.htm>.

27. Interview with Shwan Taha by the author. Istanbul, August 7, 2014.

28. Wearden, Graeme. "US Rivals 'plotting to End Oil Trading in Dollars'" *Theguardian.com*. Guardian News and Media, 06 Oct. 2009. Web. 14 July 2014.

29. "SUMMER 2007 VOLUME XIV: NUMBER 3." *Iraqi Kurdistan's Downward Spiral*. N.p., n.d. Web. 14 July 2014.

30. Ibid.

31. Interview with Shwan Taha by the author. Istanbu, August 7, 2014.

32. "Long-awaited Pan-Kurdish National Conference Postponed Indefinitely." *Ekurd*. N.p., 11 Nov. 2013. Web. 14 July 2014.

33. Interview with Osman Baydemir by the author. May 19, 2014 (New York).

34. "They're Saving Yazidis Yet Ignored by the US—why?" *CNBC*. N.p., n.d. Web. 26 Sept. 2014. <http://www.cnbc.com/id/101927791>.

35. "Five Reasons US Should Change Policies toward Syria's Kurds - Al-Monitor: The Pulse of the Middle East." *Al-Monitor*. N.p., n.d. Web. 12 Sept. 2014. <http://www.al-monitor.com/pulse/originals/2013/10/us-change-policy-syria-kurds.html>.

List of Abbreviations

Armenian Secret Army for the Liberation of Armenia (ASALA)
Central Treaty Organization (CENTO)
Committee of Union and Progress (CUP)
Democratic People's Party (DEHAP)
Democratic Society Party (DTP)
Democratic Union Party (PYD)
European Union (EU)
Foreign Terrorist Organizations (FTOs)
Global War on Terror (GWOT)
International Monetary Fund (IMF)
International Security Assistance Force (ISAF)
Islamic State of Syria and Iraq/ Islamic State (ISIS)
Justice and Development Party (AKP)
Kurdish Communities Union (KCK)
Kurdish Democratic Front (KDF)
Kurdistan Democratic Party (KDP)
Kurdish Democratic Party of Syria (KDPS)
Kurdistan Democratic Party of Syria (Provisional Leadership) (KDPS-PL)
Kurdistan Freedom and Democracy Congress (KADEK)
Kurdish Future Movement Party (KFMP)
Kurdish National Council (KNC)
Kurdistan National Parliament (KNK)
Kurdistan Patriotic Women's Association (YJKW)
Kurdistan Regional Government (KRG)
Kurdistan Society Congress (Kongra-Gel/KGK)
Kurdish Supreme Council (KSC)
Kurdistan Women's Freedom Movement (TAJK)
Kurdistan Worker's Party (PKK)
Members of Parliament (MPs)
Nationalist Movement Party (MHP)
National Liberation Front of Kurdistan (ERNK)

National Security Council (NSC)
Near Eastern Affairs (NEA)
New Counterinsurgency Strategy (COIN)
New People's Democracy Party (HADEP)
North Atlantic Treaty Organization (NATO)
NSC (National Security Council)- Turkey
Palestine Liberation Organization (PLO)
Patriotic Revolutionary Youth Movement (YDG-H)
Patriotic Union of Kurdistan (PUK)
Peace and Democracy Party (BDP)
People's Defense Force (HPG)
People's Labor Party (HEP)
People's Liberation Army of Kurdistan (ARGR)
People's Liberation Party of Turkey (THKO)
Red Army Faction (RAF)
Republicans People's Party (CHP)
Rojava Democratic Society Movement (TEV-DEM)
Society for the Ascension of Kurdistan (KTJ)
Southeastern Anatolia Development Project (GAP)
Status of Forces Agreement (SOFA)
Turkish Energy Company (TEC)
Turkish General Staff (TGS)
Turkish Grand National Assembly (TGNA)
Turkish Military Intelligence (MIT)
Turkish Petroleum Company (TPC)
United Arab Republic (UAR)
United Nations (UN)
United States Government Accountability Office (GAO)

Index